The Last Great Forest

The Last Great Forest

Japanese Multinationals and Alberta's Northern Forests

Larry Pratt and Ian Urquhart

NeWest Press Edmonton

Canadian Cataloguing in Publication Data
Pratt, Larry, 1944-
    The last great forest

    Includes bibliographical references and index
    ISBN 0-920897-77-0

    1. Forest policy—Alberta. 2. Forests and forestry—Economic aspects—Alberta. 3. Wood-pulp industry—Environmental aspects—Alberta. 4. Investments, Japanese—Alberta. I. Urquhart, Ian T. (Ian Thomas), 1955- II. Title.
SD146.A5P72 1994   338.1'749'097123   C94-910565-1

Editor for the Press: Douglas Owram
Cover design: Diane Jensen
Interior design: John Luckhurst/GDL
Maps: Mostly Maps
Financial assistance: NeWest Press gratefully acknowledges the financial assistance of The Canada Council; The Alberta Foundation for the Arts, a beneficiary of the Lottery Fund of the Government of Alberta; and The NeWest Institute for Western Canadian Studies.

Printed and bound in Canada by Best Gagné

NeWest Publishers Limited
Suite 310, 10359 - 82 Avenue
Edmonton, Alberta T6E 1Z9

Over 50% recycled paper
including 10% post
consumer fibre
Plus de 50 p. 100 de
papier recyclé dont 10 p.
100 de fibres post-
consommation.

M - Official mark of Environment Canada.
M - Marque officielle d'Environnement Canada.

For Tricia, Shaun, Rebecca, Kate, and Jean Cooper
and
Theresa, Andrea, Kali, Margret, and Hugh

Contents

Acknowledgements

Many individuals and organizations have helped us research and tell this story of political conflict in Alberta's forests. First, we would like to thank Rudy Wiebe and the board of directors of NeWest Press for the enthusiasm they showed towards publishing our manuscript. Thanks as well are owed to the valuable design and editorial assistance provided by Wendy Dawson, Eva Radford, and Diane Jensen.

Over the past several years we have received invaluable research assistance from Kimiko Abe, Lynn Cover, Janna Promislow, Michelle Spencer, Kathleen Stokes, and Marian Weber. Kathleen Stokes also played a crucial role in arranging many of the interviews we conducted. We would not have been able to benefit from their work without the financial assistance we received from the Social Sciences and Humanities Research Council of Canada and the University of Alberta.

Our study has also been shaped by the more than forty interviews we arranged with the architects, supporters, and opponents of the province's forestry strategy. We would like especially to thank the following people for the time they took to discuss Alberta's forest strategy with us: LeRoy Fjordbotten, Mike Cardinal, John McInnis, Al Adair, Leo Piquette, Fred McDougall, Al Brennan, Al McDonald, Bill Kostiw, John Brennan, Stuart Lang, Jim Morrison, Barry Mjolness, Frank Crawford, Eric Jerrard, Dr. Bruce Dancik, Dr. W. A. Fuller, Vivian Pharis, Brian Staszenski, Ed Struzik, Louise Swift, Lorraine Vetsch, Darryl Cardinal, François Cardinal, and Gerald Johnson.

Others assisted our endeavors by generously letting us consult their own research on aspects of this subject. We would like to thank Lynn Cover and Ed Struzik for their permission to cite several interviews they conducted; Fred Lennarson for making his archives on the Lubicon dispute available to us; the Japan Tropical Forest Action Network (JATAN) and the Rainforest Action Network for materials pertaining to the global operations of Mitsubishi and Honshu Paper.

The comments and criticisms of a number of people have improved the final product. Glenn Williams, Kim Sanderson, and Doug Owram, the academic editor for NeWest Press, stand out in this respect. We are also grateful to Pierre Mousseau for his assistance with the manuscript.

Finally, thanks of a different kind are owed to our families. Without their support and understanding, in particular that supplied by Tricia and Theresa, we doubt that this book would have been written.

Introduction: The Prize

IS IT NOT ASTONISHING THAT THIS BOREAL FOREST, 60 MILLION YEARS IN
THE MAKING—ACTUALLY 4.6 BILLION YEARS IN THE MAKING—SHOULD IN
THE MATTER OF A CENTURY BE THREATENED WITH TOTAL CHANGE,
AND FOR ALL WE KNOW, TOTAL DESTRUCTION, DUE TO HUMANITY'S
ACQUISITIVENESS AND IGNORANCE?
—*STAN ROWE, "BOREAL FOREST IN THE GLOBAL CONTEXT,"*
IN BOREAL FOREST CONFERENCE: PROCEEDINGS

IT'S THE ONLY PLACE LEFT IN THE FREE WORLD WHERE
THERE'S ECONOMICALLY ACCESSIBLE TIMBER OF A QUALITY THAT
CAN SUPPORT PULP MILLS.
—*JAAK PUUSEPP, PEMBERTON SECURITIES INCORPORATED*

Until the 1980s, Canada's vast northern boreal forest lived,
died, and was reincarnated in obscurity. Few appreciated
its magnitude. Few realized that the boreal forest, the taiga
as it is called on another continent, is the largest forest in
the world, a patchwork quilt blanketing nearly sixteen mil-
lion square kilometres. In Canada, this forest covers 3.24 million square kilometres—nearly one-third of the nation—and accounts for approximately 80
percent of the country's forests as it stretches from the Yukon territory in the
west to Newfoundland in the east. Despite its vastness, scientists know remarkably little about this ecosystem. The boreal forest remains a great un-
known, a wilderness shrouded in mystery and ruled by the ghosts of Native
hunters, fur traders, and bush pilots.

The history of northern settlement and industrial development hosts many
different outlooks towards this forest. For homesteaders who settled in the
northern latitudes of Canada's prairie provinces, many of whom were driven
there by the drought of the Great Depression, these virgin, forested lands
generated heartaches of their own. Muskeg and thick stands of aspen, poplar,
and spruce trees joined the harsh, unpredictable climate as obstacles to their
dreams of pushing the agricultural frontier northward. Later, as the wave of

1

petroleum exploration and development lapped at the heels of these agricultural pioneers, the forest was more nuisance than threat. In the vicinity of Fort McMurray in northeastern Alberta, the mammoth machinery used to dig bitumen out of the Athabasca tar sands literally destroyed the forest. Elsewhere, exploration crews crisscrossed the province searching for oil and gas, carving roughly 805,000 kilometres of seismic lines into the boreal landscape and leaving countless hectares of fallen trees and scarred landscapes in their wake. Finally, in the past decade, pulp and paper companies have cast much more covetous looks at these northern forests. For the forest products industry, the millions of board feet of timber and the millions of tonnes of pulp contained in these forests represented a potential gold mine. Although these attitudes are strikingly different, they shared a common purpose, an interest in taming the wilderness and in exploiting its natural features—its soil, its petroleum, its timber—for profit.

The boreal forest does inspire, however, other attitudes. For thousands of Natives, the wilderness which Western society has sought to tame is viewed as home, larder, and sanctuary. Throughout northern Canada, the subsistence or bush economy, too often dismissed by southerners as nothing more than unemployment, is a vital part of Native life. Hunting, fishing, trapping, berry and herb gathering are more than simply the keys to physical survival; they are also vital for the cultural survival of peoples who define themselves in terms of the land, who see the land as part of their soul. "Our culture," maintains a Cree chief from northeastern Alberta, "has been based upon knowledge from Mother Earth—the mountains, trees, grasses, and animals. If these are gone, then so is the Indian." The attitudes of environmentalists, many of whom live comfortable lives in large urban centres, to some extent overlap those of Native peoples. They demand that we recognize the global environmental significance of the boreal forest. The northern boreal forest is one of the lungs of our planet and plays an important role in global warming. Forests are enormous storehouses of carbon, and plans to clearcut mature forests on a massive scale must be rejected since forest clearing accelerates global warming. Other environmentalists see profit in the boreal wilderness, not in the felling of old growth timber, but in ecotourism, an unquestionably elitist enterprise where a wilderness experience comes with an expensive price tag.

This book is about the battle for supremacy between outlooks towards the boreal forest. It details a western Canadian version of the conflict taking place in the American West, a conflict between an older resource extractive economy and a new environmental economy. In both cases the question remains the same: "To whom does the West belong—the old or the new?"[1] It examines the political conflict between the visions of multinational pulp and paper companies and their allies in government on the one hand and those of Natives and environmentalists on the other hand. Such conflicts have become commonplace around the globe. In Australia and Papua New Guinea, forests are logged to supply woodchips for Japanese paper companies. In the Amazon, gold-seekers, cattle ranchers, and forestry companies clearcut tropical forests and destroy the lifestyles of indigenous peoples. In the Pacific Northwest of the United States, loggers and environmentalists battle over spotted owls and the future of the remaining stands of old growth timber. Several hundred kilometres to the north, Clayoquot Sound has joined South Moresby, Meares Island, and the Stein and Carmanah valleys as a battleground in the struggle over the future of the temperate rainforests of Canada's Pacific coast.

The setting for our book is Alberta, one of Canada's Prairie provinces, a province better known for vistas of wheatlands, vast skyscapes, or the Rocky Mountains than for those of the boreal forest's tapestry of forests, lakes, and rivers. The outbreak of Alberta's battle over the future of its vast boreal forest springs from characteristics of the province's political and economic life. The history of Alberta's political economy is marked by spectacular booms and busts, cycles which result from the economy's dependence upon wheat and petroleum production. By the 1970s, Albertans warmed to the idea that the public purse should be used on the quest for the grail of economic diversification. New industries should be sought, encouraged, and, if necessary, subsidized in order to moderate the ups and downs of the economy. This was the message that Peter Lougheed, the driven and remarkably successful Calgary lawyer who rejuvenated the Progressive Conservative party in the mid-1960s, delivered to Albertans. In the late 1960s, he criticized the Social Credit government for "coasting" on the sale of unprocessed energy resources and failing to use Alberta's oil income for capital investment to diversify the province's economy. His election as premier in 1971 put Lougheed in position to correct the complacency of his predecessors. Despite his bold rhetoric about economic diversification during the 1970s and early 1980s, the gap between words and deeds was very wide. Despite his worries that Alberta was "too vulnerable," too dependent upon the extraction and sale of depleting oil and natural gas,[2] the economic forces unleashed by two world oil shocks overwhelmed the development strategy of his government. The province's rapidly growing economy actually became more specialized, more reliant on investment and jobs derived from the oil and agricultural industries, and more vulnerable to factors that could delay or destroy investment commitments, such as high interest rates, world oil prices, or federal energy policy.[3]

In late 1985, on the eve of a free-fall in world oil prices that would intensify dramatically the already precarious state of the Alberta economy, Peter Lougheed retired from centre stage and turned the reins of power over to his understudy, Donald Getty. Premier Getty, a star quarterback for the Edmonton Eskimos who led his team to two Grey Cup victories, first entered provincial politics at Lougheed's urging in 1966. As one of the first and most trusted members of the Lougheed team, Getty was rewarded with important cabinet positions, the most significant being the portfolio of Energy and Natural Resources, a ministry which included responsibility for forestry. In 1979, Getty dropped out of politics and returned to the private sector, reportedly "anxious for a piece of the boom."[4] Like many Albertans during this boom, Getty was seduced by the illusion of an endless resource boom and over-reached himself. His excursion into private business became troubled after he became chief executive officer of Nortek Energy Corporation, an independent oil company owned by the Sparrow family of Edmonton. Falling oil prices and heavy losses landed Getty and Nortek in a difficult situation which was only reversed after a company controlled by Nova Corporation, on whose board Getty sat, reportedly bailed out Nortek.[5]

From Lougheed, Getty inherited a province mired in a deepening economic crisis. He faced a political climate dominated by the contraction of the oil industry and desperate demands for alternative sources of investment and employment. After the 1986 election, an election where the New Democratic and Liberal parties sliced into Conservative support in Edmonton and Calgary, some began to wonder if the Conservative dynasty might be in eclipse. Facing the stagnation, unemployment, and political uncertainty produced by the collapse of international energy and wheat prices in the 1980s, the Getty administration, for reasons we will discuss in chapter 2, seized upon the strategy of encouraging a massive expansion of the province's pulp and paper industry. The utilization of the province's vast stands of aspen, a species traditionally regarded as a weed by the forest industry, was the centrepiece of the province's strategy. This expansion promised to diversify the economy, create desperately needed jobs, and prop up the government's sagging political fortunes. This strategy had tremendous appeal to multinational forest companies, companies besieged elsewhere by environmentalism as well as by worries that few supplies of virgin timber remained in politically stable countries. Multinational forest companies, looking to extend their control over raw material supplies, applauded the province as it offered them long-term, secure access to millions of hectares of forest. For its part, government gave these companies timber cutting rights in an area the size of Great Britain. In many cases, it also helped finance these projects. Daishowa and Alberta-Pacific (controlled by Mitsubishi) are the focus for attention in this book in part because their projects sparked the most intense political reaction. The Lubicon Cree defied Daishowa in northwestern Alberta while in the northeast, a massive environmental protest delayed and nearly derailed the Alberta-Pacific project, one of the world's biggest single-line pulp mills. These two companies received approximately $550 million in government loans and transportation infrastructure, a significant chunk of the $1.35 billion the government committed to forestry projects in the late 1980s.

This financial assistance helped to attract the nearly four billion dollars in capital investments that were made in Alberta's pulp and paper industry after the provincial government announced its new forestry policies in 1986. Although the principal focus of this book is on Daishowa and Alberta-Pacific, these projects were certainly not the only offspring of the new corporate-state relationship in forestry. The industrialization of the forest has occurred in northern Alberta along two major river systems. On the Athabasca River system, the following expansions and new mills, all using aspen hardwood as well as softwoods, were undertaken: in 1986, Millar Western Pulp Limited commenced construction of a $205 million chemithermomechanical pulp (CTMP) mill with a capacity of 210,000 tonnes per year at Whitecourt; in 1987, Weldwood of Canada began a $416 million expansion of its 1950s bleached kraft pulp mill at Hinton, doubling its production from 600 to 1,200 tonnes daily; in 1988, Alberta Newsprint Company Limited began construction near Whitecourt of a $406 million newsprint paper mill at a rated capacity of 220,000 finished tonnes of high-quality newsprint annually; in 1989, the Alberta Energy Company started construction of a $182 million CTMP mill with a capacity of 110,000 tonnes a year at Slave Lake; and in 1990 after a lengthy environmental review process Alberta-Pacific received permission to construct its $1.3 billion, 1,500 tonnes per day bleached kraft pulp mill between Athabasca and Lac La Biche. On the Peace River system, the major new project, which commenced construction in 1988, was Daishowa Canada's Peace River Pulp Company, now owned by Daishowa and Marubeni, a $580 million bleached kraft pulp mill with a daily capacity of about 1,200 tonnes near the town of Peace River; an older mill, Procter and Gamble's bleached kraft pulp mill at Grande Prairie was scheduled to double its production, but Procter and Gamble went out of the pulp production business and sold the mill to Weyerhaeuser before the expansion could be undertaken. Also on the Peace system and in the Grande Prairie area, a consortium known as Grande Alberta Paper has proposed to construct a $1.6 billion high value-added lightweight coated paper mill, but its status as we write remains uncertain. Table 1 lists these investment projects while Table 2 details the government financial assistance the forest sector received.

Table 1: Pulp and Paper Investments in Alberta, 1986–1993

Owner	Project	Project Cost – ($ Million)	Location
Completed			
Millar Western Pulp Limited	Chemithermomechanical Pulp Mill (CTMP)	$205	Whitecourt
Alberta Energy Company Slave Lake Pulp	CTMP	$182	Slave Lake
Alberta Newsprint Company	CTMP & Newsprint Mill	$406	Whitecourt
Daishowa Canada (Daishowa-Marubeni International)	Bleached Kraft Pulp Mill (BKP)	$580	Peace River
Weldwood of Canada	BKP Expansion	$416	Hinton
Alberta-Pacific Forest Industries	BKP	$1,300	Athabasca area
Future Projects			
Grande Alberta Paper	Lightweight Coated Paper Mill	$1,600	Grande Prairie

Table 2: Government Financial Assistance to Forest Project Investments

	Pulp and Paper	Other	Total
Loan Guarantees	615	15	630
Debentures	525	25	550
Infrastructures	170	—	170
Total	**1,310**	**40**	**1,350**

In total (and with the inclusion of smaller forestry-related projects), these major investments have increased direct employment in Alberta's forest industry from about eighty-four hundred in 1985 to above twelve thousand five hundred in the early 1990s. Four thousand permanent new jobs are of course important, especially to the communities affected, but the growth in direct employment has actually been small, given the scale of the investments, because of the capital intensive nature of new pulp mills and the types of technology used in the harvesting and pulp production processes. The Canada-Alberta Partnership Agreement in Forestry, as renewed in 1992, states that Alberta's forestry industry accounts indirectly for another twenty-four thousand jobs. In the mid-eighties, about 15 percent of the eight thousand plus jobs in the Alberta forestry sector were held by persons of Native ancestry, but these are the most recent data known to us. Overall, as of 1991 the forestry industry sector accounted for about 1 percent of Alberta's employed labour force.

Despite these employment gains, for some segments of society the government's forest investment strategy was abominable. The province's enthusiasm for pulp and paper megaprojects coincided with the moment when forests started to preoccupy environmental groups around the world. This international consciousness seeped into provincial politics. Newly-minted environmental groups, many of them located in the small communities which were supposed to derive economic benefits from these projects, raised ecological objections to the plans of Daishowa and Mitsubishi. They warned that forest exploitation on such a gigantic scale would damage irreparably the ecological diversity of the forests and would accelerate global warming. Others raised concerns about the impact that toxins in pulp mill effluent would have upon northern rivers and the health of those who depend upon the Peace and Athabasca rivers for water and food. Native peoples, such as the Lubicon Cree, worried that these projects would further marginalize their position in white society. Timber cutting, on the scale needed to feed these pulp and paper mills, might compromise further their treaty rights, outstanding land claims, and traditional hunting and trapping economy.

More often than not, when we consider contemporary forest use conflicts, we focus our attention upon the environmental consequences of timber cutting and pulp mill production. In Alberta, the furore over environmental issues concerning the pulp mills distracted analysts' attention from the equally important question posed by every good detective story—*cui bono?* Who got the swag, and why? Who bears the risks in the event that one or more of the new projects fails commercially? Why did the Alberta government finance these projects, some of which are backed by some of the world's wealthiest corporations? Was direct involvement required on financial grounds, or was it deemed expedient to have the state in the project in order to socialize risks: that is, to protect private capital from a variety of risks, including those associated with the politics of the environment? While the government and its critics have invested much time and effort in the debate over the likely effects of poisonous dioxins and furans on the Athabasca and Peace rivers, very little analysis has been done on the political and corporate priorities that led the Alberta government and Japanese capital to forge a transnational developmental alliance. We argue that, in reality, if not in some people's perceptions, the political economy and the physical environment are linked inextricably and cannot be understood in isolation from one another. It may well be true, as a well-known Canadian ecologist has argued, that clearcutting forests to feed pulp mills in northern Alberta is just part of a worldwide problem of "people armed with powerful technology . . . knocking ecosystems apart and using the pieces to feed huge ever-growing industries."[6] But that does not tell us who these people are, why their powerful technology came to Alberta when it did, why they found both a generous landlord and an active partner in the Alberta government, or why they encountered fierce opposition from an environmental movement that had barely existed a few years earlier. This book addresses these questions by examining the origins of Alberta's forest strategy, the interests and requirements of the Japanese multinationals who came to Alberta in the late 1980s, and the nature of the environmentalist challenge to the developmental coalition.

Our arguments are presented as follows. Chapter 1 outlines the essential historical background for the current conflicts—the history of forest management and environmental politics in Alberta. There we meet an ideology in which forests are regarded as little more than fibre and note the longstanding nature of debates about the government's role in forest industry growth. Chapter 2 describes and analyzes the decision of Premier Getty's government to use the "visible hand of the state" to facilitate spectacular growth in the province's pulp and paper industry. Chapter 3 examines the motives which led Daishowa, a multinational known as an *enfant terrible* among Japanese pulp and paper producers, to invest in Alberta. It demonstrates well how the strategies of the Japanese paper industry fit neatly with the Getty administration's objectives and the enormous amount of trust the government gave a company with a checkered history. Chapter 4 shifts our attention to the environmental dimension of the Daishowa project. It considers whether Alberta's regulatory systems contributed to Daishowa's interest in Alberta, the nature of the opposition to Daishowa, and how political and legal institutions insulated the pulp mill proposal from many important criticisms. Chapters 5 and 6 examine the Alberta-Pacific project, a project advertised as "the world's largest single-line pulp mill."[7] Here again, we examine the motives which drew Mitsubishi, one of the world's most powerful corporations, to the forests of Alberta as well as how the provincial government came to share a considerable portion of this project's risk. Chapter 5 also analyzes the "Friends of the Mill," people who had been bypassed by earlier booms, who came to favour and lobby for the Alberta-Pacific pulp mill. Chapter 6 returns to consider the opposition to the Alberta-Pacific project. It focusses upon how the decision-making setting was massaged in order to declaw environmental critiques of the mill proposal. It also argues that the very scientific type of environmental critique which was often employed against Alberta-Pacific is self-defeating. The emphasis on science downplays the social, economic, and political forces that bring about industrial challenges to the environment in the first place and plays to the predisposition of regulators to accept technological approaches to the ecological challenges posed by pulp mill projects. We conclude the book by assessing the impact of these projects upon the province's political and economic life.

1 . Samuel P. Hays, "The New Environmental West," *Journal of Policy History*, 3 (1991), 237.

2 . John Richards and Larry Pratt, *Prairie Capitalism: Power and Influence in the New West* (Toronto: McClelland and Stewart, 1979), 165–68.

3 . Our interpretation of Alberta's economic instability closely follows Robert L. Mansell and Michael B. Percy, *Strength in Adversity: A Study of the Alberta Economy* (Western Centre for Economic Research and C. D. Howe Institute: The University of Alberta Press, 1990).

4 . Andrew Nikiforuk, "Third Down and Ten," *Report on Business Magazine*, April 1987.

5 . Ibid.

6 . Stan Rowe, "The Technology of Large Enterprises," *Parks and Wilderness*, 6 (Fall 1989).

7 . Robert Forrest, "Alberta-Pacific: Striving for World Class in a Global Market," *Pulp and Paper Journal*, Vol. 45, no. 2 (February 1992), 23.

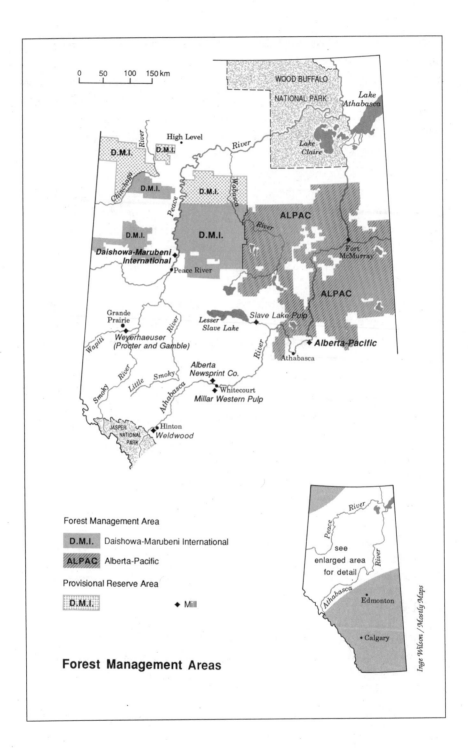

Forest Management Area

D.M.I. Daishowa-Marubeni International

ALPAC Alberta-Pacific

Provisional Reserve Area

D.M.I.   ◆ Mill

Forest Management Areas

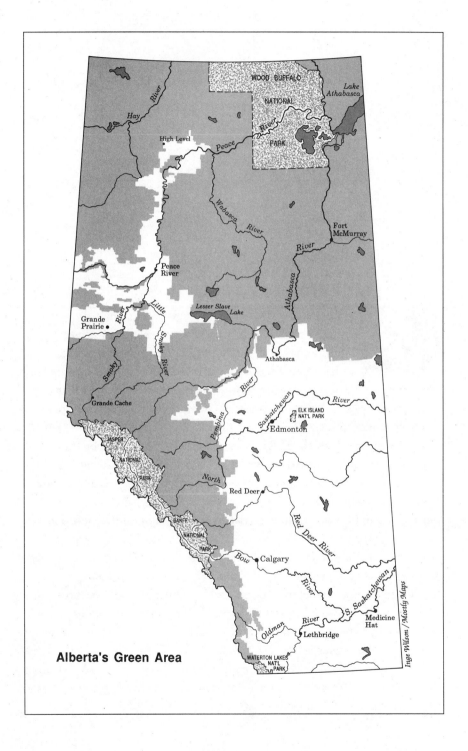

Alberta's Green Area

CHAPTER 1

The Fibre Syndrome:
A History of Forest Use in Alberta

TIMBER AND OTHER PRODUCTS OF THE FOREST ARE A CROP.
THIS IS THE UNDERLYING THOUGHT OF ALL FOREST MANAGEMENT
OR CONSERVATION WORK.

—*ALBERTA, DEPARTMENT OF LANDS AND FORESTS, ALBERTA'S FORESTS*

 The discovery of oil at Leduc in 1947 signalled the beginning of thirty-five years of steady, sometimes spectacular, economic growth in Alberta. Led by energy exploration and development, the provincial economy boomed. In looking back on this period it would be absurd to suggest that widespread, vociferous environmental protests emerged as serious obstacles to natural resource megaprojects in Alberta. Albertans were obsessed with the pursuit of rapid economic growth. This obsession was well symbolized by the enthusiasm for developing the Athabasca tar sands near Fort McMurray in northeastern Alberta. Politicians, corporate executives, and citizens all applauded the technological wizards who drafted blueprints for squeezing heavy oil, as well as jobs and profits, from the asphalt-like tar sands. Only a few doubted the propriety of schemes to destroy the natural landscape in the name of economic growth. Only a few suggested that the certainty of environmental degradation should temper the gigantic scale of tar sands exploitation.

When it came to the province's forests a similar attitude was born. The "Fibre Syndrome"—the beliefs that forests are best used for making pulp and other wood products and that the primary obligations of forest management must always be timber cutting and regeneration—grew to dominate professional and public outlooks towards the province's forest resource.[1] Yet, from the 1950s to the 1980s the province's forest products industry grew slowly, too slowly in the minds of some. Forestry consultants and senior officials of the

Alberta Forest Service alike spoke of an underutilized resource that needed development. Towards the end of the energy boom of the 1970s a leading forestry consulting firm argued that the growth of the forest products industry "should be part of the province's industrial strategy." The problem or challenge then, as it was when government first entertained major development proposals in the 1950s, was that although the province was blessed with millions of acres of virgin timber a considerable proportion of this resource bounty was economically inaccessible, "beyond the economic margin."[2] How badly did government want a larger forest products industry? This was the question policy makers faced. Would government subsidize the development of the forest products sector? If so, how extensive and generous was the provincial government prepared to be?

Mills and Managers: The First Generation

The economic potential of Alberta's forests was first appreciated during World War II. War, following on the heels of a depression which hit Alberta's lumber industry very hard, produced sharply increased demand for wood products of all sorts. Lumber production soared to its highest levels since the province received jurisdiction over natural resources in 1930. For some companies involved in other resource sectors, the profit-making possibilities of forest projects were only recognized as they tried to cope with the economic disruptions that war visited upon their operations. The birth of the province's first pulp mill lay in the efforts of North Canadian Oils, an Alberta company with coal properties in west central Alberta, to compensate for coal markets that fell victim to the war. This loss prompted the company's owners, the Ruben family, to explore the possibility of exploiting the forests surrounding their Robb coal mine. A forestry operation would help sustain their coal mining properties if North Canadian's coal could be used to fuel the project. With government approval of the idea of securing rights to timber in hand, North Canadian began to search for a partner. With no experience of its own in the pulp and paper industry, the company sought an established forest products company, one with pockets deep enough to help finance a pulp mill. The great distance between west central Alberta and American pulp and paper markets threatened to destroy the Ruben's ambitions, for it discouraged many of the companies which explored the possibility of forming a joint venture with North Canadian. Finally, the St. Regis Paper Company of New York, on the condition that it would manage the forestry operations, joined North Canadian as an equal partner in North Western Pulp and Power Limited—the province's first pulp producer. In 1954, these two companies agreed to supply 50 percent each of the equity capital needed to construct a pulp mill at Hinton, a town located in the foothills of the Rocky Mountains, 285 kilometres west of Edmonton. However, North Canadian's dreams of supplying coal to the North Western mill would not be fulfilled. Coal dust contaminated the pulp, pushing North Canadian to acquire gas rights in the Wabamun gas fields to the east and build a gas pipeline to the mill site.

Judged by the standards of the 1980s megaprojects, the original mill was a medium-sized facility. By 1966, nine years after its opening, the Hinton mill was producing 544 tonnes of bright white, bleached kraft pulp per day. This pulp, like the overwhelming majority of market pulp then produced in Canada, was shipped to markets in the United States. In 1969, North Canadian Oils sold its interest in North Western Pulp and Power to St. Regis. The Hinton mill, currently owned by Weldwood of Canada, is now a part of the holdings of the American multinational forestry giant—Champion International Corporation, the world's eleventh largest forest products company in 1991. Since it was built in 1957 the Hinton mill has undergone several expansions and modernizations. The latest expansion of this mill, completed in 1990 at a cost of $416 million, increased daily production to nearly twelve hundred tonnes per day. The government of Alberta assumed a portion of the risk of this expansion by providing Weldwood with a loan guarantee of $285 million.

Unlike the generation of new forestry projects and mill expansions born in the 1980s, the original North Western Pulp and Power mill was not showered by government grants, loans, loan guarantees, or commitments to build expensive infrastructure. This did not imply, however, that public policy was not used in the 1950s to enhance the attractiveness of building pulp mills. It did mean that Premier Ernest Manning's Social Credit government believed quite strongly that government support should be modest. Social Credit's commitment to some form of industrial development helped prompt the introduction in Alberta of the Forest Management Agreement (FMA), a significant change to the province's timber disposal system. An FMA would only be awarded to a company if it promised to build a major wood processing facility—a pulp mill, large sawmill, or plywood mill. In exchange for the commitment to build such a project, government made concessions in the areas of timber dues and tenure over the forests.

A set of "low and stable" timber dues was one of the features the North Western FMA contained to compensate for the competitive disadvantages facing a mill constructed thousands of miles from its principal markets. Stumpage—the fee government charges for the amount of timber cut on Crown lands—was negotiated between North Western and the Forest Service and generally is conceded to have been set low enough to provide an incentive for pulp company investment. The dues for coniferous pulpwood timber ranged from twelve to forty-one cents per cubic metre; deciduous pulpwood timber dues ranged from eight to twelve cents per cubic metre.[3] North Western also benefited from the fact that these dues were frozen for the twenty-one year life of the FMA. Gathering economic rent from the resource was not an important public policy objective. The province did not even receive enough revenue from industry to cover the administrative costs of managing and protecting the forest resource.[4] Investment and its associated employment, not rent collection, were the primary economic objectives of the FMA.

In most of Canada, unlike some of Canada's rivals in world pulp markets, the vast majority of the forests is owned by the Crown. In Alberta, 95 percent of the province's forest lands falls into some category of public ownership. By contrast, only 9 percent of the forest land in the southern United States, a region that accounts for more than 60 percent of American pulp production, is vested in the public sector. For the first generation of forest managers in Alberta, strengthening the private sector's tenure over the province's forest resources was a second incentive to investment offered in Alberta's FMAs. The North Western FMA initiated the practice of offering companies exclusive cutting privileges to specific types of timber in a forest management area for long periods of time. In the North Western FMA, secure tenure was offered for a minimum period of twenty-one years, a period set at twenty years in subsequent FMAs. Because FMAs could be renewed indefinitely, they offered the pulp and paper industry a very attractive potential—perpetual timber cutting privileges.

The Forest Management Agreement's injection of long term security to the province's forest management system was prompted by the belief that the province's timber allocation process blocked investment in the forest products sector. Prior to introducing FMAs the province sold timber cutting rights to the highest bidder. To some extent, competitive bidding produced destructive competition between forestry companies. In order to protect investments, timber licensees waged bidding wars against each other for the harvesting rights to timber adjacent to their established properties. This produced, in the Alberta Forest Service's opinion, "unreasonable over-bids and operating costs for many timber licensees."[5] Overbidding, in turn, led operators to cut costs wherever possible, a practice which encouraged "cut and run" operations and generally depressed investment in new machinery and equipment. Moreover, to the Forest Service the insecurity of tenure made it impossible to interest forest companies in committing themselves to reforestation programs. The province hoped that the long term, secure land tenure offered by FMAs would provide some of the incentive firms needed to come to Alberta and build major wood processing facilities and to practice an aggressive policy of reforestation after clearcutting the land. Des Crossley, North Western Pulp and Power's chief forester from 1955 to 1975, certainly regarded the tenure provided by Alberta's FMAs as an important improvement over the timber disposal arrangements then used in central Canada:

> The most significant difference between these Agreements and Alberta's was that none of the former provided for significant tenure. The industries in Ontario, and I'm pretty sure in Quebec, were provided with far more timber land than they required, and consequently far greater allowable cuts than they could utilize (on an average probably more than 3 times as much), so they really did not have any incentive to do forest management. There was always more timber over the next hill.[6]

From Crossley's assessment it would appear that, relative to provinces with established pulp and paper industries, Alberta was miserly when it came to devoting territory to the North Western Pulp and Power project. This was not the case at all. When Crossley himself first flew over the territory ceded to his company, he was "awed of its magnitude." So he should have been. Some 7,769 square kilometres of land, 80 percent of it forested with the softwood species such as lodgepole pine and spruce then preferred by pulp and paper makers, were set aside to supply the Hinton mill. In fact, the territorial concessions made in the North Western FMA were just as generous as many of the pulpwood concessions found in Ontario. Moreover, the 7,769 square kilometres set aside by the North Western FMA was a significantly larger area than some of the Ontario pulpwood agreements offered to that province's pulp and lumber barons. The principle of devoting extensive territories to timber production joined security of tenure and a favourable stumpage rate as the ingredients government first used to attract investors to the province.

This first Forest Management Agreement was more than simply a potion concocted to attract investors. It also injected, what was for the 1950s, a progressive philosophy into Alberta forestry management. Within the professional forestry community the management regime ushered in by this first FMA was well regarded. Crossley praised it as "a remarkable document for the time."[7] The North Western FMA became a model other provinces studied carefully. Nova Scotia, in fact, virtually copied the North Western FMA when it issued a timber lease to the Swedish pulp and paper firm, Stora Kopparberg in the late 1950s.[8] Bruce Dancik, the chair of the University of Alberta's Department of Forest Science, speaks highly of the first generation of forest managers in Alberta. They learned from the experiences of colleagues in other provinces and were committed to realizing the renewable potential of forests.[9] Consequently, although managers favoured clearcutting—cutting down all the trees in a harvesting area or cutblock—because it maximized the utilization of forest fibre, clearcuts in Alberta were much smaller and more tightly controlled than the clearcuts allowed in other provinces. Provincial regulations prevented the blight represented by vast contiguous clearcuts from developing. Forests were recognized for the important role they played in watershed protection and harvesting rules were designed with this role in mind. In order to encourage the effective reforestation of cutover areas, government offered incentives to companies that practiced intensive forest management. Any additional wood resulting from intensive management of forest lands could be harvested stumpage-free by companies.

An able representative of this first generation of forest managers was Reg Loomis, the province's first professional forester and the senior superintendent of Forest Management from 1953 to 1966. Loomis, who had worked previously for International Paper Company in New Brunswick, joined the Alberta Forest Surveys Division in 1950 and used aerial photographic surveys to produce the province's first forest resources inventory, an estimate of the species, ages, and distribution of Alberta's forests. Loomis regarded this inventory as one of the essential foundations needed to establish more effective forestry management in Alberta than he had encountered in eastern Canada. He advocated the principle that forestry companies must manage the forest resource on a sustained-yield basis. In the jargon of the professional forester, sustained yield is the idea that the volume of trees cut down in any given period should not be greater than the volume of new forest growth in the same period. Or, as Cliff Smith, the assistant deputy minister of the Alberta Forest Service put it more recently: "We calculate what the forest is growing, then we don't cut any more than that. It's like a bank account where you only take the interest."[10] Loomis deserves some of the credit for the references to sustained yield and perpetual yield found in the province's first FMA. The orientation he brought to forest management helps explain why, in the late 1970s, F. L. C. Reed and Associates complimented Alberta for its "positive approach" to forest management, praise which stands out in the company's generally unfavourable assessment of Canadian forestry practices.

To an important degree Crossley shared Loomis's enthusiasm for implementing the principles of sustained yield forestry. But, the issue of how much money North Western needed to spend in order to fulfill its responsibility to reforest caused friction between the company and the Forest Service. "The Forest Service couldn't care less about our costs," Crossley charged, "provided desired results are realized. As a professional forester charged with this responsibility I demand the right 'to do it my way.' At least until it has been demonstrated that my way is not producing the desired results, and one of these results is an acceptable cost."[11]

If the company's reluctance to commit the monies needed to guarantee reforestation threatened the renewability of the forest resource so too did the exploration and development practices of the petroleum industry. North Western complained bitterly that the concept of multiple use—that forestry should share access to the land with other industrial, agricultural, and recreational pursuits—badly compromised the government's commitment that the primary use of these lands would be timber production. Seismic lines, pipelines, strip mines, and grazing leases gobbled up hundreds of thousands of hectares of productive forest land. Formal requests to the minister of Lands and Forests that the government enforce existing land use protections and compensate the company for timber in its FMA destroyed by petroleum exploration were ignored. The scale of the damage caused by the petroleum industry was staggering. By 1977, 378,200 kilometres of seismic lines criss-crossed the Green Area, that portion of the province set aside to supply a secure land base for forest management. The Environment Council of Alberta estimated that more than 234,700 hectares had been "disturbed" by exploration activity, an area nearly as large as the 255,692 hectares which had been cut by logging companies between 1956 and 1976.

Letting the Market Set the Pace of Development

The indifference government showed towards the petroleum industry's waste of the province's forests was a useful metaphor for the subordinate place forestry occupied then in the province's political economy. In 1974, the value of all shipments from the sawmill and planing industry amounted to $67.6 million. Meanwhile, the value of oil and gas production was just over five billion dollars. Forestry was nothing more than a pretender to the thrones occupied by energy and agriculture, a pretender who lacked powerful societal and governmental allies. If the habits of petroleum exploration wasted trees so be it. Energy was king and the government had no intention nor need to challenge the status quo. With healthy energy and agricultural sectors in place during the 1960s the Social Credit governments of Ernest Manning and Harry Strom refused to raid the public treasury and offer prospective forestry investors more incentives than were generally available through Forest Management Agreements. This position was also typical of Peter Lougheed's Progressive Conservative cabinets throughout the 1970s and early 1980s. A single theme united these three administrations—forest development would proceed only if investors were prepared to proceed with, at most, minimal government assistance.

Social Credit's commitment to refrain from using public finances to stimulate the growth of the forest products sector was tested on several occasions in the 1960s. In 1965, MacMillan Bloedel Limited (MacBlo), the Canadian firm which dominated the British Columbia forest industry, signed an agreement with Alberta to set aside a portion of the Whitecourt forest for a planned integrated forest products complex. Four years later, MacMillan Bloedel informed the government that the customary incentives found in an FMA were not rich enough for the company to honour its prior commitment. Despite improving pulp prices, MacMillan Bloedel argued that, without financial assistance and/or tax concessions, its proposed $115 million investment would not deliver an acceptable rate of return. The company concluded:

> It therefore now appears to be of paramount importance that maximum assistance be sought, at both the federal and provincial levels, towards the reduction of the capital base at risk to the Company . . . and towards reduction of the unrealistically heavy total tax burden faced by this development from all three levels of government. Without significant assistance of this form, it is at this stage very doubtful that such a major investment at Whitecourt can be made viable at all.[12]

Before MacBlo would give the Whitecourt operation the green light, it needed "equivalent assistance"—the sorts of financial assistance which governments had bestowed upon forestry projects in Saskatchewan, Quebec, and Atlantic Canada.

When MacMillan Bloedel officials met Premier Strom in July 1969 to discuss MacBlo's doubts about the viability of the Whitecourt proposal they were asked why concerns about an unfavourable rate of return had not surfaced when the company signed the initial agreement. Increases in capital and operating costs between 1965 and 1969 were only part of the company's explanation for its change of heart. Ironically, government assistance, the very item MacBlo sought, was also a culprit. The assistance which governments around the world had lavished on pulp and paper projects was one catalyst for increased global pulp capacity. Although the generosity of governments fuelled an increase in industrial capacity which, in turn, depressed pulp prices, MacBlo argued that government financial assistance was essential to *any* new pulp and paper project. "Any pulp mills being built today," MacMillan Bloedel instructed Premier Strom, "are not profitable unless some special low cost conditions or concessions prevail. . . ."[13] If Alberta wanted a project like MacBlo was contemplating it would have to assemble a package such as the company had secured in Alabama. There, MacBlo only proceeded with its investment after receiving a basket of concessions—low-interest loans, property and sales tax exemptions, an investment tax credit, a bridge, and housing! For MacMillan Bloedel's management, southern hospitality certainly lived up to its reputation.

Premier Strom would have nothing to do with the key demands made by MacMillan Bloedel—government sharing the capital risk of the project, long term municipal tax concessions, and construction of a bridge across the Athabasca River. Nothing the company had said to the premier during their July meeting persuaded Strom to accept the suggestion that Alberta guarantee MacMillan Bloedel's bonds. "I see no reason," the premier wrote, "why the Government of Alberta would be prepared, at this time, to set such a precedent." Strom was just as adamant when it came to the bridge MacBlo wanted built across the Athabasca: "I would have to say quite frankly that we could not find it possible to spend half a million dollars of public funds to build a bridge, the use of which would be limited to your Company." The premier also would not offer MacBlo special concessions on municipal taxes. He replied bluntly: "All industry in Alberta is treated alike."[14]

Faced with the province's refusal to buy MacMillan Bloedel's favour, the company turned to explore what it called "alternative, more attractive investments." The company's urge to grow was satisfied through a global expansion program carried out during the 1970s. The United States, Great Britain, Spain, Brazil, Malaysia, Indonesia, France, and Holland all became hosts to this Canadian transnational company.

Social Credit's refusal to offer the concessions other governments were willing to offer forestry companies certainly slowed down, but did not halt altogether, the flow of investment dollars into Alberta's forest products sector. The second pulp and paper mill built in Alberta was sponsored by the American transnational, Procter and Gamble. In the mid-1960s, the Grande Prairie Chamber of Commerce began to promote the idea of bringing a pulp mill to the Grande Prairie area. The town's major industry, the British Petroleum refinery, had closed down and in the absence of major oil and gas discoveries in the region, the Chamber wanted to boost the local economy.[15] In late 1966 the Government of Alberta took out advertisements in leading pulp and paper journals offering land in the vicinity of Grande Prairie and Rocky Mountain House for pulp and paper development. Any firms with the financial and managerial capability needed to construct a pulp mill and market its production were invited to submit development proposals. Only two companies responded: McIntyre Porcupine Mines Limited, a major Canadian mining company then exploring the feasibility of exploiting the coal deposits found in the Grande Cache area, and Procter and Gamble, one of the world's giants in consumer products manufacturing. Unlike McIntyre, Procter and Gamble was a pulp and paper industry veteran. Formed in the 1830s as a partnership between two brothers-in-law, William Procter and James Gamble, Procter and Gamble began as a candle and soap making company. By 1967 this consumer products manufacturer had worldwide sales of $2.4 billion, manufacturing plants in twenty-eight countries, and forty thousand employees. The company's involvement in pulp and paper production began in the early 1920s with the creation of the Buckeye Cellulose Corporation, a wholly owned subsidiary. In the 1950s the company expanded aggressively in this sector. During the Korean War the United States urged corporate America to expand cellulose production and offered tax incentives to firms that would construct new plants. Procter and Gamble responded by building a huge pulp mill in Foley, Florida, a mill large enough to meet 5 percent of world demand. The purchase of Charmin Paper Products in 1957 marked the establishment of a paper products division within the company. This division grew rapidly thoughout the late 1950s and 1960s as the demand for tissues and disposable diapers outraced supply. Edward Harness, a future company president, felt that a secure future in the paper business depended upon the company's ability to control a major portion of the long-fibred pulp which the company's products depended upon. This search for a secure pulp supply eventually led the company to Alberta, the only jurisdiction willing to offer Procter and Gamble a twenty year renewable timber berth.[16] At public hearings held to discuss the two competing proposals, Procter and Gamble emphasized its impressive forest products pedigree and its belief that the trees from the Grande Prairie region had excellent pulp making qualities for many of the company's paper products.

Compared to the many concessions MacBlo coveted, Procter and Gamble's public demands were modest. The company expected that any FMA it concluded with the province would contain terms which were generally as favourable as those found in already existing FMAS. The absence of a provincial sales tax represented an important cost consideration and the company asked for a guarantee that "this current favorable tax climate for pulp mill investment" would not be taken away. Furthermore, the company's willingness to proceed hinged upon the province's willingness to upgrade the area's transportation infrastructure. It was necessary, the company argued, for the province to fulfill the commitment to complete the Alberta Resources Railway to Grande Prairie, pave local highways, upgrade the Wapiti River bridge, and build a bridge over Big Mountain Creek. In correspondence with J. Donovan Ross, the province's minister of Lands and Forests, the company worried about the availability of construction labour over the timeframe needed to build the mill and "the currently excessive interest cost in funding such a project."[17] If Procter and Gamble was satisfied with the terms offered by the province the company proposed to build a six hundred tonne per day bleached kraft pulp mill. The price tag attached to this mill in the summer of 1967 was estimated at more than fifty million dollars. Once the mill was completed and operating in 1973 the total construction cost had jumped to over one hundred million dollars. By 1977 the company employed approximately eight hundred workers directly and another three hundred workers through various types of service contracts. While the provincial government did not assist the company in project financing, the federal Department of Regional Economic Expansion was more generous and gave the company a grant of twelve million dollars, on the condition that the mill would hire local people, including Natives.[18]

Throughout the 1970s the Grande Prairie mill was a picture of stability. The mill, unlike many other Canadian pulp and paper companies, operated continuously when pulp markets were poor between 1976 and 1978. At the same time, production expanded. The company added a 100 million board foot sawmill to its operations in 1980 and boosted its pulp capacity to 820 tonnes per day. By the end of the 1980s, however, as low pulp prices and a rising tide of environmentalism buffeted pulp and paper makers, Procter and Gamble abandoned grandiose expansion plans to double the capacity of the Grande Prairie mill and to build a new lumber mill in Manning. These last acts were merely a prelude to a much more fundamental decision the United States parent was about to make—selling all of its North American pulp assets.

Two months before the Grande Prairie mill shipped its first pulp to Procter and Gamble's paper making plants in the United States, the Alberta Forest Service held public hearings to consider forestry proposals for the Whitecourt-Fox Creek area. After evaluating the timber found in this area the Forest Service determined that, rather than a pulp mill, "a lumber complex of some type would be much more useful to the Province. . . ." In the fall of 1972 the Lougheed government had invited interested companies to submit development proposals. Simpson Timber, a private Seattle-based corporation, outbid several companies, including the giant American multinational Weyerhaeuser, for rights to an FMA in the Whitecourt area. In return for this FMA, Simpson agreed first to build one of the largest sawmill complexes in Alberta. In order to appease concerns for public participation, particularly participation by Albertans in this venture, Simpson Timber sold Alberta Energy Company a 40 percent joint venture interest in the project it was building near Whitecourt. Like so many of the promises of future development that have accompanied forest company bids in Alberta's history, nothing came of Simpson Timber's 1973 promises of future phases to its operations that would utilize the forest resource more fully and employ more Albertans in the process. By 1981, the American parent had lost its appetite for Alberta's forests, and Alberta Energy became the sole owner of the Blue Ridge forestry complex when it purchased Simpson Timber for twenty-four million dollars. The move to acquire Simpson Timber was one of two significant moves Alberta Energy made that year into the forests products sector. Alberta Energy also purchased a 28 percent interest in British Columbia Forest Products (B. C. Forest Products) from Noranda Mines for just over $217 million. The company's shareholders would come to regret this second purchase. Five years later, Alberta sold all of its shares in

B. C. Forest Products, losing nearly sixty-five million dollars in the process.

The Blue Ridge lumber complex represented the last major new forest project the province would see until Progressive Conservative Premier Donald Getty aggressively promoted Alberta's forests in the latter half of the 1980s. The Forest Service continued to seek forestry investment and to advertise the availability of thousands of square miles to the forest products industry but market circumstances conspired against the interest the government's foresters had in increasing the utilization of the province's timber. In the summer of 1979, on what was possibly the last occasion where the Forest Service invited the public to listen to and comment upon the development proposals of forest companies, public hearings considered forest company plans for the timber resources in the Berland-Fox Creek area. A dozen companies vied with each other in public for government approval to exploit some or all of the forest lands earmarked for the timber industry. Every possible element of the Canadian business community came to the towns of Fox Creek and Grande Cache to make a salespitch to the MLAs and senior Forest Service personnel who convened these hearings. Local independent sawmill operators were well represented at these hearings. Some, such as Mostowich Lumber Limited, had worked in this area for decades, growing from a husband and wife operation which used a portable sawmill to produce 150 thousand board feet in 1945 to a firm that, by 1956, was processing 5 million board feet per year. Others, such as Northroad Lumber and Building Supplies, had just started operations. All the small operators were driven by the same concern—the Forest Service was not giving them access to the volumes of timber they needed in order to grow. At the other end of the spectrum sat giant integrated firms. Alberta's established pulp mills, St. Regis and Procter and Gamble, were there. They were joined by B. C. Forest Products, one of the firms then dominating the British Columbia forest industry. Even Nelson Skalbania, the flamboyant, Vancouver entrepreneur who won and lost fortunes with amazing speed and had negligible experience in the forest products sector came to Alberta in search of fibre.

Among these proposals, the B. C. Forest Products plan stood out as one of the most ambitious. Its promises were grand, perhaps predictably so given the aggressive expansionary posture the firm had struck in the Canadian forest industry in the 1970s. To satisfy the government's insistence that the coal mining town of Grande Cache should benefit from the use of this timber area, the company offered a twenty-five million dollar sawmill in Grande Cache, a sawmill that would employ 225 workers and churn out 120 million board feet of lumber every year. The Grande Cache sawmill was not, however, the centre-piece of the proposal. The priority it received in the B. C. Forest Products proposal was designed to satisfy the government's political interests in diversi-fying the economy of a one-industry town. The heart of the B. C. Forest Prod-ucts initiative rested in its plans for Obed, a village perched near the highest point on the Yellowhead Highway midway between Edson and Hinton. There, an instant town would be born. A sawmill nearly as large and nearly as expen-sive as that planned for Grande Cache was proposed. More significantly, the company planned to spend $165 million and build a five hundred tonne per day newsprint plant in Obed as well. In total, B. C. Forest Products pledged to invest $230 million and create more than one thousand permanent jobs if it was granted exclusive harvesting rights to the unallocated timber within the Berland-Fox Creek area. In July 1980 B. C. Forest Products received the prize which brought it to Alberta—an FMA conferring these exclusive rights. Apart from the Grande Cache sawmill, a perpetual money loser, B. C. Forest Prod-ucts never proceeded with the other elements of its development scheme. Buf-feted by the falling pulp prices of the 1982 recession, a large debt-load in-curred through rapid expansion and accentuated by high interest rates, and substantial corporate losses in 1982 and 1983, B. C. Forest Products reneged on the major development commitments of its FMA. Market conditions crip-pled its grand design. In default of the FMA's key provisions, the province stripped the company of its rights to the Berland-Fox Creek area.

The recession of the early 1980s claimed other forestry megaproject schemes as victims. The government's efforts to attract a large pulp mill to exploit the one million hectare Brazeau Timber Development Area in west central Alberta came to nothing as well. In the summer of 1982 the forestry caucus heard the proposals of several suitors. The most grandiose plans were Makin Project Initiators' offer of a one hundred and sixty million dollar pulp and paper mill and a $970 million integrated forestry operation proposed by Atco Limited and Northwoods Mills Limited—a Noranda subsidiary. Again, the combination of depressed markets and skyrocketing interest rates proved to be an insurmountable obstacle to the megaproject dream.

The slow, sometimes stumbling, pace of development, marked by unkept promises and scaled down projects, was due then to a variety of factors. Pulp prices during the 1970s generally were too low to justify the high capital costs of building new facilities. Procter and Gamble used this rationale to argue against the construction in the Grande Cache area of either a bleached kraft pulp mill or the newsprint mill B. C. Forest Products proposed:

The capital cost of an economical-sized bleached kraft pulp mill would be in the range of 300 to 400 million dollars in today's costs. Since it requires some four to five years to design, engineer, and construct a pulp mill, the final cost of such a facility near Grande Cache could well approach one half billion dollars. Today's pulp mill prices simply will not justify this magnitude of an investment, and forecasts of prices and market conditions, as well as cost escalations, do not indicate that the future will be much better.[19]

Even allowing for a healthy measure of self-interest in Procter and Gamble's position—as a purchaser of softwood chips there was a commercial logic to limiting the number of outlets for pulp chips—the company's doubts about the commercial viability of pulp mills were shared by others. A forestry economics consulting firm, hired by the province to recommend an optimum forest industry development strategy, concluded in 1977 that kraft pulp prices were too low to attract new investments. Prices would have to rise by more than 20 percent before new mills would begin to look attractive. St. Regis Corporation, one of B. C. Forest Products' competitors for the Berland-Fox Creek timber area, argued that the viability of the pulp mill and paper making facilities it proposed to add to its Hinton facilities depended upon the higher profit margins the proposal's associated lumber mills would deliver. Integrated forestry operations were like meat packing plants. "Our proposal . . . ," explained a senior St. Regis official, "needs the lumber produced from the best parts of the resource to offset the wood unsuitable for sawmill operation that is processed into pulp and paper just as a meat packing plant's viability depends on the top cuts of offset the hamburger [sic] . . . ."[20]

The lustre of megaproject development was also tarnished by the energy boom that Alberta experienced after the oil crisis of 1973. The frantic rush to find oil and pump it out of the ground drove labour costs skyward. Alberta's reputation as a relatively low wage jurisdiction was cracking under the pressure this boom was having upon the construction sector. For example, average weekly earnings in construction rose by 38 percent in the twelve months stretching from June 1975 to June 1976. Forestry labour costs were undoubtedly going to be inflated for as long as the boom lasted. For the pulp and paper industry these circumstances generally made investment unattractive—unless public financing could be massaged from government. As the consulting firm of Paul H. Jones and Associates suggested: "In the near future neither Canadian nor foreign companies are likely to consider investment in new pulp and paper facilities in Canada unless there is substantial public funding of any such new ventures to pay the costs of financing."[21]

This observation returns us to a point made earlier—the reluctance of the provincial government to play the role of financier. We have already seen the refusal of the Social Credit government to underwrite MacMillan Bloedel's proposal. There are signs from the early 1980s that the Lougheed government, despite its professed commitment to the diversification of the provincial economy, was also determined not to play the financier's role. Companies and the proponents of pulp mill projects sought, but were refused, government financial assistance. John Zaozirny, the province's minister of Energy and Natural Resources, reportedly rejected in 1984 a request from the municipality of Fox Creek that the province extend a loan guarantee to the troubled B. C. Forest Products project.[22] Makin's failure to proceed with a pulp mill in Drayton Valley offers a well-publicized example of the province's refusal to come to the aid of an interested investor. In February 1985 Stewart Behie, Makin Pulp and Paper Limited's vice president, warned that it would take its $365 million project out of Alberta unless the province offered his company an FMA and a $41 million loan guarantee. Behie explained that the FMA was needed in order to attract equity partners and that the international banking community insisted upon government loan guarantees. The government's response was blunt. "We are not in the philanthropic business," replied Hugh Planche, the province's economic development minister. Without assurances from Makin that its project had secure funding the government would not lend financial assistance to the company. The project died.

To some extent this reluctance to assist the forest industry, even as energy prices weakened, reflected the government's confidence that the bloom would soon return to the energy economy. This attitude was a holdover from the late 1970s, a time when the government and its advisors believed that an employment crisis was unlikely to appear in the province until at least 1995. The counsel of the late 1970s, adopt a "hands off" approach to the forestry sector, remained popular. This approach called for the government to retain the essence of its regulatory system, allow development to proceed according to the cues of the market, and avoid extensive public involvement in the manufacturing side of the forestry sector. Until the mid-1980s there also was not any political imperative for the Lougheed government to adopt anything other than a "hands-off" approach. Lougheed's administration enjoyed unparalleled political support throughout Alberta, support that resulted from more than simply rosy economic times. After his first election and with his treasury awash in petrodollars Lougheed was in a perfect position to practice a shrewd type of political budgeting. Political support was purchased through explosive public sector expenditure growth that was timed to coincide with provincial election campaigns.

If the late 1980s was to be a period when the provincial government raided its coffers in order to accelerate the pace of pulp mill development, in the 1970s this dubious role was more often than not played by the federal government. The first Alberta project to benefit from federal financial assistance was, as noted earlier, the Procter and Gamble mill in Grande Prairie. As in the MacMillan Bloedel case, the province was not interested in contributing to the mill's financing. The one financial concession that Procter and Gamble did win was a cost-sharing agreement with the Lougheed government to install pollution abatement technology to meet new environmental standards. The company argued that they were the only company in Canada that had to meet these standards and won Lougheed's approval to contribute 50 percent of the seven million dollar cost of installing the new technology.[23] The federal government proved to be more sympathetic to easing whatever strain financing this project placed upon Procter and Gamble. The company received a grant of twelve million dollars from Canada for building the Grande Prairie mill.

Financing a portion of the Procter and Gamble project was not the last Alberta forest products venture aided by the federal treasury. The Department of Regional Economic Expansion (DREE) believed that the forests offered an important possible foundation for increasing employment and economic production in the Lesser Slave Lake Special Area. "At the present time," reported DREE's minister, "my Department can help to build on that foundation by assisting in studies of the resource base and the market possibilities and by providing incentives for private investment in wood-using processing and manufacturing facilities."[24] The federal government went on to sponsor several other wood processing projects in the 1970s. According to one forestry consulting firm, the federal assistance offered to Alberta Aspen Board Limited and North American Stud Mills Limited, two firms established in the Lesser Slave Lake area which exploited the province's underutilized stocks of aspen, was ill-considered. "Federal financing," concluded Jones and Associates, "appears to have been granted in the absence of feasibility studies for the two separate units." Soon after these two companies opened their doors, they failed.

An appeal to DREE became a common feature of proposals to exploit Alberta's forests in the early 1970s. In September 1972, when the Whitecourt-Fox Creek area was placed on the timber development market three of the five proposals made to the Alberta Forest Service were either contingent upon receiving DREE assistance or certainly hoped to win some level of federal subsidization for the planned facilities. Weyerhaeuser Canada Limited was one of two suitors who made their development proposals contingent upon receiving federal subsidization. Simpson Timber, a private Seattle-based corporation that ultimately won an FMA for the Whitecourt timber block, felt that its intentions fit the aims of DREE and signalled its intention to try to take advantage of this potential source of capital. The other successful applicant, Fox Creek Lumber Limited, a consortium of four Alberta sawmill operators, did not plan to apply for DREE assistance since their proposal to develop the Fox Creek timber block fell outside DREE's geographical boundaries. Only North Canadian Forest Industries Limited, wholly owned by Canfor, disavowed any interest in seeking the assistance of the DREE.

The public hearings held in 1973 regarding the forestry proposals for the Whitecourt-Fox Creek area offered a window into the competition between firms for timber exploitation rights, a window that government by the decade's end would be anxious to close. In this competition, the interest in DREE funding was used by North Canadian Forest Industries to question the economic viability of the projects offered by its competitors. Senior North Canadian officials urged provincial politicians and senior forestry officials to regard suspiciously proposals that referred to DREE assistance. Were these projects economically marginal? Could they stand alone without government aid? A senior North Canadian official summarized his position by noting that "those who feel that DREE grants were important to their projects are acknowledging that to some extent their projects do not stand on their own feet economically." While companies refused to concede that their proposals were only viable with DREE support, one senior official from Simpson Timber pointed out that the criteria the Alberta Forest Service proposed to use to judge this competition—harvesting large volumes of small trees and utilizing poplar—increased the economic risks of development and justified his company's interest in DREE funding. The timber of the Whitecourt-Fox Creek area still was "beyond the economic margin." "I think a logical conclusion," Simpson Timber argued, "is that if the conversion of the kind of volumes and the kind of timber in this location, the utilization of poplar, was not a difficult task, this timber probably would have been allocated for use a long time ago."[25]

David versus Goliath

When Alberta's forestry development potential was debated in the 1970s more was at issue than whether or not the market should set the pace for development. Conflict also swirled around the issue of the industry's structure and whether or not government should reinforce or modify the established pattern. In the mid-1970s, a small number of companies dominated the wood processing sector. Seven companies processed approximately 80 percent of all the roundwood cut in the province and two-thirds of this output was shipped in a primary form to the United States. Corporate ownership structures strengthened the pull of American markets since four of the leading seven companies in the province were controlled by Americans. When the government advertised timber development areas in the 1970s questions arose about what place the Forest Service intended Alberta capital to play in this industry. Among small, independent sawmill operators the perception flourished that government wanted to turn this resource over to the large, integrated operators. Local independent operators urged government to regard suspiciously the declarations large companies, irrespective of nationality, made when they sought Alberta timber. Instead, the Forest Service was lobbied to endorse the plans of smaller Alberta-owned businesses. Those who favoured increased timber access for small operators employed statements Lougheed's Conservatives had made while in opposition to support their demands, such as the following excerpt from one of Dr. Hugh Horner's speeches:

> It seems to me we need a whole new policy for Alberta forests. It's about time we looked after our own people. The local sawmill operator has endured the hardship of initiating his industry, some of them over a very long term of up to 25 years. We say "give him a chance," don't ignore his efforts.[26]

Small companies, many with deep roots in rural Alberta, professed to have a sensitivity and commitment to rural Albertans which large corporations lacked.

Small communities were their homes and they would not betray rural Alberta's dreams of economic diversification:

It is interesting to note that at or near the same time we received our rights to operate our quotas, MacMillan Bloedel had an opportunity to operate nearly 4 million acres of Alberta forest land near Whitecourt. They made great promises. Because these promises did not materialize, millions of dollars of revenue were lost by the Province as well as the people of this area. Let us not be fooled again by the fiery words of a giant. If we take our development slowly, of the kind we know can succeed, we can progressively develop our forest and our town.[27]

The source of the independents' frustration was the decision of government to reserve timber areas for pulp and paper projects. The complaints of Mac Millar, one of the principals of Western Construction and Lumber Company, were typical. This enterprise, later renamed Millar Western Industries Limited and destined in the late 1980s to receive a very generous government loan for a pulp mill in Whitecourt, had cut timber in the Whitecourt area since 1923. Between 1956 and 1966 Millar's company repeatedly asked the Forest Service for additional timber in this area. The government refused because the Forest Service "was in negotiation with various companies concerning a possible pulp mill and they did not wish to release any timber for sale in the area."

From a distance, it appeared that the province's timber quota system, introduced in 1966, should have solved Millar's problems. The timber quota system broadened the guarantee of secure, long-term forest access first offered by the Forestry Management Agreements. Each quota gave its holder the right to harvest a designated percentage of an area's annual allowable cut for renewable periods of twenty years. But, according to Millar, the quota system created problems for any company interested in expansion. A company's quota basically equalled the share of an area's production taken by the operator between April 1960 and March 1964. Millar complained that, since his company had been refused timber between 1956 and 1966, the quota system did not give him the timber he needed to expand his operations. With large companies entering the industry promising permanent employment to seasonal forestry workers, Millar's competitiveness hinged upon his ability to get enough timber so that he too could operate on a year-round basis. Other possible roads to expansion had proved to be dead ends for his company. While it was possible to purchase the quotas held by other operators, quota-holders were generally unwilling to part with them. This placed Millar in "a rather desperate" situation. He urged the Foresty Caucus to find a solution:

> before there is a massive allocation of our timber resources. . . . Surely after over 20 years of requesting more timber we might get a favourable reply now. We are an Alberta company owned and operated by Albertans employing Albertans for over the last 50 years.[28]

Later events in the mid-1980s would add a measure of irony to Millar's Alberta-first rhetoric. With his own thirst for growth quenched by the government's agreement to finance more than one-half of his new pulp mill complex in Whitecourt, Millar apparently was content to see the province allocate the majority of the province's remaining forests to foreign multinationals.

Whether the venue for examining forestry development proposals was Whitecourt and Fox Creek in 1973 or Fox Creek and Grande Cache in 1979, Millar's sentiment was shared widely. Several regional economic development boards, town councils, and chambers of commerce rallied to the side of smaller, already established, sawmill owners. Arguments that the arrival of pulp mills in Alberta led to the extinction of independent, small quota holders struck a receptive chord in these small communities. The animosity and resentment the independents felt towards government and large corporations occasionally bubbled to the surface during public hearings. Gerald Hecht, the owner of Northroad Lumber and Building Supplies complained:

> I figure right now myself there is enough big companies around us without letting any more in to take up what is left [sic]. In the future, I think we should think about the future years to come. What the hell are our children going to do? If they want timber, where are they going to get it? What is going to be left?[29]

The anger of small operators highlighted the crossroads that Alberta's forest industry had reached and the Forest Service's refusal to take the path favouring the smaller independents. Jones and Associates issued warnings that additional sawmill quotas "in areas with pulp and paper potential" could kill any prospects of pulp and paper development. Such warnings simply strengthened the resolve of Fred McDougall, the province's deputy minister of renewable resources, to ensure that the province set aside the timber needed to feed integrated forest products complexes. McDougall, a native Albertan who, after graduating from the University of New Brunswick, had spent most of his professional life in the Alberta Forest Service, gained a reputation among the independents as a manager who had eyes only for the major integrated forest products companies.

Did a government have to allocate millions of hectares of forest lands to a company in order to promote pulp and paper development? Developments in British Columbia suggest that this generosity was not always required. The pulp industry which developed during the 1960s in the interior of British Columbia did so despite the fact that most of the allowable cut had already been allocated to sawmill companies. In 1962, the British Columbia government added the Pulpwood Harvesting Area Agreement to its forest management system. Through this device the British Columbia government effectively superimposed a pulp industry upon the Interior's established sawmilling economy. Under these agreements pulp companies were required to purchase the chips and logging residues produced by sawmills. Sawmills responded eagerly to the opportunities these agreements created for them and invested in the log debarking and chipping equipment needed to take advantage of the new situation. The overwhelming response of sawmill operators to the government's creation of a chip market proved to be an economic boon to the pulp companies who were able to purchase chips from sawmills for less than it would have cost them to manufacture their own chips. So confident in these arrangements were three of the five pulp ventures started via these pulpwood agreements that they never incorporated debarking and chipping facilities into their complexes. Whatever concerns might have remained about security of wood supply also were addressed by the minister's commitment to direct the chips produced in a harvesting area to the pulp companies. According to the Pearse Commission on Forest Resources, the Pulpwood Harvesting Area Agreement, was in principle, an ingenious device. It has facilitated the establishment and growth of the Interior pulp industry while at the same time providing a substantial stimulus to the pre-existing sawmilling industry. Thus the forest industry was encouraged to achieve the advantages of integration, without necessarily inducing horizontal integration and concentration of resource rights in a few large firms. The resulting implications for fuller utilization of timber and for resource management generally have been profound.[30]

During the rounds of public hearings held in the 1970s, Alberta's foresters

and politicians were reminded that independent sawmills could supply whatever chips pulp mills required. When Weyerhaeuser lobbied the forestry caucus for timber rights in the Whitecourt-Fox Creek area in 1973 the company
pointed out that the existence of its huge 1,250 tonne per day Kamloops pulp
mill depended entirely upon the chips the mill purchased from forty-two in-
dependently owned sawmills. In 1979, North Canadian Forest Industries, a
Canfor (Canadian Forest Products) subsidiary, cited its British Columbia experience when it urged the government to base the expansion of the pulp sector on chips produced by sawmills:

In B. C. Canfor produces 1,822 tonnes of pulp and paper per day from
three pulp mills which are totally dependent on residue chips from the
lumber and the plywood industry. We have found that we can operate
these three pulp mills entirely on residue chips where only 28 percent of
the chips are from the Canfor affiliated mills and 72 percent is secured
from outside purchases. For the two Prince George pulp mills . . . 83
percent is secured from outside purchases.[31]

Could the Pulpwood Harvesting Area Agreement model have been adapted to
the Alberta setting? An obstacle to adapting the division of labour characteristic of the sawmilling and pulp sectors in the British Columbia Interior arguably arose out of Alberta's interest in increasing the harvest of previously
underutilized deciduous species, particularly aspen poplar. In 1976, the forest
industry took only 4 percent of the annual allowable cut for deciduous species.
When the Forest Service advertised provincial timber development areas it
stressed the importance of utilizing all available fibre resources. Until lumber
markets changed there was no incentive for sawmill operators to turn away
from spruce and other preferred conifers to species such as aspen. The reluctance of sawmills to utilize aspen did not mean, however, that integrated pulp
production offered a more likely route to the extensive use of aspen. There too
the market was the constraint. Alberta's distance from final markets under-
mined the competitiveness of hardwood pulp production. Market conditions
had to change before the Pulpwood Harvesting Area Agreement model could
provide an alternative approach to allocating the province's resources between
the pulp and sawmilling sectors.

On the Periphery: Forestry and
the Environmental Movement

The use of the phrase "fibre syndrome" to summarize the prevailing attitudes towards the forests during the postwar economic boom suggests that a critique of forestry development did not figure prominently in the repertoire of environmental groups. "The issues of the 70s," recalled one of the founders of STOP (Save Tomorrow Oppose Pollution), a high-profile Edmonton-based environmental group during the 1970s, "were mainly ones of emissions—what's legal to put out of your smokestack and into the water."[32] Technology was viewed as a useful ally in the battle against emissions. Environmentalists, using a phrase that Alberta Environment would use years later in regards to pulp mills, demanded that corporations adopt the "best available technology" in order to mitigate pollution. This preoccupation on the part of some environmentalists complemented the public's perceptions of where the most serious environmental problems lay. In 1974, when a sample of Albertans was asked to identify the most serious environmental problem in the province 50 percent of the respondents mentioned pollution in one form or another. Only 9 percent mentioned the misuse of the province's lands and forests by industry.

The peripheral position of forestry within Alberta's environmental politics was illustrated in other ways as well. First, in terms of public and group interest, opportunities to address the environmental consequences of forestry practices were neither catalysts for the formation of environmental groups nor for extensive group activity. In 1978, the Environment Council of Alberta (ECA) travelled across the province and held well-publicized public hearings into the environmental effects of forestry operations in Alberta. The strength of public concern regarding forestry practices differed greatly from one part of the province to the next. Few concerns were expressed in northern Alberta, more concerns were heard in the Slave Lake and Lac La Biche areas, while the most intense concerns were expressed in the eastern slopes region of the Rocky Mountains. As a prelude to these hearings the council commissioned a comprehensive series of information bulletins and invited at least fifteen hundred individuals and groups to participate in its information meetings and public hearings. While 188 briefs were presented to the ECA during its five weeks of hearings the vast majority of submissions came from individual citizens or ad hoc collections of local residents. Little formal group formation resulted from this public hearing process. Only seven environmental groups, all formed well in advance of the announcement of the ECA investigation, participated in these hearings.

Despite their small numbers, conservation and environmental groups none-theless offered fundamental critiques of the province's forest use policies. The Alberta Fish and Game Association (AFGA), the province's oldest conservation group, argued that key commitments in the province's forest policy—inte-grated resource management and multiple use—were essentially empty. Its call for a Co-ordinated Resource Management Plan asked McDougall's offi-cials to respect the principle of multiple use by assigning greater importance to values associated with alternative forest uses such as wilderness preservation and wildlife enhancement. The AFGA's agenda also included the recommenda-tion that timber cutting practices be modified wherever the dominant use of land would be logging. Its opposition to clearcutting prompted its endorse-ment of selective harvesting. Where clearcutting was unavoidable the size of clearcuts should be irregular and narrower than three hundred yards to pro-tect aesthetic and wildlife values.

The distinction of offering the most fundamental challenge to the growth of the forest industry probably belonged to the Alberta Wilderness Associa-tion (AWA). Created in 1968 out of anger over the damage the energy industry was doing to the eastern slopes, the AWA's founders were people who depended upon wilderness for their livelihood—ranchers, guides, and outfitters—as well as wilderness recreational enthusiasts. Its fundamental interest—wilderness preservation—was beyond the reach of technological solutions. In its brief the AWA attacked the fibre syndrome. The AWA, joined by the National and Provin-cial Parks Association of Canada (NPPA), also had asked the government to ensure that some wilderness would be protected when decisions were made regarding the future of the forests of the western Swan Hills. "The main con-flict which the Government must resolve," argued the AWA/NPPA, "is between the wilderness value of the western Swan Hills and the activities of the forest industry."[33] By 1978 the provincial government had resolved this conflict—in favour of the forest industry. Virtually all of the land in the western Swan Hills was allocated to timber companies. No effort was made to accommodate even a portion of the approximately 1036 square kilometre recreational wilderness proposed by the AWA/NPPAC. Consequently, the AWA urged the Environment Council of Alberta to recommend that the government reexamine the quota and FMA timber allocations in that area and to place an eight- to fifteen-year moratorium on extensive cutting.

The ECA hearings underlined two features of forestry's initial standing within environmental politics in Alberta. First, only a handful of environmental organizations were concerned about the growth of the forest industry in Alberta. Second, these groups offered a very similar, somewhat narrow, critique of the forest industry. All focussed upon the fibre syndrome and criticized foresters, in both the public and private sectors, for paying insufficient attention to the value of forests as locales for recreational activity, wilderness, and wildlife.

The government's reaction to the ECA final report and recommendations confirms the opinion that, by the late 1970s, the government was deaf to the ECA's counsel. As the rush to authorize pulp and paper mill developments in the mid-1980s demonstrated, the recommendations that government not subsidize pulp mill projects and that new pulp mills should be designed to provide zero pollution to provincial waterways were ignored. Similarly, the call for public input into how forest lands should be used *before* specific industrial use proposals were either invited or entertained, was ignored totally—with fateful consequences for policy a decade hence. The notion that the primary use of forests should be anything other than fibre production scandalized Alberta's policy makers. "Where," complained Fred McDougall five years after the ECA report, "can we log? There's a limit as to how much can be left to the undisturbed wilderness."[34]

No sooner had the ECA issued its final report and recommendations than the AWA, the AFGA, and the NPPA were given the opportunity to focus their critique, not upon forestry operations in the abstract, but instead upon a much more tangible target—the invitation to forest companies for development proposals for the Berland-Fox Creek area in west central Alberta. The marginal stature of the ECA within the provincial government was signalled by the cabinet's willingness to let the Department of Energy and Natural Resources issue this invitation in November 1978—months before the release of the ECA recommendations. Ostensibly, the Berland-Fox Creek hearings were held to make information available to the public and to secure the public's views on the desirability of specific proposals. Yet, the real commitment appears to have been only to symbolic participation—the structure of the hearing process made it difficult for members of the public to participate knowledgeably. The AWA, for example, was frustrated in its efforts to receive information from the Alberta Forest Service and the Department of Recreation and Parks. Moreover, the AWA did not receive summaries of the timber development proposals until the hearings were only one week away!

In its brief to the Berland-Fox Creek public hearings the AWA reiterated its view that basic land use alternatives must be debated publicly before forest companies were invited to submit development proposals. The protection of wildlands and wildlife habitat had to be designated as the primary management objective in a portion of this area. "What is necessary for the Fox Creek/ Berland area," the AWA insisted, "is a completely new approach to land management—one that does not lock up all of the land for a single prime use, while trying to accommodate as many of the other uses as is possible under various compromises." An environmental impact assessment—one that would consider the effects of timber harvesting on the soil, watershed, grazing, fisheries, wildlife, wildlife habitat, and recreation resources—should be completed and subjected to public comment before the forest service made any firm commitment on an annual allowable cut of timber from this area. Similar concerns were raised in presentations from the AFGA and the National and Provincial Parks Association. The AFGA used these public hearings to renew its quest for a coordinated management plan. The NPPA urged the government to introduce a land use zoning system where forestry would be declared unsuitable in certain areas because it would lead to erosion or intrude upon critical fish and wildlife habitat.

Ironically, these arguments received considerable support from the Fish and Wildlife division, one of the agencies encompassed under the umbrella of the very prodevelopment Department of Energy and Natural Resources. In February 1978 all of the government's wildlife staff in the Edson district were killed in a tragic plane crash. The task of rebuilding the Fish and Wildlife presence in the Edson area was given to Michael Bloomfield, a freshly recruited biologist who during his years in the Alberta public service was instrumental in efforts to protect Alberta's caribou population. Able to recruit his own staff, Bloomfield assembled a team that began to accumulate baseline information on the fish and wildlife resources of the Berland area. The hope of these officials was that, with this information in hand, they could persuade government to commit to more than just timber and petroleum extraction in this area. Baseline information regarding the area's fish and wildlife resources could be used to seek a commitment that forest development would not intrude upon critical wildlife habitat in the Berland area. Certain areas would have to be placed beyond the reach of the forest companies. The presentation Bloomfield made at the Berland-Fox Creek hearings, authorized by his division, argued that Fish and Wildlife needed more funds and personnel to study the area's game populations and their habitat requirements before timber allocations were made. In blunt language the paper warned that the province's fisheries and wildlife would be threatened in the future unless the existing approach to land management was changed. "In light of the intensity of regional and provincial development," Fish and Wildlife argued, "it would be impossible and irresponsible to continue to use this approach. The proposed logging developments can not be evaluated in an isolated manner and the review process must seriously consider the implications of other activities within the boundaries of the proposal and in adjacent areas."[35]

Government responded to Bloomfield's work in two totally different ways. The formal response was what we would expect when public servants turn in excellent performances—a letter of commendation and a double increment salary raise. The informal response was more ominous. He was ordered to Edmonton to meet with senior department officials. There, Bloomfield claims that he was warned that he was in danger of going too far in his advocacy of multiple use resource management. His enthusiasm for this approach to resource use issues conflicted with the department's interest in finding a forest company that would take on the job of building an integrated forest products complex and bring development to this corner of Alberta. Bloomfield alleges that senior department officials made it very clear that they never wanted to see his Fox Creek performance repeated. Moreover, he alleges that after the Berland-Fox Creek hearings senior officials in the department took a variety of steps that ultimately drove him out of the public service.[36] His division's reward for believing that portions of forests should be used for something other than fodder for hungry sawmills and pulp mills, according to Vivian Pharis of the AWA, was to have its jurisdiction "essentially squelched. They have never been able to say no to development since 1979. . . . "[37] Both outcomes were suggestive of the primary lesson the Alberta Forest Service and others within the government who favoured forestry megaprojects learned from both the ECA hearings and the Berland-Fox Creek hearings—public examination of proposals for timber area developments invites criticism of the fibre syndrome, criticism that is heretical for those who believe the syndrome is a sign of health, not of sickness. Although the voices of critics of forestry megaprojects were seldom heard by the public, the government moved to ensure that the stage provided for these critics by the Berland-Fox Creek hearings would be dismantled permanently. "The province was so upset by the fact that the public, like us," recalled Pharis, "came and spoke out, that the Fish and Wildlife Division spoke out at it that it decided then and there to curtail that kind of public involvement in any further forest decisions and that's why we have had all these massive agreements signed basically in secret."[38] Little wonder that Pharis regards these public hearings as a real turning point in terms of the way forestry, fish, and wildlife issues were handled in Alberta.

1. The phrase was coined by the Environment Council of Alberta in its study of the environmental effects of forestry operations in Alberta. For a discussion see Alberta, Environment Council of Alberta, *The Environmental Effects of Forestry Operations in Alberta: Report and Recommendations* (Edmonton: Douglas Printing, 1979), 96–98.
2. F. L. C. Reed & Associates, *Forest Management in Canada, Volume 1* (Environment Canada, Canadian Forestry Service, 1978), 39, 10.
3. O. C. 1250/54, section 9. These figures are metric equivalents. The dues in the original FMA were calculated by the cord. In 1956, section 9 of the FMA was modified to allow the coniferous timber dues schedule to be waived with the approval of both parties and instead levy a timber dues of twenty-one cents per cubic metre for all species of softwood.
4. W. R. Hanson, *Forest Utilization and its Environmental Effects in Alberta* (study prepared for the Environment Conservation Authority, Spring 1973), 47.
5. Alberta, Environment Conservation Authority, *Perspectives II: The Forest Industry in Alberta* (Environment Conservation Authority: November 1977), 14.
6. Desmond I. Crossley, "We Did It Our Way" (as interviewed by Peter J. Murphy and James M. Parker, the University of Alberta, September 1985), Manuscript Group 84–69, University of Alberta Archives, 19.
7. Crossley, "We Did it Our Way," 16.
8. Peter Clancy, Department of Political Science, St. Francis Xavier University, letter to author, 23 September 1993.
9. Dr. Bruce Dancik, interview with author, Edmonton, Alberta, 3 May 1991.
10. Eric A. Bailey, "Good Forest Management for the Future," *Environment Views*, 12:2 (September 1989), 11.
11. Crossley, "We Did It Our Way," 16.
12. MacMillan Bloedel Limited, "Summary Review—Plans for Whitecourt Development—as of April 1969," 4. See J. O. Hemmingsen, executive vice president, MacMillan Bloedel Limited, letter to the Honourable H. E. Strom, premier, 1 May 1969.
13. J. O. Hemmingsen, executive vice president, MacMillan Bloedel Limited, letter to the Honourable H. E. Strom, premier, 17 July 1969.
14. Honourable Harry E. Strom, letter to J. O. Hemmingsen, executive vice president, MacMillan Bloedel Limited, 13 August 1969.
15. Elmer Borstad, interview with Kathleen Stokes, Grande Prairie, Alberta, 24 July 1992.

16. Jerrard helped negotiate Procter and Gamble's initial agreement with Alberta. Eric Jerrard, former public and governmental relations manager, Procter and Gamble, interview with Kathleen Stokes, Grande Prairie, 31 August 1992.
17. Edward G. Harness, vice president, the Proctor and Gamble Company, letter to Arnold J. Donovan, Minister of Lands and Forests, 12 September 1969.
18. Jerrard interview.
19. David Shores, vice president and manager of Western Operations, Procter and Gamble Cellulose Limited in Alberta, Energy and Natural Resources, Alberta Forest Service, *Public Hearings on Proposed Timber Developments, Berland-Fox Creek Area, Volume 2* (1979), 220. Constructing a TMP mill he went on to observe would be "highly questionable" and "flirting with economic disaster."
20. Ken Hall, vice president and general manager, St. Regis (Alberta) Ltd., in Alberta, Energy and Natural Resources, Alberta Forest Service, *Public Hearings on Proposed Timber Developments, Berland-Fox Creek Area, Volume 1* (1979), 91.
21. Paul H. Jones & Associates Limited, *Alberta Forest Industry Development Prospects (prepared for the Alberta Forest Service)*, Vancouver, 1977, 44.
22. David Holehouse, "Print Mill Spreads Seeds of Discontent in Fox Creek," *The Edmonton Journal*, 23 March 1988.
23. Jerrard interview.
24. Canada, Department of Regional Economic Expansion, *Alberta: Economic Circumstances and Opportunities*, 1973, 39.
25. Alberta, Department of Lands and Forests, Alberta Forest Service, *Public Hearings on Proposed Timber Developments Whitecourt-Fox Creek Area, June 4, 5 1973*, 84.
26. Ibid, 97.
27. Mel Meunier, Manager, Fox Creek Lumber, in Alberta Forest Service, *Public Hearings on Proposed Timber Developments Whitecourt-Fox Creek Area, June 4, 5 1973*, 13.
28. Mac Millar, Western Construction and Lumber Company Limited, in Alberta Forest Service, *Public Hearings on Proposed Timber Developments Whitecourt-Fox Creek Area, June 4, 5, 1973*, 48.
29. Alberta Forest Service, *Public Hearings on Proposed Timber Developments, Berland-Fox Creek Area, Volume 1*, 270.
30. British Columbia, Royal Commission on Forest Resources, *Timber Rights and Forest Policy in British Columbia, Volume 1* (Victoria: Queen's Printer, 1976), 107.
31. Roy Bickell, vice president and general manager, North Canadian Forest Industries Limited, *Public Hearings on Proposed Timber Developments, Berland-Fox Creek Area, Volume 1* (1979), 246.
32. Louise Swift, interview with author, 2 June 1992.
33. Alberta Wilderness Association and National & Provincial Parks Association, *The Western Swan Hills—Alberta's Forgotten Wilderness* (1976), 24.
34. "No Retreat Planned from Forest Logging," *Calgary Herald*, 7 March 1984.

CHAPTER 2

The Visible Hand:
Forestry and Diversification

ADAM SMITH'S INVISIBLE HAND WILL NOT BUILD PULP MILLS,
PARTICULARLY IN THE KINDS OF FOREST AREAS THAT REMAIN AVAILABLE
IN CANADA FOR EXPLOITATION. IT REQUIRES A GREAT DEAL OF
COORDINATION BETWEEN PRIVATE INTERESTS AND PUBLIC INTEREST,
AND THE PUBLIC INTEREST BEING WILLING TO TAKE A RISK FOR
DEVELOPMENT. THAT RISK HAS PRIMARILY POLITICAL DIMENSIONS FOR
THE PUBLIC SECTOR, BUT FINANCIAL DIMENSIONS FOR
THE PRIVATE SECTOR.
—GEORGE F. LANDEGGER, "INVESTMENT IN CANADA: AN INDUSTRIAL
PROSPECTIVE," *FORUM ON FOREST INVESTMENT*

 The story of Alberta's forestry strategy after 1985 is, in large measure, the story of the industry's move into the commercial development of the province's northern hardwood resource—mainly trembling aspen. Alberta's largest ecoregion—the boreal mixed wood forest—encompasses 43 percent of the province and blankets most of the province north of Edmonton. The principal commercial softwood, or coniferous, species are white spruce and lodgepole pine and the main hardwood, or deciduous, trees are two species of poplar—aspen and balsam. Trembling aspen is the dominant hardwood, making up 32 percent of the province's total growing stock, but until the early 1980s its commercial potential in Alberta was basically nil. Aspen was dismissed as a "weed," a nuisance that (or so it was implied) had no utility or economic value, and hence was not worth conserving. According to one school of thought, aspen only became attractive to industry when a technological breakthrough allowed the conversion of hardwoods into an attractive pulp finish to be used in making fine paper and other products.

A good deal of important forest products research was indeed carried out in Alberta on aspen and its commercial uses, but we would argue that developments in world markets and changes in provincial policy were more important than resolving the technical problems involved in using short-fibred hardwoods in pulping. No major technological breakthrough occurred. As was the case with the commercial exploitation of the tar sands in north-east Alberta, the basic technology involved in upgrading the resource was known: it was the cost and risks of producing and transporting synthetic oil and hardwood pulp on a very large scale in remote northern Alberta that were the true unknowns. Could these commodities compete with alternatives from around the world, and could investors be found with the control of capital, technology, and markets? Pulp production from eucalyptus hardwoods had been feasible in Tasmania and other jurisdictions since the 1940s, while aspen had been adopted for pulp mills in Minnesota and elsewhere well before the Japanese and others invested in new mills in northern Alberta. Paper makers had discovered that the use of hardwood pulp not only could decrease costs but also could enhance certain paper qualities.

Following the "chip shock" of 1979-80, when the major Japanese paper producers were surprised by a doubling of the price of the softwood chips which they purchased from the American forest industry, users of market pulp initiated a shift away from higher-cost traditional softwood suppliers, such as Scandinavia and the United States Pacific Northwest, towards lower-cost plantation eucalyptus in South America, Spain, and Portugal. For the paper industry, the issue was not so much whether aspen could be used to make good pulp as it was whether it could be done in remote northern Alberta, far from the principal markets, and cheaply enough to compete with Brazil and other producers for a share of the growing market in hardwood pulps. The Environment Council of Alberta correctly noted at the end of the 1970s that world market conditions, not technological limits, posed the most serious obstacle to aspen developments: hardwood pulp was in substantial demand for a number of products, "but there are still plentiful hardwood supplies closer to final markets able to undersell the Alberta product." Only when the supply of softwoods in North America became tighter and market prices for hardwoods increased would the commercial exploitation of Alberta's immense aspen forests be viable; and even then it would be debatable whether multinational and Canadian pulp and paper corporations would invest without a good deal of government support and risk insurance. The industry's view, as the chairman of Parsons and Whittemore put it, was that "Adam Smith's invisible hand will not build pulp mills, particularly in the kinds of forest areas that remain available in Canada for exploitation"; but the Environment Council thought that costly government assistance to the forest industry should be unnecessary:

At some time in the future, the attraction of aspen conveniently located to markets and transportation will balance off against distant and inaccessible softwoods. No unusual measures or levels of assistance will be necessary to utilize aspen as a substitute for softwoods. Market forces will bring forth the processing capacity and the necessary harvesting equipment with only the normal ongoing programs of assistance to research and development.[1]

The Environment Council's stress on market forces was perhaps naive—it neglected the controversial issue of who was to build and pay for the very costly transportation infrastructure that would be required to move pulp and other forest products from the north to markets. But *laissez-faire* on forestry was not unpalatable advice in the context of the great energy boom of the late seventies. The council's report was published in 1979, at a moment when the Alberta economy was already overheating because of rising energy prices and the impact of new oil, oil sands, and natural gas investments on costs in construction, engineering, and services. In such circumstances, the government of Alberta was not likely to stress the economy even further by sponsoring major capital spending on forestry projects, driving up labour and other costs to the disadvantage of the oil and gas sector. During the boom years, and indeed until late 1981, when signs of the coming bust in the oil industry first appeared, Alberta's unemployment rate stood at 3 percent or less; there was little or no room for the expansion of the forestry sector until oil and gas and their ancillary industries cooled off.

Whether the government of Alberta was interested in forestry expansion seems to have depended as well on the individual who held the premier's office. We have seen that neither Ernest Manning nor Harry Strom, the two postwar Social Credit premiers, had much interest in giving financial concessions to multinational forest companies proposing major projects in Alberta—not even to those who thought Social Credit must match the generosity of Alabama! For not only were big forestry investments unnecessary while oil and gas spending remained high, but such concessions would also likely trig-

ger similar controversial demands for aid from other sectors of business. Social Credit preferred a policy of extending renewable Forest Management
Agreements (FMAS) covering large timber hinterlands in exchange for corporate commitments to invest in industrial forestry projects: access to resources
and security of tenure in exchange for jobs and regional growth. Peter
Lougheed's four Conservative administrations, covering the period from August 1971 to the end of 1985, by and large retained the hands-off policy for
forestry (although Lougheed was much more interventionist in his economic
policies than his Social Credit predecessors had been). Concrete forestry development proposals were debated within and outside the Lougheed government during the oil boom period, but the industry was really of marginal interest to provincial Conservative governments until the mid-eighties when
Lougheed departed Alberta politics and world oil prices collapsed. As a Calgary
politician close to the petroleum industry who was interested in economic
diversification via higher technologies and energy-linked industries such as
petrochemicals, Lougheed evinced little interest in the relatively small forestry sector—certainly he never saw it as a significant part of the foundation
for Alberta's economic strategy—and in Lougheed's government, nothing of
importance happened without the premier's interest and approval. It was not
that Lougheed, unlike his successor, Don Getty, disapproved of government
intervention in the provincial economy (as some of his colleagues and advisors
have told us); Lougheed's governments intervened frequently in the economy.
Rather, forestry was never one of Lougheed's interests and priorities.

The prospect of waiting, in the words of the Environment Council, for
"some time in the future" for major new developments in forestry did not
please the government's top forestry officials, many of whom apparently believed that Alberta's forests were being undervalued and underutilized in part
because of the forest industry's relative lack of political support in a province
dominated by energy and agricultural interests. There was probably some truth
in this. Alberta's frustrated foresters, led by Fred McDougall, the provincial
deputy minister of renewable resources until the late 1980s when he resigned
and moved to head up Weyerhaeuser's operations in Alberta, were ambitious
professionals who resented the lowly status of Alberta's forestry sector relative
to oil and gas, a pecking order that was duplicated in their own circumstances
within the provincial bureaucracy. McDougall, who strenuously objects to the
appellation of "bureaucrat" when applied to professional foresters, did not even
head up his own department until early 1986. Prior to that date, when Don

Getty began to set forth his own economic policies, forestry was part of the renewable resources division—with fish—within the old Department of Energy and Natural Resources.

During the conflict over Getty's encouragement of pulp mills in northern Alberta, Fred McDougall became a sort of *bête noir* of environmentalists, who saw him as the backroom Rasputin exercising his baleful influence on Getty, the last of Alberta's tsars. Such reputations go with the territory in forestry policy-making, but it is fair to emphasize that, whatever his influence, McDougall was not indifferent to the ecological effects of rapid growth. He believed that only when the conventional oil and gas resources of Alberta were fully developed would the province begin to exploit its underused forests; but until then, when the interests of the oil and forestry industries conflicted, it was the trees that would get knocked down because of the oil industry's much greater economic and political clout. Better perhaps than anyone else in government, McDougall realized—and spoke in public about—how destructive some oil industry work had been to Alberta's forestry resources, and how the province's petroleum laws and regulations validated and even encouraged the destruction. McDougall estimated that hasty and ill-planned oil and gas activities had resulted in the loss of a *million* acres of Alberta forests over a forty year period, of which four hundred thousand acres contained productive softwoods.[2] We have already noted that the oil industry's environmental record has received little attention from Alberta's "green" movement, even though oil and gas activities—roads, seismic, drilling, and so on—left scars all over the province. Compared to the uproar in the late 1980s over the pulp mills and forestry projects, the oil companies' rampage in parts of the north of Alberta during the energy boom went largely unreported. Near Fort McMurray on the Athabasca River, the massive Syncrude oil sands project, bigger by far than any existing or proposed pulp mill and a major disruptive force in the same boreal forest ecosystem, was all but ignored by environmentalists when it went into production at the end of the seventies. The urban middle class which had grown up in Alberta over four decades of petroleum development did not have an interest in criticizing oil's environmental practices.

In the McDougall years, Alberta's forest management policies were based on several key assumptions as to how the province as Crown owner of the northern hardwood resources could compensate for its relative disadvantages—the great distances from the world's markets, the lack of transportation infrastructure, the lack of commercial interest in aspen—and compete with other jurisdictions for new capital investments, if market conditions improved. The assumptions require some brief description if we are to understand Don Getty's forestry initiative.

First, in order to realize the economies of scale required to lower the costs of harvesting aspen and manufacturing pulp in northern Alberta, large international forestry companies with a longer time horizon than that of local operators would be needed as investors; and to attract such firms, with their capital, know-how, and technologies, a secure forestry tenure system was the first prerequisite. Without security of tenure, for which Alberta's renewable twenty year FMAs and timber quotas were explicitly designed, longer term investments would not be made, banks would not loan capital and the forests would go uncut. Without a guarantee of access to fibre supply over a lengthy period, it was argued, the forest industry would be of the cut-and-run variety and that would only reinforce the instability of the northern communities. International forestry companies were vertically integrated, and they typically offered an internal market with their investment: for example, as part of the negotiation with government over terms, a major Japanese corporation might commit to the purchase of, say, 60 percent of the total production of pulp from a new mill, rain or shine, for export to its own paper mills in Japan. Large integrated forestry firms such as Weyerhaeuser or Daishowa were thought to have a capacity to weather downturns in the business cycle that independent operators did not enjoy—a key consideration in that forestry development was about jobs and offering stability to northern communities. In effect, through the FMAs the provincial government intended to turn over the long-term economic and environmental management of the great northern forests of Alberta to the biggest transnational firms in exchange for jobs, stability, and the development of some value-added industry, especially pulp and paper mills.

Second, because the objective was to realize large capital investments in integrated forestry/pulp and paper complexes, it was essential to avoid fragmenting the resource—for example, by allocating significant parts of it to sawmills and other small users—and to keep sufficient volumes in contiguous timber blocks, or timber development areas, to attract multinational companies looking for long-term fibre supplies and sites to manufacture pulp in accessible, stable locations. Withholding timber would not only prevent fragmentation of the resource, it would also inhibit the growth of Alberta capital in the forestry sector; and that would be resented. Small Alberta-based forestry operations, independent loggers and contractors, and Native communities using the forests all represented a threat to Fred McDougall's strategy of reserving the very large timber development areas for the integrated majors. They were each trying to get a small share of what the Crown needed to attract big capital. For their part, some of the owners of independent sawmills and other businesses that needed increased access to the resource in order to expand their operations thought the government's withholding of timber was deliberately designed to wipe out the smaller forestry companies. Whether this was accurate or not (we return to these charges later in the chapter), it was surely strange that Alberta-owned forestry businesses—of which there were several hundred—found themselves unable to obtain rights to additional supplies of timber from a government that was always complaining that the vast forestry resources in Alberta were badly "underutilized."

Third, the lack of essential transportation infrastructure in northern Alberta was understood to be the largest barrier to multinational investments in forestry; removing it would require very expensive commitments by Alberta of front-end government spending on "roads to resources," bridges, rail spurs, and so on in several regions of the north. Industries other than forestry— construction, engineering, agriculture, and oil and gas—would potentially gain from new infrastructure, but the costs to be borne by taxpayers would be high. "Most of our Alberta timber available for development is in Northern Alberta and is difficult to access," the forestry division noted in a 1985 policy paper, which, though it was prepared for cabinet, did not estimate the full costs. "Transportation infrastructure is required to establish a permanent road network and good rail access from the resource to the mill and from the mill to the market. As forest products are extremely heavy, bulky and expensive to move, manufacturing should take place in close proximity to the resource. In most cases, sites for potential plants are inadequately serviced by road and rail infrastructure."[3]

The fourth and most controversial assumption concerned Alberta's stance on direct financial assistance or subsidies to big forestry projects. Given the disadvantages facing the forest industry in the province, should the Alberta government socialize more of the costs and risks by using its financial resources to provide direct assistance to major projects in the form of grants, loan guarantees, equity investments, subordinated loans, and so forth? Without financial incentives and risk insurance—which, as Fred McDougall's staff pointed out in their position paper for cabinet, were offered by many jurisdictions competing for forestry investments—would it be feasible to develop world-scale forest product operations in Alberta? Here there were important shifts in government policy because of the province's rapidly deteriorating economic situation, and the direction of the change was not towards fiscal prudence. After 1981, the Alberta economy was struck by the twin shocks of falling world oil prices and the high interest rates generated by the monetarist policies of the American government; and the effects of these external events were quickly felt in a sharp decline in new investment, increased unemployment, and a succession of large and small business failures. One consequence of this was that Alberta's bargaining power relative to that of transnational capital declined after 1981, and the provincial government began to use the public finances—including part of the Alberta Heritage Savings Trust Fund—to attract new investments and to foster economic diversification projects. With the advantage of hindsight we can see that the provincial Conservatives were proposing to open the door wide to all sorts of unproductive "rent-seeking" behaviour by the private sector at a moment when the government's own revenue position was about to change dramatically and for the worse.

A crucial moment in this process occurred in July 1984 when the Lougheed government published a White Paper proposing a more interventionist industrial policy for Alberta. In its endorsement of public financial assistance for diversification, the White Paper would become an important element in the forestry and pulp mill initiatives of the Getty government. The White Paper was about jobs and new investments, and it had its origins in a decision taken by Lougheed's cabinet in 1983 to develop an "updated and integrated industrial strategy" in the pursuit of a diversified economy. It was the government's role, and not the market's, to select the winning industries and then to channel public assistance; indeed, the White Paper barely disguised Lougheed's distrust of the operations of open markets:

> We do not need to concern ourselves about the transition from "smoke stacks" to silicon chips. Our problems are more oriented to selecting strategies which will encourage some industries to locate here which will *complement* our existing strength yet further diversify our economic base. The selection of these industries may be difficult and the initiatives needed to bring the developments here imaginative. Yet the government should be involved in this strategic policy since financial or other assistance may be necessary.[4]

Lougheed later stressed that the diversification strategy was not designed to broaden Alberta's tax base by reducing the province's dependence on unstable oil revenues. "Diversification was to stabilize employment in this province, not to strengthen the fiscal structure. It was never the view that economic diversification in the medium term would affect the revenue stream."[5] The White Paper conveyed the same message: in the interest of economic diversification, the province would provide financial inducements, spend on infrastructure, and forego the collection of revenues in return for new investments and jobs. The emphasis would be on "present job activity and deferred revenue flows," especially in the financing of big projects such as oil sands plants, heavy oil upgraders, and other resource ventures such as pulp mills.

Although the forestry industry did not get special emphasis in the 1984 White Paper, Don Getty's forestry initiative was a direct extension of earlier decisions taken by Peter Lougheed's cabinet in favour of a more interventionist approach to industrial strategy.

In November 1985 Getty returned to politics after some difficult and chastening years trying to make money in the oil business in the United States and Canada. Lougheed had stepped down as premier, and Getty had been persuaded by the provincial Conservative establishment to come back to succeed the man who had been his political mentor for nearly twenty years. Getty shared most of Lougheed's views on the need for a more diversified economy, but he was more interested than his predecessor in trying to use the underdeveloped forestry sector as a tool of economic policy. Forestry, tourism, and technology/research were the three areas identified by Getty's government in early 1986 as the leading sectors of its industrial strategy. Getty's role was decisive in selecting forestry: he made the commitment to create the interdepartmental machinery required for the accelerated approval of development proposals; he agreed to finance costly infrastructure in the north; and he was the politician who authorized the use of high-risk loan guarantees, debentures, and other forms of financial support in negotiating with the multinational forestry companies.[6] Why forestry? Pulp prices were strong after 1985, Getty liked resource megaprojects, he was looking for stable alternatives to oil and gas, and he was familiar with the prodevelopment views of the forestry service, of which he had been in charge in the late seventies when, as a senior minister in Lougheed's cabinet, he had had responsibility for Energy and Natural Resources. Unlike Lougheed, Getty was a well-known former football star and politician from Edmonton, a city whose natural hinterland is in the north, with its great and tempting resource wealth. A departmental discussion paper first circulated by forestry officials in May 1985 argued that "a vast potential exists for the utilization of the hardwood resource" if the government were prepared to provide incentives and bear the costs of developing new infrastructure. The main constraints were said to be the absence of good road and rail infrastructure, the high capital costs and financing limits, lack of access to the timber resources, freight rates, and the growth of protectionism in the United States, the major market. The document was badly flawed in that it did not estimate the full financial costs of the strategy to the government, did not discuss the likely impact of multiple pulp mills on the northern river systems, did not predict the effects on the North West Territories, and did not even estimate the probable employment benefits. The likely costs, in short, were scarcely mentioned; the conclusion was ebullient.

> Alberta's forests are capable of supporting several significant pulp and paper developments. . . . However, the high capital cost of new pulp operations has proven to be an impediment to development. The government is prepared to consider assistance to pulp and paper developers where such support is required to bring an economically viable project forward...[a limit of $200 million per project is proposed]. Modernization of the sawmill and panelboard industries, transportation and marketing intitiatives and the development of pulp and paper facilities will position Alberta well to capture the opportunities which will develop with recovering markets in North America and expanding opportunities in the Pacific Rim.[7]

The Visible Hand

Alberta's northern forest industry initiative was described by one of its architects as "a planned government economic strategy."[8] He meant that it was the state rather than the private sector that conceived and orchestrated the plan to put the immense and allegedly underutilized forests of the north of Alberta under the exclusive management of a handful of Canadian and transnational companies in return for commitments of jobs, technology, and access to world markets. Choosing this strategy of forestry exploitation, with its huge economies of scale, its forced-growth timetables, and its areas of risk and uncertainty required government to become a partner with transnational capital. Here the operative word is "required," for *if* the provincial government chose to pursue the megaproject strategy of stimulating and diversifying the economy via forestry investments (and there was nothing inevitable about its decision to do so), then it would of necessity be drawn into commitments that would take it well beyond its legal obligations in forestry management. Policy planners understood this requirement for growing state involvement, but they did not foresee how little control they would have over the consequences of what they were proposing to do.

It was a strategy made possible, first, by the Crown's ownership of 95 percent of the province's forest resources; second, by the Getty cabinet's willingness to fund expensive infrastructure in northern Alberta and to get into risky financial support for big forestry projects in order to surmount some of the high costs and the physical constraints involved in opening up the province's vast but inaccessible stands of hardwood timber to the international forest products industry. The problem was not so much one of technical feasibility as it was a conflict in political economy. Given the constraints of distance and the lack of infrastructure in the north, who would bear the costs and risks of developing the new forestry staples and connecting the remotely situated pulp mills to North American and overseas markets? After Don Getty's accession to office the answer was clear: if Adam Smith's invisible hand would not build world-scale pulp mills on Alberta's northern frontier, then the visible hand of the state would become directly involved.

The nature and location of the resource, then, not ideology, provided the basic motive for extensive state intervention in the development of Alberta's forestry frontier. Whether particular forms of government assistance were wise or excessive can be legitimately debated, but once the basic decision had been taken to exploit the northern hardwoods and to use the forestry sector for broad economic purposes, the government and the public finances were sure to play a major role. Canada's north remains a hard frontier on which transplanted doctrines such as *laissez-faire* tend to wither and die. A British Columbian forestry consultant had noted at the close of the 1970s that Canada had reached the end of an era of extensive development of its coniferous forests and faced shortages of logs and pulpwood; in many parts of the country the constraints of distance, cost, and effort "would preclude the opening up of the more distant stands. Without public funds these forests will not likely be opened up for many years."[9] There were options available to governments and industry during the 1980s other than a strategy of opening up Canada's remaining frontier timber reserves—for example, to promote a much more intensive management of those forests already under development—but in any early push to cut and upgrade northern hardwoods such as aspen and balsam poplar the role of "public funds" was bound to loom large. As had happened so frequently in Canada's economic history, the shift to the new export staples would be pioneered and heavily subsidized by the public sector. To borrow a distinction made in a famous essay on the state in Canada's economic history, development of the aspen forests of northern Alberta would be "largely induced rather than autonomous" and "contingent on state action" because of the necessity of providing the indispensable and very costly transportation infrastructure.[10] The Alberta government was advised by several consultants in the mid-eighties that pulp, newsprint, and certain value-added paper products could possibly be manufactured in some areas of northern Alberta at acceptable rates of return, *but* big and risky investments in pulp and paper manufacturing would not proceed without the provincial government's involvement, including, perhaps, politically controversial financial aid. For instance, a 1987 report by EKONO Consultants on the feasibility of value-added paper manufacturing facilities in Alberta pointed to the high capital cost of building new paper mills relative to other corporate options:

> The investor profiled as being best able to invest in such a project will have large capital resources. He also will most likely have the option of adding onto an existing [paper] mill somewhere else than in Alberta. It is generally accepted that exercising such an option would cost 25 to 40 percent less than a greenfield mill. The implication is clear: if an investor is to be attracted to Alberta to build a greenfield mill a subvention by the province may be required to reduce the investor's capital outlay to the point where the profitability is high enough to balance the main risk factors of market price and volume fluctuations.[11]

Thus, a "value-added" strategy of encouraging higher processing of resources via, say, paper manufacturing or—in the case of natural gas—petrochemicals could involve the government in wasteful concessions to industry on financing, the price of the resource, royalties and taxes, and pollution controls. This point is not well understood by the public or, it seems, by many politicians: it is hard to persuade Canadians that in some cases they may be better off economically and ecologically if they simply produce and trade resources such as crude oil and natural gas than if they require them to be processed into chemicals or plastics and use the Crown's ownership of the resource to keep the cost of the resource below market value. In order to obtain the smelting, the refining, the petrochemical industries, and the like, governments have traded away the surpluses or rents generated by the publicly owned resource base in return for the prestige, a few good jobs, and the pollution. The Conservative governments in Alberta have pursued a neomercantilist value-added approach to resource use since Peter Lougheed's earliest years as premier, typically justifying it on the popular but dubious and potentially expensive grounds that their children and grandchildren should never have to leave Alberta to seek employment; northern Albertan politicians insist that resources should be processed up north so that northerners should not have to move to Edmonton or Calgary for work; and Peace River politicians insist that "their" forest resources not be upgraded near Grande Prairie, less than three hours away by car! As we will show, this obsession with catch-up industrialization has cost Alberta jobs and economic surpluses. The government's fixation with the processing of forestry resources in the late 1980s led Alberta into a strategy that allowed a handful of transnational companies to acquire immense timber hinterlands in northern Alberta, at the expense of the many existing forest companies and sawmills that account for most of the employment in that sector and now have very limited prospects of growth. At the end of the day, as political economists such as Eric Kierans and John McDougall have cautioned Canadians, an excessive preoccupation with the upgrading of natural resources can result in excess refining capacity, the surrender of economic rents, and the transfer of pollution-causing industries from the industrial core areas to the resource-producing areas.[12] Nevertheless, even if it makes little economic sense, the demand of the producing regions such as northern Alberta for more of the "value-added" from resource exploitation has always had real political appeal; and no fair analysis of the forestry policies of the Getty cabinet can neglect this factor.

In the mid-eighties, economic and political pressures were also pushing the Alberta government into a much more activist role in the economy. In this wider context forestry was only one sector affected in the search for major new investments in industries other than oil and agriculture. Public opinion and the media strongly—and quite uncritically—demanded the diversification of the economy *and* looked to government for the solutions. For the first time since the election of Peter Lougheed's Conservatives in August 1971, the provincial Tories were being seriously challenged at the polls, and by the New Democrats, a party campaigning for large-scale public investment and commodity price regulation as a response to Alberta's deepening economic crisis. Don Getty's misfortune was that his first year as premier happened to be the same year that Alberta experienced all of the hazards and instabilities associated with small, cyclical resource-based economies. We noted in the introduction that the economic crisis that struck Alberta in the first few months of 1986 was caused by the unanticipated fall in world oil prices from twenty-seven dollars (US) per barrel to below ten dollars (US) per barrel and by dramatic declines in international prices for grain and other important agricultural commodities. Ironically, Canadian oil and gas prices, having been closely regulated by Ottawa for more than a decade for the advantage of consumers, had been largely deregulated via the Western Accord in 1985; deregulation now exposed the oil and gas industries and the province to the full force of the collapse in world prices and the attendant instability in markets. Even with the very large royalty and tax reductions implemented by Alberta and the federal authorities to offset the price fall, up to fifty thousand oil and related jobs were lost in Alberta after the petroleum industry suffered an unprecedented loss of nearly ten billion dollars in revenues in 1985–86. It was the *real oil crisis*, and no government could have prevented it. With the sharp rise in unemployment came greater numbers of welfare recipients, bankruptcies and small business failures, office vacancies, food banks, and much other misery. These social trends and the grim interpretations of them by opposition politicians and the media during the spring 1986 provincial election campaign intensified the pressures on the Getty government to accelerate its support for stimulus and economic diversification even while it was simultaneously trying to cushion oil, gas, and grain producers from the full costs of adjustment to the disastrously low international prices—it is not clear whether Getty realized that a number of his costly short-term measures, for example, shielding small oil and gas producers from the impact of world prices, would work against market-induced diversification by delaying the industry's adjustment to external realities. In any event, the government clearly had concluded that it needed economic stimulus in order to be reelected.

Getty's Conservative cabinet tended to equate economic development with big resource projects. Capital investment and public spending on megaprojects and related infrastructure could provide some new jobs and stability—especially in areas such as the north and Edmonton where the New Democrats were strong and challenging the Conservatives on the left and, as Getty himself noted, there was a demand for government intervention:

In the south they're telling me, be tough, get the deficit under control, and stay out of our hair, reduce government. You come up [north] and somewhere around Ponoka it starts to change. You hit Edmonton and it's different. In Edmonton, it's "do something, get us jobs, take care of us." You move further north, the farmers of the north, they really want big government involvement.[13]

That clamour for "big government involvement" from farmers and other northerners—including Conservative MLAS—was the consequence of the economic instability and vulnerability that by the mid-eighties plagued all northern Alberta communities. The mood was grim—despair on the farms, desperation in the towns and smaller cities. Dependent on variable income, employment, and taxes generated by oil, natural gas, and agriculture, these communities now lobbied Getty's cabinet to stabilize and diversify the regional economy of the north with new industries and large projects. The decline of the energy industries in the north went well beyond a drop in exploration and development activity, though that was certainly a fact of life after world oil prices fell after 1981 and then plunged much further in 1986. The unstable oil market forced the cancellation of several major energy projects favoured by the Lougheed and Getty cabinets, notably the huge Alsands venture north of Fort McMurray and Shell's proposed oil sands recovery project at Peace River, and it also encouraged the oil and gas industries to use up their conventional oil and gas reserves without replacing them. Across the north the biggest conventional oil and gas fields that had gone into production in the fifties and sixties—such as Swan Hills, Rainbow, Judy Creek, and a number of others—were in irreversible decline by 1986; so that the north-of-Edmonton region, which in the mid-seventies had been producing close to half of Alberta's crude oil produced by major fields, was producing less than 30 percent a decade later. The northern share of Alberta's remaining conventional reserves of oil and gas also dropped off. Whereas the northern region of the province accounted for 51.2 percent of Alberta's recoverable crude oil reserves in 1976, a decade later the northern share had fallen to 35.1 percent; while the north's share of Alberta's marketable gas reserves fell from 13.3 percent in 1971 to 6.3 percent in 1986.[14] For northern communities all of this meant smaller tax bases, less income, fewer jobs, and a greater anxiety about their future. Northern Alberta, like the frontier of many another Canadian province, was now sending its most promising young people away from the region, and many people expected the government in Edmonton somehow to reverse the trend.

A northern cabinet minister, referring to the sharp downturn in the Alberta economy in 1986, defended the government's interventions on grounds that had nothing to do with economic diversification. "We were struggling to keep some degree of business activity going. There were some deliberate attempts to move away from what was considered the norm of private sector/public works—of, say, 70 percent private sector/30 percent government capital works in the total package—and almost reversing that to ensure some protection for jobs, and some balance to get us through this downturn."[15] He might have said, with John Maynard Keynes, that in the long run we are all dead. This short-run philosophy of jobs for today held the voters, or most of them. The Conservatives managed to win the provincial election of 8 May 1986, but the New Democrats swept Edmonton and gained seats in Calgary and some rural constituencies. It was in part to satisfy their electoral pledges that led the Alberta government to borrow $3 billion and to opt for the stimulative effects of a large fiscal deficit ($2.5 billion and, as events subsequently developed, the first in a string of such deficits). Such intervention and borrowing also flowed from the unstable and vulnerable structure of Alberta's resource-driven economy. Confronting massive layoffs and farm and business bankruptcies, Alberta and the federal Conservative government struck a number of agreements and policy changes that injected several billion dollars into the grain and energy sectors of the economy, thereby forestalling an even harsher downturn. They deserved more credit than they have received for having done so. But it is true that rather than begin adjusting expenditures to the new revenue structure, the Getty cabinet also began to spend heavily in a few select areas that promised early results in the search for a more diversified economic base. There was no economic plan; there was not even a coherent rationale for the areas chosen: forestry, tourism, high technology. It was very much an ad hoc winners and losers approach to intervention based on what Getty called "judgement calls." He had not even read Lougheed's 1984 White Paper, Getty insisted.[16]

Getty understood economic development as a process driven by large capital investments negotiated and, if necessary, guaranteed by government, and he preferred huge resource projects like the Syncrude oil sands venture near Fort McMurray (he had been closely involved with Peter Lougheed in the province's negotiations from 1973 to 1975 with the multinationals leading to the building of Syncrude) because of the big impact they had on the total provincial economy and especially on employment. The construction industry, which accounted for better than 10 percent of Alberta's work force in 1981, nearly twice the Canadian average, and several of whose leading firms were prominent financial contributors to the provincial Conservative party, was lobbying for work. If oil sands megaprojects and *in situ* heavy oil upgraders, backed by loan guarantees and other government assistance, were not feasible, forestry would do. Forestry, that is, as conceived by Fred McDougall, involving big projects and capital investments in return for secure long-term access to new fibre. When Getty announced the first of the big new pulp projects, Millar Western's mill in Whitecourt, he enthused: "This resource is almost like the oilsands. It's even better than the oilsands, it's all over the province."[17] But who would get to use the resource?

Who Gets the Forests?

In early 1986 the Getty government set up a separate Department of Forestry, Lands and Wildlife (new ministries were also established for tourism and technology), with Don Sparrow as minister and a mandate from Getty "to double the output" of the forest industry in Alberta.[18] Don Sparrow, who died in July 1993 in a car accident, was then close to Getty; Getty had worked for the Sparrow family's oil company in the first half of the 1980s. Don Sparrow ran Forestry until late 1987, when he was moved by Getty to another anointed portfolio, Tourism; his successor at Forestry, Lands and Wildlife was southern rancher LeRoy Fjordbotten, and it was Fjordbotten who implemented much of the policy. Also in 1986, the Alberta government set up a small new agency, the Forest Industry Development Division (FIDD), within Forestry, Lands and Wildlife and gave it the mandate and promise of financial support to find major new investors willing "to upgrade and utilize Alberta's vast uncommitted forest resources for a variety of forest products." Getty selected one of Fred McDougall's deputies, J. A. "Al" Brennan, a career forester who had moved from Newfoundland to Alberta in the seventies, as Executive Officer of FIDD. With the premier's backing, Brennan would operate a "one-stop" service for potential forestry investors, shepherding them around the government bureaucracy and providing them with access to the central policy-makers. He could arrange financial assistance if required.

Brennan came across as a man in a hurry: he thought Alberta had a window of just a few years to get its major forestry investments in place, for once the cyclical forest products industry entered another downturn in the early nineties, capital investment would dry up. That the development of several new mills in Alberta would contribute to the surplus capacity in pulp and hasten the downturn did not faze him: Alberta's new mills would survive any shakeout. Brennan had few good things to say about Alberta's "green movement." He worried that the growth of environmentalism in Alberta—"All those people running around dressed up like trees!"—would derail the forestry strategy before it left the station, for political stability and a reputation for keeping its promises to international business were among Alberta's strongest cards. Al Brennan praised Getty as the politician who had been receptive to new ideas and willing to spend on infrastructure and financial assistance for forestry projects, steps which, he thought, Peter Lougheed would not have taken.[19] Like McDougall, Sparrow, and Getty, Brennan was a supporter of the rapid commercial development of the northern boreal forests and of using government financial assistance in the competition for international capital. The main rationale for such assistance, we recall from the Forestry Discussion Paper that launched the strategy, was not so much that it was needed as it was that everybody else did it; Alberta had to be competitive. Such assistance would be offered "flexibly," Brennan said:

> Financial support was not constrained by a rigid set of rules or regulations but was designed to provide flexible assistance as long as the proponent could demonstrate a need. Grants were generally not provided except for the development of key infrastructure. Assistance designed to prop up projects which were not viable would not be provided. While no particular form of assistance was rejected automatically, the Government tended to be supportive of loan guarantees and, if necessary, participating debentures.[20]

On several projects the levels of financial support would run into hundreds of millions of dollars, a great deal of public money for a government with so little experience with the industry. Except for infrastructure, grants were not used because of the requirement that all assistance must be non-countervailable— that is, safely out of reach of a protectionist United States Congress.[21] This was the period of Canada's softwood lumber dispute with the United States, and Alberta plainly feared that the use of grants might lead to further protectionist actions, this time directed against its new pulp and paper projects. That does not mean, however, that Alberta was somehow avoiding risks in using loan guarantees, participating debentures, and subordinated loans instead of grants in implementing its strategy.

To whom was FIDD itself really accountable, and why was it given so much discretion to operate outside the normal financial "rules and regulations," which exist for very good reasons? If FIDD's one-stop service was intended to expedite the approval of major projects, the approach also appears to have circumvented or reduced the controls of the provincial treasurer and others charged with the prudent management of the province's financial resources. At the very least, it is fair to say that some of FIDD's recommendations for financial support to forestry projects involved rather hasty assessments leading the province to accept high financial risks for unimpressive economic gains. Still, the premier and the rest of the cabinet were ultimately responsible for the decisions. They set the process in motion, and in doing so ruled out many alternative ways of managing the forest that would not have required the aid of the state.

Was financial assistance even necessary? The government wanted to use a forestry boom to stimulate growth, generating employment and industrial spinoffs, and to do so without the constraints of bureaucracy and prolonged interdepartmental negotiations. But if the international forest industry needed new sources of fibre, and the province owned such a valuable source and controlled the access to it, why was it necessary to socialize the risks of the forest companies who agreed to invest? FIDD's Al Brennan justified the government's financial risk-sharing as follows:

> Attracting the huge capital investment necessary for pulp and paper development requires security of timber tenure within a forestry management agreement. Sharing the risk of such investments might be necessary to encourage private investment. In the past, the Alberta Government has been reluctant to get involved in sharing the risk of such capital investments despite competing with other jurisdictions where such financial support was more common.
>
> The enticement by government to financially participate in some of the projects had an important psychological effect. While sharing the risk with private investment, it also sent a very strong signal that the government was strongly committed to the projects. Government became, in effect, a stakeholder in the project.[22]

The logic is dubious, the thesis suspect. While the first sentence in the Brennan quotation is quite right, what follows it is unfounded speculation about what "might" be required beyond what clearly *is* required to attract capital investment: namely, access to the resource and security of tenure within some type of long-term lease. For any forestry company, as one executive put it, such tenure and timber supply "are the fundamental assets by which potential investors or lenders judge the viability of a company. In most cases these tenures are included in present and prospective trust deeds as security for loans."[23] If that is what the investor and bank really need, why offer more? There is, as we shall show, ample reason to believe that Alberta offered too much and asked too little in its negotiations with the transnationals. In addition, the statement is evidence of real intellectual confusion within the Alberta government over its own role in economic development. For the role of a "stakeholder" in big and highly risky resource projects is not necessarily an appropriate one for a government that also has obligations to be a prudent manager of public finances and a careful steward of the physical environment. The Alberta government had adopted this same "risk-sharing" strategy fifteen years earlier in negotiations with the Syncrude consortium of multinational oil companies. It ended up sharing all of the risks and not much of the profits. Employed in a scattergun approach to entire industries, the difficulties with it are obvious. No matter what jurisdictions like Brazil or Spain do, a vaguely defined policy of using public financial resources to produce a "psychological" effect on such a volatile industry as forestry is a license to raid the treasury and expose taxpayers to risks that the private sector does not bear. When such indulgence coincides with politicians piously admonishing workers and the public to practice restraint, one outcome is likely to be a growing, corrosive cynicism about government and its transparent class bias.

The power of internationally mobile capital to play off resource-owning jurisdictions against one another derives in no small part from the willingness of relatively small governments such as Alberta's to play loose with the public finances in bargaining with transnational corporations. The Alberta government had no effective control over its spending when Don Getty took over, and his indulgence in loan guarantees, tax and royalty incentives, and other subsidies at a time when the province's revenue position was deteriorating made matters worse. Milking traditional prairie suspicions of the banking system, Getty vowed that, "I'm not going to wait for the banks" in diversifying the economy. If the chartered banks were not willing to finance some of the forestry projects, he would use the financial strength of the Heritage Savings Trust Fund to do so. But how far should the premier go in lowering the risks and on *whose* behalf? Some public expenditure on infrastructure for resources may well be required and legitimate, particularly if new roads and bridges have other uses than to serve the interests of a single megaproject. But if government financial support in the form of a very large debenture on generous terms is necessary to secure bank financing for the construction of the world's biggest pulp mill, is the project commercially viable? If it *is* judged to be viable, then why offer such support at all? Is its real purpose to lower the cost of capital to the transnational firms or is it needed to shield them and the banks from future financial and political risks? We argue throughout this book that in their dealings with jurisdictions such as Alberta, transnational forestry firms are primarily motivated by their need to secure long-term supplies of low-cost fibre in stable areas in order to manufacture products, to expand their domestic paper mills and market shares and, of course, to accumulate capital; if Alberta's forestry resources are competitive with those of, say, Australia or Spain, then why should public monies be offered in financing the construction of big projects the profits from which these firms alone will own? If the answer is that such "inducements" are now required as a cost of doing business with transnational pulp and paper firms, which have other places to invest their capital, one response is to say that there are also plenty of other ways to manage a forest and to find other investors.

Finally, if the state is to be a direct "stakeholder" in massive resource projects, who will regulate the stakeholders? Once the government has, at an early stage of the bargaining, promised hundreds of millions of dollars in financing to capital in order to send "the very strong signal" that it is strongly committed to such a project, it obviously builds up a cumulative interest in its commercial success. What, after all, would opposition politicians and the media say of a government that had made such an investment if the project subsequently failed, especially if it failed because of shifts in public policy on, say, environmental questions? Intervention breeds further intervention: a mill that is threatened by surplus productive capacity and low prices will use its workers' jobs, the reliance of rural communities on the mill's continuing operations, and the state's past support to secure further assistance. In such admittedly difficult circumstances, how can the state credibly fulfil its obligations to carry out public environmental reviews and to act as stewards of publicly-owned resources? Can the same department of the same government be steward *and* huckster of the forests?

As of the mid-eighties, most of Alberta's northern forests had not been allocated to any commercial interests. Who would gain access to the resource? Who would get the rights to use the aspen? This was the central issue in the political economy of Alberta's forest industry. The provincial government controlled access to the resource, but many interests were vying for the rights to use it. Would the last great forest in North America remain open to Alberta-based and Canadian capital and to Native communities in the region, or would it be reserved for transnational capital? The Alberta forestry policy envisioned a rapid transition to a state of affairs where the northern forests would be committed, via administrative discretion rather than auction, to a few major companies proposing large projects with some value-added content and jobs. Public ownership of the forests gave the Alberta government all the powers it needed to do this; had some of the forests been privately owned, as in the southern United States, there would have been more than one landlord and more than one vision of forestry development, and independent Alberta-based forestry operators might then have had a chance to expand by controlling more of the resource.

That, however, was antithetical to the prevailing philosophy of the Alberta government—and, perhaps, much of the public—that in the management of natural resources, bigger operations are better operations. In order to realize the economies of scale required to lower the costs of harvesting aspen and manufacturing pulp in northern Alberta, large international forestry companies with a longer time-horizon than local sawmills and wood manufacturers would be needed as investors and forestry managers. Implicit in the policy was an expectation of a dramatic growth in concentration in Alberta's forest products industry: the government wanted the biggest integrated firms because they controlled the markets, technology, and expertise and also because they had the size to weather downturns in the business cycle. But would a policy of allocating the resource to the integrated majors and denying it to the small and medium-sized players actually result in what the province wanted— "full utilization" of the forests? Not necessarily, for if all the wood supplies ended up in a few hands there would be no guarantees the FMA holders would develop the forests at the rate desired by the government or that wood products would flow to the uses of highest return. And beyond the issue of utilization, one effect of tying so much of the forests to the consumption of a handful of pulp mills owned by a few major firms would be major losses in diversity and innovation.

In a province covered with vast forests and supposedly under-utilized timber areas, local sawmills and wood manufacturers found themselves short of wood supplies. To get a timber reserve from which to expand their operations and add new employees, the independents found themselves paying much more in auctions than the majors paid on their Forest Management Agreements. Some independent operators, such as Frank Crawford, a sawmill owner with a timber quota north of Athabasca, thought the government's policy was designed to wipe out the smaller forestry companies. "Under McDougall small owners couldn't get any timber. McDougall gave it all to the outside companies. He wanted to phase the little guys out so he could deal with the big players. . . . The province was always looking for industry. The big timber quotas went to the big companies and they didn't have to pay anything for them. It was the small companies that had to pay."[24] Among the independents there was talk that the government had a master-plan to force the smaller operators out. There may not have been a master plan, but if they could not get wood or had to pay an exorbitant price for it in this province of "underutilized" forests, it may have amounted to the same thing.

The resentment of the small players over their limited access to the forest resources was not a new issue. During public hearings in 1979 on proposed timber development in the Berland-Fox Creek area, Craig Corser, then a sawmill owner from Edson, worried that too many Albertans seemed content to assume "that one of the majors will once again be granted an immense FMA, and in return, will confer employment and prosperity upon us. I wonder if these Albertans have considered that there may be an alternative approach to development. Rather than have a single company administer a massive injection of capital, the possibility exists for the timber resource in question to be developed in a slower, more orderly fashion, with a large number of companies investing smaller amounts of money."[25] In 1992, after the forests had been given away, a spokesman for Alberta's independent sawmillers noted that for "every cubic metre of wood harvested the employment generated by these operators is double that of large pulp mills and it is not done on the backs of taxpayers with large grants and giveaways." Using tougher language in public than the Alberta government is used to hearing from provincial business, the sawmillers' spokesman identified unequal access to the forestry resources as the central issue:

Alberta's independent sawmillers are currently in trouble; not because of markets or technology but because of the unfair competitive advantage bestowed upon the multinationals by the provincial government. The province has given management agreement areas to these companies in return for the promise of new jobs. Many of these companies seem to have sufficient clout to persuade the government to change the rules of the game in their favour at will. By comparison, the smaller independents need to acquire their cutting rights through competitive bid. They are told there is not enough surplus wood for them to expand while at the same time more mega-projects are being entertained....Why are we giving away our resources to outside interests when we have home-grown expertise with a proven track record?[26]

The independents were not well-organized and their lobbying seems to have been singularly ineffective, but they appear to have had a good case. That the policy of favouring big projects in the allocation of hardwood timber and public financial assistance worked against the expansion of Alberta capital in the forestry industries is incontrovertible. The policy implied that many sawmillers and other forest products businesses would be absorbed by the multinationals' pulp mills or that they would end up doing the latter's bidding. Who controls the resource determines the nature of the industry. The government was certainly interested in developing supplier industries within Alberta that would build linkages with the big pulp mills, but it acted as if the existing firms in the forestry industry, many of which remain important to the smaller communities of the province, were either an irritant or did not even exist. The rules of the game allowed only a few to grow. "It's taken away our ability to expand," said the owner of a medium-sized sawmill operation, Spray Lake Sawmills, based in Cochrane, northwest of Calgary. This mill, founded in 1943, employs 100 to 125 people and contracts with another 50 in the woodlands, roughly the same employment created by one of the smaller pulp mills. In the 1980s Spray Lake wanted to double its output of lumber but could not acquire the necessary supply of wood. When the owner attempted to expand his operations to the north, he was informed by the government that "we are saving the wood for a major development in the Rocky Mountain House area."[27] The independents argued that employment in the forestry sector would actually increase very little under the government's strategy because modern pulp and paper mills are highly automated and capital intensive, employing only the specially trained and highly skilled, whereas sawmills provide stable employment for local (often including Native) workers. On this basis, the government should ensure a wood supply for those sawmills interested in expansion. But as the government saw the issue, the independents were too small and undercapitalized to take on the major forestry and pulp projects it wanted for economic stimulus and diversification; if the resource was to be fully utilized, the transnationals would have to be enticed to invest. This would mean giving each of them financial aid that was not available to the independents plus exclusive access to a large portion of the remaining uncommitted reserve of hardwood fibre.

There was one important exception to the trend in favour of the transnationals. At least one Alberta-based company with established interests and know-how in forestry understood the political climate and used the visible hand of the state to vault itself into the business of producing and marketing pulp. Ironically, Hugh MacKenzie "Mac" Millar, one of the owners of this corporate group, Millar Western Industries, reportedly opposed the government's plans for financial assistance to pulp and paper projects when, at some early point in the process, Al Brennan and other officials ran the strategy past the Alberta Forest Products Association.[28] Because of the high financial and technological barriers to entry into the modern pulp industry, even Alberta's biggest sawmill and lumber operations could not hope to acquire the financial support or the wood supply to move up to pulp production without special political agreements with the province. Only a political strategy, involving corporate support for the government's forestry expansion plans in return for government aid on financing and increased access to wood supply, would allow Alberta capital to make it into the major leagues. There were historical precedents for such special arrangements with local business in Alberta, especially when a corporation was able to appeal to powerful politicians by identifying itself as a flagship of a government policy. For instance, in the 1970s the Lougheed Conservative government formed an alliance with management-controlled Alberta Gas Trunk Line (subsequently renamed Nova) in order to get Alberta-based capital into the production of petrochemicals from natural gas derivatives; the government supported the empire-building ambitions of the corporation on the unspoken premise that this privileged entity was also advancing the interests of the government in province-building and industrial development.[29] Such a political strategy is a risky course for a company to pursue, for politicians are fickle and move on and governments are wont to change their priorities to suit the fashions of the day. Where are the Canadian petroleum companies which, seeking privileged status, shrewdly linked their strategies to the Trudeau government's National Energy Program in 1980? Like the House of Medici, bankers to many sovereigns in Europe during the fifteenth century Renaissance, they found out too late that princely *raison d'état* is a poor substitute for profit, and they were abandoned by their patrons.

In the case of forestry, if there was a locally-owned entity in Alberta that would play the private/public role, it was Millar Western Industries at Whitecourt, a town of about sixty-five hundred people located some 180 kilometres northwest of Edmonton. This private family-owned group of companies, with interests in lumber, heavy construction, and industrial chemicals, was founded in 1906 by J.W. Millar, an enterprising blacksmith who expanded into lumber and railway grading and eventually established Millar Western's sawmill/planer complex at Whitecourt. It was among Alberta's largest, fastest-growing forest product companies but, like many lumber producers attempting to expand, it was constrained by ceilings on the amount of timber it could cut. By the early eighties, Millar Western had modernized its sawmill but, having reached the limits of its available sawlogs—it held rights to cut softwood timber in the Whitecourt and Slave Lake forests, with an annual allowable cut of about five hundred thousand cubic metres, but no rights to utilize hardwoods—it would be difficult to grow further without becoming an integrated company. Millar Western realized that new timber development areas would only be allocated to those interests that intended to use aspen as well as the available softwoods in their operations, with clear preference given to pulp producers. The writing was on the wall for the independents. One of the Millars explained: "As the trend of government today is the total utilization of the resource, it follows that the smaller operators are going to be phased out."[30] Confronted with a choice between a limited future in lumber with restricted access to timber supplies and expansion via forward integration into pulp production with increased access to hardwood and softwood fibres, Millar Western opted to become an integrated company. It could not have happened without the backing of the Getty government in Edmonton. MacKenzie Millar, president of Millar Western Pulp, recalled: "The government encouraged us; it wanted pulp mills built."[31] It did more than encourage; it made it possible. On the other hand, Millar Western was the breakthrough that Getty's entire forest policy needed. Surprisingly, nobody asked why this one Alberta-based company should have received such privileged treatment or whether it would be returning to the government's door looking for additional assistance.

Millar Western's deal with the Getty government was announced by the premier in April 1986 during the provincial election campaign. Although the media, with its usual flair for originality and deep analysis, greeted the announcement as an "election goody," Millar Western's project was important because it was the first of the new pulp mills to be launched in response to the diversification strategy. At a point when the Alberta economy was being battered by falling agricultural and energy prices, Getty could argue that Millar Western—a third-generation Alberta firm—was initiating a new value-added approach to economic development. The company planned to build a bleached chemithermomechanical pulp (CTMP) mill capable of producing 240,000 metric tonnes of market pulp per year. Much smaller in cost and scale (and environmental impact) than the big kraft pulp mills favoured by the majors, the Millar Western mill would be built for about $190 million and go into production in 1988. Financing of the project was made possible by the Alberta government, which purchased $120 million in interest-bearing debentures in order to share the risk and to enable the Millars to negotiate favourable terms with their bankers. The debentures must be repaid with 10 percent interest by 2004. Millar Western also received, in return for its investment, significantly greater access to hardwood and softwood timber areas in the Whitecourt and Slave Lake forest; this permitted the company to introduce new technologies and processes into its sawmill complex, which is now part of an integrated operation. Technology came from the giant Philadelphia-based Scott Paper Company, which wanted a pulp project that would take its patented alkaline peroxide bleaching system from the laboratory into commercial application.[32] Millar Western's process involves no discharge of organochlorines, including dioxins or furans—the toxic substances that nearly derailed the huge Alberta-Pacific project in the Athabasca region in 1990–91. An advantage of CTMP mills is that they can manufacture ninety tonnes of pulp from one hundred tonnes of wood, twice the yield of the kraft process, and the product has enjoyed an eighty to one hundred dollars-per-tonne cost advantage in some markets. The Millar Western mill works two production lines, one that uses 100 percent softwood furnish and produces pulp for tissues, towels, and diapers; the other designed to use a furnish of mostly aspen to yield a pulp for printing and writing grade paper.

Apart from any commercial strengths, the chemithermomechanical pulping technology used by Millar Western has certain environmental advantages that help to explain why this and other CTMP mills did not generate the intense political opposition in Alberta that greeted the subsequent kraft mill proposals. The advantages centre primarily on the issue of water pollution. First, CTMP mills do not have the great thirst for fresh water that kraft mills do. Second, and more importantly, although Millar Western's Whitecourt mill, like its kraft counterparts, produces an effluent that robs oxygen from and darkens the waters into which it is dumped, the mill does not pollute the nearby Athabasca River with organochlorines, those chemical compounds linked by some researchers to cancer and other human health concerns. The organochlorine-free quality of a CTMP mill's effluent is a result of a key difference between the bleaching processes used in the two types of pulp production. Unlike kraft mills, CTMP mills do not use chlorine or chlorine dioxide to bleach brown pulp. Instead, Millar Western uses Scott Paper's alkaline peroxide bleaching process to produce a high-yield pulp which, in the case of its 100 percent-aspen product, is marketed for papermakers in the United States, Europe, Mexico, Japan, and elsewhere and is reported to be highly competitive with bleached kraft pulp. Soon after startup of the Whitecourt mill, Millar Western launched its second CTMP mill, an all-aspen, $250-million, 240,000 metric tonne-per-year project at Meadow Lake, Saskatchewan, in which the Saskatchewan government invested between $50 and $60 million.[33] At Meadow Lake, because of low water flow in the Beaver River, the company employed a closed-cycle, zero-effluent process. The mill evaporates all of its liquid effluent and produces only solid waste—a dream come true for those environmentalists whose concerns centre on the water pollution generated by mills. Meadow Lake's 100 percent-aspen alkaline peroxide pulp stands up well in competition with kraft pulps, performs well with recycled papers, and is used for smoothness, formation, and printability.[34] Ultimately, though, for CTMP pulp to continue to capture an increasing share of world market pulp sales—by 1991, its share of the world market pulp industry stood at 10 percent, twice its 1981 share—producers such as Millar Western must search for new technologies to overcome the continuing scepticism in some markets over the weakness and dinginess of CTMP pulp when compared to kraft pulps.

Canada's economic history is littered with examples of political entrepreneurship such as Millar Western's foray into pulp production. Some have succeeded, many have failed: we do not see a simple moral in a complex history of business and politics. If Millar Western (or another of the smaller pulp or newsprint mills) succeeds despite the soft markets and weak prices of the early 1990s, its success will likely be attributed to the vision and hard work of the entrepreneurs—the Millar family of Whitecourt—who saw their opportunity to expand and took it. If the company fails, the failure will in all likelihood be blamed on the Getty government's decision to subsidize Millar Western's pulp mill and to intervene in the industry at all. The historical reality, as we have seen, is more complicated and morally ambiguous than these black-or-white scenarios would suggest. The Getty government confronted a real economic crisis in 1986 after world oil and grain prices collapsed, and Alberta public opinion was strongly behind the decision to force the pace of economic diversification. It was the systemic economic crisis, not ideology or party or personalities, that led the Alberta government into the forestry and pulp mill initiative sketched in this chapter. The northern aspen forests were to be *fully utilized*, and from this an empire of pulp, newsprint, and fine paper mills was to be constructed and Alberta's oil-dependent economy made less variable and vulnerable. Multinational investments would be needed, and to get them the government of Alberta would promote, build infrastructure, offer financing, and provide renewable twenty-year management agreements, or secure tenure, over vast tracts of northern forest. There was not much room for the small independents in this vision: a few would try to use government support to get into the bigger leagues, others would go out of business.

Whether the entire forestry strategy and intervention will succeed is a question taken up in later chapters. Here we will say that the Getty government's policy was based upon assumptions and forecasts that, with hindsight's advantage, do not appear to have been reliable or solid. But the policy was a gamble undertaken in a situation of uncertainty, and we shall see that it was to generate political consequences that nobody anticipated.

1. Environment Council of Alberta, *The Environmental Effects of Forestry Operations in Alberta: Report and Recommendations* (Edmonton: Douglas Printing, 1979), 103.
2. Speech of F.W. McDougall to the Canadian Institute of Forestry, Rocky Mountain Section. Grande Prairie, 5 and 6 February 1982.
3. Government of Alberta, "Forest Industry Development Position Paper," 28 May 1985 (revised 3 February 1986).
4. Government of Alberta, *Proposal for an Industrial and Science Strategy for Albertans, 1985-1990* (Edmonton, 1984), 39.
5. "Alberta Tories Are on the Run," *Financial Post*, 20 July 1992.
6. Our sources on Getty's role include two of the architects of the forestry initiative. Interviews with Fred McDougall, 21 May 1991 and J.A. Brennan, 9 May 1991.

7 . Government of Alberta, "Forest Industry Development Position Paper."

8 . Brennan, "Stimulating Investment," 2.

9 . Peter Woodbridge, "Canada's Future Role as a Supplier of Wood Products," *Forest Products Research Society Proceedings, Timber Supply: Issues and Options,* 2–4 October (1979), 97.

10 . H. G. J. Aitken, "Defensive Expansion: The State and Economic Growth in Canada," *Approaches to Canadian Economic History,* W.T. Easterbrook and M.H. Watkins, eds. (Toronto: McClelland and Stewart, 1967), 221.

11 . EKONO Consultants Ltd., *A Prospectus For Value Added Paper Manufacturing in the Province of Alberta,* 1987.

12 . See the 1973 Kierans Report, *Report on Natural Resources Policy in Manitoba.* Prepared for the Secretariat for the Planning and Priorities Committee of Cabinet, Winnipeg; and John N. McDougall, "Natural Resources and National Politics: A Look at Three Canadian Resource Industries," *The Politics of Economic Policy,* G. Bruce Doern, ed. (Toronto: University of Toronto Press, 1985). (This study is Vol. 40 of the studies produced for the research program of the Royal Commission on the Economic Union and Development Prospects for Canada.)

13 . *The Edmonton Journal,* 22 March 1987, B2.

14 . Northern Alberta Development Council, *Trends in Northern Alberta: A Statistical Overview 1970-1990* (March 1990), Sec.O.

15 . Interview with Al Adair, 14 November 1991.

16 . "Getty Won't Follow Lougheed's Economic Dream," *Calgary Herald,* 6 February 1986, A20.

17 . "Millar Western Cashes in on Provincial Initiative . . . ," *Canadian Forest Industries,* September 1988.

18 . "Sparrow Wants to Double Output of Alberta's Forest Industry," *British Columbia Lumberman* 71, no. 4 (April 1987).

19 . Interview with J. A. Brennan, 9 May 1991.

20 . Brennan, "Stimulating Investment," 9-10.

21 . "Alberta Company Will Build $185–Million Greenfield Market CTMP Mill at Whitecourt," *Pulp and Paper Journal* May/June 1986, 8.

22 . Ibid., 13.

23 . See the comments by R. V. Smith, head of MacMillan Bloedel in 1986, as cited in Jeremy Wilson, "Wilderness Politics in BC: The Business Dominated State and the Containment of Environmentalism," *Policy Communities and Public Policy in Canada: A Structural Approach,* W. Coleman and G. Skogstad, eds. (Mississauga: Copp Clark, 1990).

24 . Interview with Frank Crawford, 28 May 1992.

25 . Alberta Department of Energy and Natural Resources, *Public Hearings on Proposed Timber Developments in the Berland-Fox Area, Fox Creek* 1 (1979), 415.

26 . Barry Mjolsness, president, Independent Sawmillers of Alberta, in a letter to *The Edmonton Journal,* 9 August 1992.

27 . Interview with Barry Mjolsness, 10 August 1993.

28 . Interview with Al Brennan, 9 May 1991.

29 . On Alberta in the seventies, see Larry Pratt, "The State and Province-Building: Alberta's Development Strategy," *The Canadian State*, Leo Panitch, ed. (Toronto: University Press, 1977).

30 . *Canadian Forest Industries*, September 1988.

31 . *Pulp and Paper Canada* 89, no. 10 (1988), 27.

32 . Mark Stevenson, "Meet Millar Western, the Mr. Clean of the Pulp Industry," *Financial Times of Canada*, 29 June 1992, 6.

33 . Ken L. Patrick, "Millar Western Launches Plans for Second BCTMP Mill in Saskatchewan," *Pulp and Paper*, May 1990.

34 . Ibid., 78.

CHAPTER 3

Daishowa: Good Buddhists
of Fuji City

YOU HAVE TO REMEMBER THAT WE THINK DAISHOWA IS A FINE
COMPANY. THE SAITO FAMILY ARE PEOPLE YOU CAN WORK WITH AND
TRUST. THEY'RE BUDDHISTS, YOU KNOW.
—*FORMER MINISTER OF FORESTRY, LAND AND WILDLIFE LEROY FJORDBOTTEN*
IN CONVERSATION WITH THE AUTHORS

THE LARGER-THAN-LIFE ARE SUDDENLY BEING CUT DOWN TO SIZE.
[DAISHOWA'S] RYOEI SAITO, EXTRAVAGANT COLLECTOR OF VAN GOGH,
RENOIR AND RODIN, APOSTLE OF BUSINESS EXPANSION, BANE OF
ENVIRONMENTALISTS FROM SYDNEY TO SHIZUOKA, AND THE "EMPEROR"
OF A GOOD CHUNK OF MID-JAPAN SUFFERED THE HUMILIATION OF
ARREST ON BRIBERY CHARGES ON 11 NOVEMBER.
—*THE FAR EASTERN ECONOMIC REVIEW, 25 NOVEMBER 1993*

 Alberta wanted to attract the investment of the forest indus-
try transnationals from Japan and other countries of the
Pacific Rim, and it had reason to expect some success. The
paper industries of East Asia were expanding by the mid-
eighties and the supply of pulp was increasingly tight. Following the so-called "chip shock" of 1979–80, when American producers of
softwood chips exploited Japan's heavy dependence on supplies from the United
States Pacific Northwest and dramatically increased their prices, the Japanese
pulp and paper industry, supported by the Ministry of International Trade and
Industry (MITI), had adopted a long-term strategy of diversifying the supply of
raw materials by developing new sources of fibre overseas. Up to the recession
of the early 1990s, each wave of expansion in Japan's paper industry—and they
were steady due to the continuing revolution in office and information technologies—prompted outward searches for long-term, reliable wood supplies.

74

From the 1960s onward, North America had been the favoured source of supply. '

In the early eighties, MITI's Industrial Structural Council attempted to organize a long-term strategy for Japan's pulp and paper industry, then languishing in a deep recession caused by the two oil price shocks and weak international pulp prices. MITI identified two major problems that had to be addressed before Japan's major pulp and paper producers could continue to expand. In the first place, the paper industry in Japan suffered from a chronic problem of surplus capacity caused by overinvestment, of spending far too much on new plant and equipment; the overinvestment resulted, MITI said, from the tendency of the big paper producers to try to expand their market shares in Japan, from MITI's lack of success in trying to rationalize and eliminate the less profitable firms, and from the absence of a dominant company that could impose order on the fifteen or so largest pulp and paper producers (the Japanese industry had been forcibly broken up by the Americans during the postwar occupation). MITI, which had succeeded in imposing order or "administrative guidance" in steel and several other big Japanese industries, was clearly frustrated by the growth-driven paper industry's endemic problem of excess capacity:

> The government has carried out directly and indirectly the administrative guidance about the industry's investment in facilities and equipment, but the effects of the guidance have not been sufficient because of the producers' fierce competition of their market shares and their desire to expand their production. If the producers do not change these problematic attitudes, the leadership of the government will continue to be ineffective.[1]

MITI was not able to reorganize the Japanese pulp and paper industry. To skip ahead of our story, in the early 1990s after a new cycle of big investments by pulp and paper companies (including in Alberta), another crisis of excess capacity was visited on the industry around the world. MITI's efforts to limit new Japanese investment in plant and equipment in pulp and paper ended in 1988, and it was still unable to engineer a rationalization of this very unstable sector.[2] Because of the growing economic interdependence of Japan and western Canada, the crisis of the early nineties demonstrated the vulnerability of Alberta's forestry and pulp industries to what the head of MITI's paper, pulp, and printing division called "Japanese paper companies . . . doing stupid things by selling more and making more losses."[3]

The second basic problem identified by MITI in the early 1980s was that of securing a more diversified supply of raw materials and partially-processed commodities—such as pulp—from overseas. The Japanese expected to encounter tight supplies and high prices of raw materials—softwood chips, hardwood chips, or even pulp—for paper production throughout the eighties, and MITI strongly emphasized the need to expand the use of recycled paper and to reduce consumption. Still, overseas chips and pulp would be absolutely essential. Diversifying supply was linked to the problem of getting prices down and improving the costs of Japanese capital, and after being gouged on woodchips by the Americans the government did not intend to rely on market forces alone:

> We must emphasize [said MITI] the necessity of diversification of the overseas sources of supply of woodchips and of increasing the independence of the industry. It is still fresh in our memory that the industry's large dependence on a particular supply area placed the industry in a very disadvantageous position when the industry negotiated with suppliers about the price-hikes of wood chips. The prices of imported wood chips increased rapidly, and in addition the excessive competition among the Japanese producers confused the import picture. Not only the price of woodchips but also the prices of finished goods increased, resulting in instability in both the industry and the Japanese economy.[4]

Also used as a strategy in coping with the oil crisis, one of Japan's tools in coping with the political economy of outward dependence on raw materials was to promote foreign direct investment by Japanese transnationals to bring on new supplies, particularly in politically stable jurisdictions—Canada, Australia, and some Asian countries—thereby weakening the power of resource owners to dictate prices. Relying on foreign investment via transnational companies rather than on trade alone to secure supplies of raw or semiprocessed materials would give the integrated Japanese firms far more stability and control over the entire process of production; in turn, this would help stabilize the Japanese business system. MITI wanted the *sogoshosha*, the big trading companies like Mitsubishi, Mitsui, and Marubeni, and the Japanese banks more closely involved in joint ventures and the sharing of risks overseas; and it encouraged the industry in diversifying its supplies to adopt the strategy known as development and import, or D and I, in which integrated Japanese companies agree to develop, partially upgrade and market within their own global systems up to 100 percent of resources in return for guarantees that the crude oil, woodchips, pulp, and so on can then be imported by Japan where the higher value-added activity occurs. This, as we mentioned in the case of Alberta's strategy, can be very attractive to the resource owner as well. Some of the risks involved in D and I arose from the need for very big front-end capital investments in resource projects and long periods waiting for returns, while others were associated with nationalism and the demands of host countries for a larger share of the benefits of resource development. But the strategy had served the interests of resource-scarce Japan, and MITI saw it as essential in resolving the paper industry's problems. The Japanese government, MITI noted, "should support the D and I of the industry with financial assistance as much as possible because of the importance of the industry as suppliers of paper to the Japanese economy. ... The Japanese industrial users of paper, the trading companies and the main banks of the paper producers should establish a full-scale back-up system for the industry's D and I."[5]

MITI's essential message was that the Japanese paper industry needed to internationalize much more of its system of production if it intended to keep expanding and to resolve the dilemma of resource scarcity. It must form partnerships with local governments and business interests and come to terms with resource nationalism in fibre-producing states: the industry should accommodate the desire of host governments to have more of the value-added production occur in their own jurisdictions—to produce pulp, for instance, rather than woodchips. As the scale, costs, and risks of pulp production increased, the economics pointed to closer cooperation and partnerships between the integrated companies and the governments of fibre-producing jurisdictions. The highest level of industrial activities and technical improvement—and the Japanese, who tend to think of the world political economy in hierarchical terms, had a definite international division of labour in mind—would still occur in the paper mills of Japan. The Japanese government wanted to see some pulp production, together with pollution-intensive chemical and heavy industries, shifted to overseas sites for reasons of ecology and rising costs. Japan's stringent environmental controls, high energy costs, and prohibitive land values precluded further domestic growth in forestry exploitation or pulp production. To expand paper output and to grow, the Japanese industry needed to acquire new long-term supplies of fibre and new sites for pulp production.

This is why the Getty forestry initiative appealed to some firms and, it seems probable, to MITI when they heard about it from Al Brennan and other Alberta officials in 1986. Alberta's enormous uncommitted reserves of northern aspen mixed with softwoods, secured through renewable twenty-year forestry management agreements, could offer a Japanese investor and its banks the assurance of up to one hundred years of secure supply of high quality pulp. Along with rising pulp prices and forecasts of tight supplies, these were the interests that led a number of Japan's transnationals to northern Alberta in the 1980s. Among the Canadian provinces, conservative, free enterprise Alberta was attractive because of the extent of the uncommitted resources and because the Japanese wanted political stability and continuity as an aspect of their security of tenure. By 1986–87 its labour costs were below those in British Columbia and other provinces, and forestry-related environmentalism was still relatively weak and tame in Alberta. Japan's timing was heavily influenced by the rapid appreciation of the yen after the so-called Plaza Agreement of 1985 between the United States and Japan. The strong yen was a short run factor that made it attractive for Japanese companies to acquire or build new overseas assets such as pulp mills; a new mill could be built or bought in North America in the late 1980s for half what it would cost in Japan. All of these factors reinforced MITI's case for internationalization. By extension, they should also have given fibre-producing areas such as Alberta a good deal of bargaining power.

Armed with promotional materials, including a mawkish video translated into Japanese, Korean, and Chinese extolling Alberta's abundant low-cost hardwood supply, the excellent pulp-making qualities of aspen, the plentiful and reasonably-priced energy resources, its probusiness government and its "excellent labour climate," Forestry Minister LeRoy Fjordbotten, Al Brennan, and other Alberta officials toured East Asia in 1986–87 looking for capital investment.[6] There they contacted several leading paper producers, including Daishowa, Oji Paper, Honshu Paper, and major trading companies like Mitsubishi. Trade and investment missions to the Pacific Rim had become almost routine in the Alberta government since Premier Lougheed's official tour of the region in 1983, but Alberta was now in a position to provide much practical advice and detailed information concerning the provincial government's interest in attracting investments in major forestry and pulp and paper projects. Now Alberta was giving out its phone number: actively bidding for investment, offering to pay for expensive road, rail, and other infrastructure and to assist with project financing.

Japan's second-largest pulp and paper producer, Daishowa Paper Manufacturing Company Limited of Fuji City, was one of the targets of Alberta's promotion. The company had six big paper mills with forty or so paper machines to supply, and by 1987 it was embarked on a major program of international expansion. In some ways, Daishowa and Alberta seemed made for one another: certainly their views of the Japanese/Canadian division of labour were congruent, and both had reputations as big spenders with great expectations. With three billion dollars (US) in sales and record profits in 1986, Daishowa already had an established presence in British Columbia and was about to embark on an ambitious, even grandiose, plan of "globalization" that would see it making seven large foreign investments—mostly in Canada and the United States—worth 3.5 billion dollars (US) between 1986 and 1991. Behind this burst of growth abroad, most of which was financed via debt, was a corporate strategy of securing within Daishowa's own system of production sufficient long-term fibre supplies and pulp to feed its expanding network of paper mills in Japan. Daishowa's controlling shareholders, the Saito family, spoke publicly of the need to shift overseas more of the company's lower-value (and pollution-intensive) productive activities.[7] The company has a reputation as a maverick: for MITI, Daishowa is the *enfant terrible* of Japan's paper industry, an aggressive risk-taker whose investment binges and attempts to seize market share from its competitors are held by some to be partly responsible for the industry's chronic problems of excess capacity.[8] Actually, Daishowa's aggressiveness and independence make it a convenient scapegoat for an entire industry that has a history of "disaster myopia"—of failing to learn from past calamities, of excessive and unrealistic optimism, of discounting risks and assuming, like complacent homeowners in a floodplain, that today's good fortune is bound to continue indefinitely. The international petroleum industry's inability to see that oil prices, which had reached unheard-of heights during the two oil shocks of 1973–74 and 1979–80, must decline in the 1980s because of weakening demand and the emergence of new supply was a classic case of disaster myopia; so too was the imprudent lending of the big Western banks to a handful of resource-rich and newly industrializing nations in Latin America, Eastern Europe, and Asia, most of which borrowers fell into arrears and approached the brink of default in 1982–83.[9] In these cases and in the international pulp and paper industry's big expansion in the late 1980s, obsessions with growth in assets or market share replaced a prudent interest in solvency. Daishowa's lack of financial prudence was well known in the business and ought to have set off alarm bells, but it did not do so because Alberta's negotiators were transfixed by the myth of Japan's invincibility.

Daishowa was founded by Chiichiro Saito in the early 1920s as a raw materials brokerage company to supply Japan's paper industry. The Saito family, whose net worth today is reckoned to be around one billion dollars (US),[10] has always resisted attempts to diminish its control over Daishowa and has taken on additional debt rather than issuing new equity for expansion. (Between 1987 and 1990 Daishowa doubled its debt to three billion dollars (US), more than five times shareholders' equity.) The ruling patriarch of the modern paper manufacturing giant is the founder's son, Ryoei Saito, in the early 1990s the still ruling "Honorary Chairman" of Daishowa who is known to some as the "Shogun of Shizuoka" Prefecture. It was Ryoei Saito who took control of Daishowa after World War II and built it into a fully integrated pulp, paper, and paperboard manufacturer that today produces about 10 percent of Japan's total paper and paperboard production. He led his family-controlled, publicly traded company in a violent struggle against the dominant members of the Japanese paper industry, Oji Paper Company, Jujo Paper Company, and Honshu Paper Company. This trio had been created from Oji Paper, part of the great Mitsui *zaibatsu*, when Oji was split up at the end of World War II. Daishowa began building new paper mills in 1950 and used aggressive price cutting to gain market share at the expense of its rivals; simultaneously, Saito protected his investments with political connections, large contributions—and, it is alleged, bribes—to the Liberal Democratic Party (LDP), which governed Japan until its electoral defeat in July 1993. The fall of the LDP commenced the fall and disgrace of the seventy-seven-year-old honourary chairman, if not of the company itself. Strongly supported by a population disgusted with constant scandals, Japan's new reform-minded government instructed prosecutors to investigate many of the big corporations and executives who had kept the LDP in power so long.

On 11 November 1993, the elder Saito was hauled off by police under the glare of television cameras and arrested for corruption, his home and offices raided by investigators from the Tokyo Public Prosecutors' Office, all of his influence and conduct exposed in the popular press. For a man who had, back in 1975, been treated with kid gloves when called to testify before parliament on why Daishowa had been poisoning Shizuoka's groundwater by dumping untreated sludge from its mills, all of this must have been mortifying.[11] Recall that this was the great Japanese industrialist whose judgement, power, and wealth the Alberta government was counting upon for Daishowa's success. Had there been no warning signs?

It was the same Ryoei Saito who had amazed the art world in 1990 by purchasing two paintings, a van Gogh and a Renoir, for an astounding 160.6 million dollars (US), and later promised to have the paintings put in his coffin "and burned with me when I die."[12] (After a predictable uproar in the international art world, he retracted). Saito, his brothers, and his sons tightly controlled Daishowa's empire from their Fuji City and Tokyo head offices, even though it is a publicly-traded company with shareholders other than the family, and they appear to delegate little real decision-making authority to those who ostensibly run the company's foreign subsidiaries. A common criticism of the eldest Saito is that he often made little distinction between his personal wealth and that of Daishowa and that he had a habit of extravagant and reckless risk-taking. It was alleged that he used one billion dollars (US) of Daishowa's money to buy up art galleries, foundations, golf courses, and works by Marc Chagall and other great artists. In the late 1970s, just when the cyclical paper industry was about to enter a period of excess productive capacity, the elder Saito committed hundreds of millions of dollars to new plant and equipment. Daishowa's debt soared, and in 1981 the company's main bank and largest minority shareholder, Sumitomo Bank Limited, moved in to take temporary control of the firm, relegating Ryoei Saito to a ceremonial status. A consequence of this affair, which Alberta surely understood, was that after this Daishowa had no main bank to support its aggressive strategies.

Many Daishowa assets, including golf courses and much of the art collection, were sold to bring the debt under control before the Saito family was allowed to resume its traditional authority over the company's affairs. Perhaps some of these events and the emotional wear and tear caused by environmental and aboriginal resistance to Daishowa's operations explain the defensiveness of Daishowa's executives overseas: in Alberta at least, the company has sometimes appeared hectoring and arrogant, as when it lectured the popular mayor of Edmonton, Jan Reimer, for giving public support to the Lubicon Indians, and totally out of touch with local opinion, as when it insisted on its rights to log in Wood Buffalo National Park in northeastern Alberta. We return to these issues in the next chapter.

We can see a pattern in Daishowa's past history of aggressive expansion, of becoming over-extended because of the Saito family's habits of empire-building (but also because of the unstable structure of Japan's paper industry). As of late 1993, it owed banks Y478 billion, a debt so large that it threatens the survival of some of its biggest creditors. How did this happen? Acting upon the philosophy that bigger is better, Daishowa has tended to borrow heavily to finance growth, with an emphasis on building assets rather than a good bottom line. It was a leader in the internationalization of the Japanese pulp and paper companies, developing over a period of twenty-five years a stable source of raw material supply for its mills in Japan through large investments overseas. As an independent paper producer without long-term supplies of raw materials or so-called "captive pulp"—pulp produced and sold within the same vertically integrated company—Daishowa needed to develop its own supply of lower-cost fibre rather than purchase it from its competitors. Daishowa was the first Japanese pulp and paper company to import softwood chips from the United States (in 1965), and in 1967 it went into a joint venture with a small Australian timber company to form Harris-Daishowa, a company producing eucalyptus hardwood chips in New South Wales for export to Daishowa's mills in Japan. Conservationists used the arrangement as a symbol of Australia's "slash and burn" approach to resource use. From an early date Harris-Daishowa has been accused by some Australians of underpricing the woodchips it sells to its Japanese parent and of paying minimal royalties and taxes. And, predictably, there is the issue of who gets the value added. Economic nationalists argue that Daishowa, having initially committed itself to upgrade resources in Australia, failed to integrate its woodchip operation into an Australian pulp and paper industry; as an Australian Broadcast Corporation report concluded in 1988:

> Figures supplied by the Japan Trade Centre indicate that of the major exporters of woodchips to Japan, Australia receives the lowest price per tonne. This is despite the fact that we are the largest exporter and produce the most uniform, highest quality chips. . . . So nationally, we now appear to be locked into a low value added, raw material exporting industry, with little prospect of any further processing. And as the more labour intensive saw log industry continues its decline, so forest jobs will keep disappearing.[13]

The Australian critics of Harris-Daishowa, like many Canadian critics of the forest products industry, are plainly ambivalent about the alternatives: some (nationalists) want the industrialization of the forests, the value-added jobs, and the wealth they associate with processing the raw materials into pulp and paper, but under Australian ownership; while others (environmentalists) do not want the "dirty, highly polluting industry" of pulp manufacturing in Australia at all.[14] The underlying argument is not just about Japanese ownership, it is also about the wisdom of using forestry resources in a strategy of industrialization. There is no easy solution to the argument in Australia or anywhere else.

Shortly after its move to Australia, Daishowa arrived in Canada, forming an alliance with one of Japan's big trading companies, Marubeni Corporation, to become partners with Weldwood of Canada in the Cariboo Pulp and Paper Company, producing softwood bleached kraft pulp at Quesnel, British Columbia, 650 kilometres north of Vancouver. Cariboo went into production in 1972. In 1978 Daishowa set up a Canadian subsidiary, Daishowa Canada, in Vancouver, and in 1981 its Quesnel pulp operations were expanded via a joint venture with West Fraser Timber Company: the Quesnel River Pulp Mill, producing thermomechanical pulp (TMP) and bleached chemithermomechanical pulp (CTMP). A major modernization and expansion of this facility was carried out in 1988 when a third pulping line was added, increasing capacity by 50 percent and making Quesnel River Pulp one of the largest TMP/CTMP mills in the world. Modernization of pulp mills means, among other things, automation via the introduction of labour-saving technologies throughout the entire pulping process; at Quesnel River Pulp, the cost of the expansion was sixty-five million dollars and it produced just twenty new jobs, bringing the total workforce to one hundred. Of the 150,000 tonnes of pulp marketed by Quesnel River Pulp in Japan annually, Daishowa Paper Manufacturing takes 80 percent for the production of newsprint. The parent company notes in its own history, published in Japan in 1991 (but not translated into English), that the then-Social Credit government of British Columbia "enthusiastically welcomed" the Quesnel expansion, providing 50 percent discounts on electricity costs and a number of tax incentives. It is doubtful whether these incentives had much influence on Daishowa's decision to expand the Quesnel River Pulp complex. Its main motive in expanding its Quesnel operation and making new investments in Canada was "to secure the supply of pulp in light of the tight supply of pulp in the world market. In addition, the low price of trees and electricity in Canada increased the profitability of Daishowa." What Daishowa really needed was low-cost captive pulp, not tax breaks.

It was anticipated that the domestic [Japanese] consumption of pulp would increase by 5.3 percent from the previous year's consumption. Therefore, securing the supply of pulp in the world market was a very important issue for Japanese paper producers. Our company decided to take advantage of our production sites in North America. We had to cope with the prospective production increases of Shiraoi and Yoshinaga factories by the production in North America.[15]

Daishowa argues that the key to successful foreign investment in Canada lies in the corporation's active role in local society. When Daishowa joins and supports local societies, local employees come to feel themselves to be part of Daishowa (instead of a labour force in an adversarial relationship with the company). Having successfully integrated local employees into Daishowa's system of production, the company is then capable of practising what it modestly calls "Daishowism" (the literal translation of *Daishowaisumu*)—that is, high-quality, low-cost expansion of capacity.[16] Less kindly, "Daishowism" could also be called acting imprudently on the basis of limited resources and extravagant disaster myopia.

In the late 1980s, Daishowa went on an extraordinary investment binge in North America, apparently in a bid to acquire new properties while the yen's appreciation against the dollar made it cheap to do so. As an independent, Daishowa did this without the backing of any of Japan's major trading companies or, it would seem, the support of the big Japanese banks. Daishowa grandly referred to its "globalization strategy," although its foreign investment was centred on a handful of developed, politically stable countries—Canada, Australia, the United States. In 1988 alone, Daishowa bought a mill that produced telephone directories in Port Angeles, Washington; spent 631 million dollars (Cdn.) to buy a newsprint mill and kraft pulp mill complex at Quebec City from British-owned Reed International (the price was called an "outrageous sum by Canadian Standards"[17]); and announced its decision to spend 550 million dollars (Cdn.) to construct a 340,000 tonne-per-year bleached kraft pulp mill near the town of Peace River in the northwest of Alberta. The latter was to prove a costly commitment of Daishowa's resources. Although Daishowa had been approached by Canadian Forest Products Limited (Canfor), a Vancouver-based corporation with large sawmills at High Level and Grande Prairie, to build a jointly-owned pulp mill near Peace River, "Honourable Chairman" Ryoei Saito took the decision to construct and operate the new pulp mill on the basis of 100 percent control. That decision was based on an optimistic view of future pulp prices. Curiously, the Daishowa corporate history gives no credit at all to the Getty government for its decision to take up the Peace River investment. It states that the opening of the Peace River mill would commemorate the hundred-year anniversary of the birth of Daishowa's founder, Chiichiro Saito, and the fiftieth anniversary of the company's founding. But what drove the investment at Peace River was the company's projected requirement for more of its own captive kraft pulp in its Japanese paper mills. Quality pulp produced at Peace River would be blended with domestic deinked pulp at Daishowa's new Number 4 paper machine at Iwanuma Mill in northern Japan to produce six hundred tonnes per day of newsprint. Daishowa had examined other sources of short-fibre hardwoods (it already had experience pulping hardwoods such as eucalyptus in Asia and Australia), but these had all been rejected because of supply limitations: according to the company itself, "the single most compelling reason for the choice of northern Alberta was the abundant wood supply in an accessible location. Each year 1.3 million cubic metres of hardwood timber will be required to supply 70 percent of the fibre needs of the Peace River mill."[18] The company believed that the forest management area offered by Alberta would give it a century of fibre supply; the area was larger than Kyushou, one of Japan's four main islands. In 1989, the then president of Daishowa Forest Products Limited, Koichi Kitigawa, linked the Peace River mill to the company's expansion in Japan:

When we get into a new mill facility we try to make sure that 50 percent of the product will be captive in that we will increase production of our pulping facilities with the understanding that paper will be manufactured in Japan, and that we will add paper machines as required, as we increase pulp production. In Japan demand is growing faster than in North America.[19]

There was no auction for the northwest forests, indeed there were no real public hearings of any kind on the proposed mill. The provincial government and the local community badly wanted Daishowa's investment, in part because of the collapse of oil and gas exploration in northwest Alberta and the postponement of a major *in situ* heavy oil project also planned for Peace River. The Getty government wanted to have its forestry strategy validated by one of the big pulp and paper transnationals, believing that Daishowa's investment would force the rest of the industry to take a serious look at Alberta. The fear of exclusion from an important new source of supply is sometimes enough to prompt integrated transnational companies to invest as a form of long-term insurance. This was, in fact, what happened after Daishowa's go-ahead announcement in February 1988. Even though it received financial support only for infrastructure, Daishowa's decision triggered a large number of proposals for new forest industry investments or expansions of existing pulp mills in Alberta. It was not financial support but the prospect of securing a supply of high-quality fibre for the expansion of productive capacity that led some of the world's biggest forest companies to the Alberta government.

Bargaining and the Viability of the Industry

Since the Alberta government controlled the access to the resources and the companies were anticipating tight supplies, it should have been able to negotiate a favourable agreement with Daishowa. (In 1992, financially-strapped Daishowa sold half of the Peace River pulp mill and its other Alberta assets to Marubeni, the Japanese trading company, forming Daishowa-Marubeni International, for an undisclosed sum. While the sale exposed Daishowa's precarious financial position, it did not alter existing arrangements between Alberta and the pulp mill owners.) Did Alberta use its control over resources to negotiate a tough agreement? The Japanese company obtained a renewable twenty-year FMA to harvest an area of more than twenty-four thousand square kilometres plus an agreement to spend sixty-five million dollars on roads, rail access, and a new bridge across the Peace River at the mill site sixteen kilometres downstream from the town of Peace River (the site is not nearly far enough downstream to prevent the town from suffering a good deal of air pollution from the mill). Alberta, the federal government, and Daishowa shared the thirty million dollar cost of building the new bridge even though—as anyone who has visited the site can see—the location is advantageous only to the pulp mill, and then mainly in the winter logging months. Apart from the infrastructure costs, Daishowa received no direct government assistance in the financing of the mill, raising the obvious question of why Alberta would then offer risky incentives to subsequent projects such as the Alberta-Pacific pulp mill near Athabasca and others. Daishowa's willingness to invest without loan guarantees or other government incentives was very good evidence that on some of the other mills Alberta had offered more public money and had assumed more risks than was necessary.

A larger issue is whether the Alberta government liquidated its forest assets for short term political gain (and economic stimulus) at the expense of long term sustainable development as well as future resource revenues. Recall that the Forestry Department and the Getty cabinet were interested in the "large-scale utilization" of the aspen resource, believing that this "would make a major contribution to the diversification of the forest products industry, and hence to the rejuvenation and diversification of the Provincial economy as well."[20] The FMA negotiated with Daishowa gives heavy emphasis to Alberta's desire for rapid and full utilization of the resource and to the drive for value-added industries:

WHEREAS it is anticipated that the initial production of pulp and paper products may be increased to 2,000 air dry metric tonnes or more of pulp per day as markets and other circumstances warrant; and...

WHEREAS the Minister desires to provide for the fullest possible economic utilization of forest stands and stable employment in local communities, and to ensure a perpetual supply of benefits and products while maintaining a forest environment of high quality by maximizing the value of the timber resource base and ensuring that it yields an uninterrupted flow of timber over time.[21]

Using the incentive of increased access to the resource in return for more investment, the government withheld an area of Crown timber within the FMA—the "5-year reserve area for second mill"—from Daishowa's overall cutting area. Over and above the timberlands allotted to the one thousand tonnes-per-day kraft pulp mill, Daishowa's FMA linked the company's access to additional Crown timber to the construction of further pulping facilities and/or a paper mill. The company agreed to double the capacity of the kraft mill to two thousand tonnes-per-day by 1996 in return for access to timber reserved by the minister; and it agreed to commence construction by 1996 of either a CTMP mill with a capacity of 500 tonnes of pulp per day or a paper machine with an initial rated capacity of 220,000 finished metric tonnes of paper annually. When either of these commence construction, the remaining timber reserve area is to be released for Daishowa.[22]

Nothing better reflects the government's unfounded expectations than this grandiose and unsustainable plan of industrialization in the Peace River region. Putting aside the environmental impacts of the proposed mills, the government's strategy flew in the face of certain basic realities concerning the location of pulp and paper production. The economics of paper production and transportation dictate that the higher value papers are made closer to the paper user in the United States, Japan, or Europe. Further, the structure of labour supply and wages gives countries with high population densities like Japan a competitive advantage over Canada in the production of value-added commodities such as paper. This industrial pattern or division of labour is determined by costs and distance and is reinforced, as evidenced by the quotations cited in this chapter, by the corporate strategies of the big Japanese paper producers and the policy of the Japanese government. Alberta's bureaucracy—which is not economically illiterate—knew these facts, and the province knew as well that it lacked the leverage to coerce Daishowa into doing things that were against its business interests. For what interest would Daishowa have in investing in a paper industry in remote northern Alberta, a strategy that would be bound to conflict with the interests of its paper-producing empire in Japan? At most, Daishowa had committed itself in the FMA to do a feasibility study of an expansion, a CTMP plant, a paper mill; meanwhile, it had more than enough timber to run its new one thousand tonnes-per-day Peace River Pulp Mill for many years. Accepting these commitments at face value, the Alberta government acted like a young and innocent woman who, having surrendered her chastity to a rich stranger for a few roses and the promise of a happy life, is surprised to learn that she has already given away all that really interested her suitor.

Daishowa-Marubeni International's bleached kraft pulp mill near Peace River town is a most impressive operation; highly automated and using state-of-the-art technologies that allow it to employ only about 330 workers at the mill, it was designed to produce 245,000 tonnes-per-year of hardwood bleached kraft pulp and 95,000 tonnes-per-year of high brightness softwood bleached kraft. The pulp mill is run by technology—all areas of the operation are tied into a centralized computerized system—and flexible work teams are used (there is no union) along with a low manning concept. The mill consumes 1.8 million cubic metres of aspen hardwood each year, harvested from scattered blocks totalling about eighty square kilometres within the vast twenty-five thousand square kilometre, twenty-year FMA. The mill produces 70 percent hardwood chips and purchases the other 30 percent in softwood chips from local saw-mills, including its own operation at High Level (purchased from Canfor), 275 kilometres north of Peace River. The company uses independent contractors to supply it with hardwoods, and this (seasonal) work has created another three hundred jobs in the woodlands. In sum, it is estimated that Daishowa-Marubeni's operation is responsible for approximately fourteen hundred direct and indirect jobs in northern Alberta.

Even though Daishowa-Marubeni's operation is highly capital intensive and uses much labour-saving technology, the importance of these skilled jobs cannot be disputed. They are important to Peace River and the region, to Alberta and, of course, to the workers themselves and their families. Given the downturns in oil and agriculture described earlier, such jobs would obviously represent a positive development provided they were sustainable over the longer term. But our analysis suggests there are very serious questions about the Peace River pulp mill's viability—indeed, there are strong doubts as to the economic viability of *all* primary pulp production in northern Alberta in the long run—and we do not believe that the jobs associated with this activity can be regarded as secure. They could, however, become a liability if the Japanese transnationals hold the jobs as hostage in bargaining with the province for additional financial concessions. Our pessimism is based on the following factors.

The success of the Daishowa-Marubeni mill, the Alberta-Pacific mill, and the smaller pulp and newsprint operations built recently in Alberta ultimately depends on their ability to remain competitive and maintain market share against global competitors. According to one study, the competitiveness of bleached kraft market pulp in Alberta ranks behind Brazil, Chile, the southern United States, and the Inland Empire.[23] Alberta's ability to maintain its market share depends on its ability to keep its costs in line with those of its major competitors. The important components of cost upon which the pulp industry competes are: fibre, labour, electricity, and delivery (transportation of the product). The major market for noncaptive pulp (that is, market pulp) from Alberta is the northeastern United States. As a remote supplier to this market, Alberta faces transportation charges that are high relative to the delivery costs carried by other suppliers of wood pulp with which it competes, namely eastern Canada and southeastern United States. Most captive pulp (that is, pulp moving within integrated corporate systems) in Alberta goes to Japan; thus, we expect that tropical wood pulps enjoy at least the same advantage over Alberta with respect to delivery costs. Moreover, the wage structure in many of the countries directly competing with Alberta also erodes the competitiveness of most North American and Scandinavian (Norscan) fibres: labour costs in the Canadian pulp and paper sector average about twenty-one dollars (US) per hour, while in Brazil and Chile they are estimated to be closer to six dollars (US) per hour.

While Canadian pulp producers have in the past enjoyed significant advantages with respect to fibre and energy costs, Canada's position as a leading low cost supplier is being eroded as major supply centres shift and continue to shift over the next twenty years in response to these changes. In particular, Brazil, Chile, Indonesia, and the Iberian peninsula have joined the traditional Norscan countries as major suppliers of wood fibre to the world's pulp and paper industries. Tropical hardwoods such as eucalyptus grown on plantations have rotation cycles of just seven years, whereas aspen's is a minimum of sixty years. In a jurisdiction such as Brazil pulp production of 500,000 tonnes per year can be supplied from just 50,000 hectares of forest, whereas Daishowa-Marubeni draws on some 2.5 million hectares of northwest Alberta's forests for its daily production of about 1,000 tonnes of pulp. All of this is reason to question the assertion that Alberta's new kraft pulp mills are actually "low cost" at all: low cost relative to what and where? Daishowa-Marubeni's costs of production and its other operating costs are not public; however, those of a similar but larger (and better located) kraft pulp mill, Alberta-Pacific (ALPAC) near Athabasca, were published in a share prospectus in 1991. While ALPAC speaks of "favourable" unit operating costs owing to its economies of scale, reduced chemical needs, energy self-sufficiency, and the low cost of fibre due to flat terrain, uniform tree size, and other factors, the mill's projected operating costs are really not especially favourable in an environment of surplus capacity in which—since 1990—world pulp prices have declined to less than $430 US per tonne (or about $510 Cdn.). ALPAC's cost of production is estimated at $286 Cdn. per tonne, but its full unit operating costs also include its cost of capital ($137 Cdn. per tonne), discounts extended under its pulp sales agreement with Mitsubishi ($30 Cdn. per tonne), and delivery costs ($99 Cdn. per tonne) for a total unit operating cost of $552 Cdn. per tonne.[24] Daishowa-Marubeni's operating costs are unlikely to be lower than ALPAC's (in fact, most of its costs are likely to be higher because Daishowa-Marubeni's is a smaller mill in a more remote location), and it is clear that neither operation can be profitable until—and *if*—pulp prices rise significantly.

Predicting the potential impact of the fast-growing eucalyptus stocks on overall capacity and price in the wood pulp industry is problematic. Commercially, eucalyptus has been used in significant quantities since the early seventies, but it has emerged as more of a threat in the last decade as major commitments have been undertaken for hardwood plantations in South America and Asia. Virgin pulp production is expected to increase by seventy-eight million tonnes over the next twenty years, with hardwood pulp commanding the largest share of the new growth.[25] For world pulp prices to rise there will have to be some offsetting growth in demand, but while the emergence of sophisticated economies in many developing nations is expected to drive growth in the paper market, population and GNP growth in the industrialized countries are not expected to match the rates of growth achieved in the previous two decades. Moreover, technological changes which enhance paper strength and reduce packaging requirements are expected to dampen demand.

The multifaceted structural change taking place in the world pulp and paper industry makes it very difficult to predict pulp prices past the near future. The market pulp industry is notorious for its highly cyclical and volatile nature. And because of the magnitude of the capital investments in new productive capacity, the industry is also subject to severe debt crises during its downturns—Crestbrook (of ALPAC) and Daishowa-Marubeni are both excellent examples of this feature of the industry, one that frequently leads to instability and new forms of state intervention. When plans were being made for the building of the northern Alberta pulp mills in 1987–89, pulp prices were on the upswing of a cycle; in fact, they were at a historical peak in 1989 at over $600 US per tonne, and then commenced a sharp decline to the $430 US per tonne range. The investments made during the peak of the cycle contributed to the surplus productive capacity that depressed prices several years later. There being little realistic prospect of an early revival in the price, the long run growth potential of the northern forest is indeed limited. While it is quite true that these modern and state-of-the-art Alberta mills are in much better shape to survive a shakeout of the industry than are many older, eastern Canadian pulp mills, ultimately the western Canadian industry's survival depends on its ability to compete with the developing countries under the conditions that we have sketched.

The psychology of booms is a familiar theme in western Canada's history, and the Peace River region has had its share of such booms and their outcomes. During three years of rising pulp prices in the late 1980s, the Alberta government and the pulp and paper companies uncritically adopted a euphoric view of the future and entered into commitments that on a more realistic view of Alberta's options never should have been entertained. The full consequences of the decisions taken then have yet to manifest themselves, but a reckoning is inevitable. Not only had Alberta a good deal of experience with the euphoria of booms in the petroleum industry, but, it is worth pointing out, the province was warned by some forest industry observers that investments in new bleached kraft pulp mills should not be encouraged because of the high capital costs and uncertain product prices that are characteristic of the pulp industry. The Getty government not only ignored such warnings, it also plunged into the building of a pulp industry in northern Alberta with many financial inducements and no second thoughts. One consequence of this impolitic behaviour is that Daishowa-Marubeni International's Peace River state-of-the-art mill, important though it is to the region's economy and its people, may be a disaster looking for a time and place to happen.

1 . Japan, Ministry of International Trade and Industry, "The View of the Pulp and Paper Industry in the 1980s," Pulp and Paper Committee of the Industrial Structural Council, Kimiko Abe, trans. (30 March 1984).
2 . Jonathan Friedland, "Writing on the Wall," *Far Eastern Economic Review* (29 October 1992), 76–78.
3 . Ibid., 77.
4 . MITI, "The View of the Pulp and Paper Industry in the 1980s."
5 . Ibid.
6 . Interview with J.A. Brennan, 9 May 1991. "Privately, the message to US and offshore investors was: labour costs are low and there is a good work ethic."
7 . See the remarks by Takashi Saito, Daishowa's president, in *Nihan Keizai Shinbun*, 21 August 1988. Kimiko Abe, trans.
8 . Friedland, "Writing on the Wall"; and "Debt-ridden Daishowa Restructures," *The Nikkei Weekly*, 7 September 1991.
9 . See Benjamin J. Cohen, *In Whose Interest?* (New Haven: Yale University Press for the Council on Foreign Relations, 1986), Chap. 2.
10 . "Daishowa Paper Manufacturing Co., Ltd.," *International Directory of Company Histories* 4, A. Hast, ed. (Chicago: St. James Press, 1991), 268–70.
11 . "The Bigger They Are," *Far Eastern Economic Review*, 25 November 1993, 55.
12 . "Shogun of Shizuoka: Japanese Tycoon Who Dazzled Art World Hits a Rough Patch," *Wall Street Journal*, 28 May 1991, Sec. A, 1.
13 . Gordon Taylor and Peter Hunt, "Report on Harris-Daishowa and the Economics of Woodchipping," "Earthworm," Australian Broadcast Corporation, Radio National, 30 August 1988.
14 . Ibid.
15 . "The Positive Reaction to Internationalization," chapter 7 of Daishowa Paper Manufacturing's *Fifty Year History*, Kimiko Abe, trans. (Tokyo: May 1991).
16 . Ibid.

17 . *The Globe and Mail*, 14 June 1988, B1 and B4.
18 . James P. Morrison (Daishowa Canada), "Daishowa—A Successful Diversification Initiative," Focus Alberta: A Global Trade and Investment Forum of *The Financial Post*, Edmonton, 1989.
19 . "Japan in Canada," *Pulp & Paper Journal* (September 1989), 26-31
20 . Alberta Forest Service and Canadian Forest Service, *Proceedings of the Workshop on Aspen Pulp, Paper, and Chemicals*, Al Wong and Ted Szabo eds., Edmonton, 1987.
21 . Alberta Forests Act, Forest Management Agreement: Government of Alberta and Daishowa Canada Co. Ltd. (O.C. 424/89), 3 August 1989.
22 . Ibid., see especially Sec. 37.
23 . Woodbridge, Reed and Assoc., *Canada's Forest Industry: The Next Twenty Years* 6, Canadian Forest Service (Ottawa, 1988).
24 . Derived from a 1991 Prospectus of Crestbrook Forest Industries on the offering of 3,920,000 Common Shares.
25 . Based on Woodbridge, Reed and Associates, *Canada's Forest Industry: The Next Twenty Years*, Canadian Forest Service (Ottawa, 1988), especially Vol. 3.

CHAPTER 4

No Peace in the Valley:
The Environment, Daishowa,
and the Lubicons

A SOCIETY WITHOUT ANY OBJECTIVE LEGAL SCALE IS A TERRIBLE ONE
INDEED. BUT A SOCIETY WITH NO OTHER SCALE BUT THE LEGAL ONE IS
NOT QUITE WORTHY OF MAN EITHER.
—*ALEXANDER SOLZHENITSYN*

BECAUSE JUST AS GOOD MORALS, IF THEY ARE TO BE MAINTAINED, HAVE
NEED OF THE LAWS, SO THE LAWS, IF THEY ARE TO BE OBSERVED, HAVE
NEED OF GOOD MORALS.
—*NICCOLÒ MACHIAVELLI, DISCOURSES*

 Daishowa Canada's proposal to build a pulp mill near the
town of Peace River marked a watershed in the politics of
timber exploitation in Alberta. For the first time the provincial government had secured an investment commitment
from a major Japanese transnational forest products com-
pany. Attracted by promises of an inexpensive, abundant, long-term supply of
fibre and government-financed transportation infrastructure Daishowa's presence lent credibility to the provincial government's forest diversification venture. If Daishowa invested in Alberta other multinational firms were likely to
follow. Turning to environmental politics, the Daishowa project also marked a
watershed. Just as Daishowa's joint sponsorship in New South Wales twenty
years earlier of a woodchip export plant to fuel its Japanese mills' hunger for
fibre led to "a conservation explosion" in Australia, so too did the company's
Peace River venture serve as a catalyst for strengthening the environmental
movement in Alberta. Between 1986 and 1989 at least eighteen forestry-ori-

ented environmental groups, many centred in the communities affected most directly by pulp and paper mill developments, were born in Alberta. The significance of the government's forest strategy to the overall growth of an environmental politics is demonstrated by a fact found in the Alberta Environmental Directory—nearly one-half of the environmental groups born during this period claimed forestry as a key interest. In hindsight the Daishowa project sat perched at the threshold of two very different environmental worlds. To Daishowa's advantage its Peace River gambit faced little organized opposition during the seven months it took the province to consider and approve the company's proposal. While helping to close the door on one era in forestry politics the Daishowa project simultaneously helped open the door onto another—one characterized by more intense opposition from Natives and environmentalists.

The Regulatory Incentive to Invest

There was, as noted earlier, an important environmental dimension to the interest Japanese pulp and paper companies showed in overseas expansion in the 1980s. Strict Japanese environmental regulations were cited by Daishowa officials as an important constraint upon the company's ability to add pulp and paper mill capacity in Japan.[1] Exporting *Kogai*—pollution—as well as fine papers, automobiles, and high-technology products to other countries thus became an important element of Japanese corporate strategy.[2] Japanese corporations, eager to avoid domestic political conflict, transferred pollution-generating operations to less developed countries. In Alberta, politicians bristled at any comparison of Alberta with Third World nations and joined the Canadian representatives of Japanese transnationals to try to discredit the idea that a more lenient regulatory environment in the province played some role in attracting Japanese pulp and paper investment. Forestry minister LeRoy Fjordbotten, in a seven page rebuttal to Andrew Nikiforuk and Ed Struzik's "yellow journalism"—their attack on the province's forestry initiative—blasted this idea as "ridiculous." "Alberta," he insisted, "is on the leading edge of environmental standards."[3] Koichi Kitagawa, Daishowa Canada's vice-president and general manager, emphasized to audiences in the Peace River region that: "Alberta Environment standards are toughest in Canada but Daishowa is willing to cooperate to minimize effect in Peace River."[4]

Both men knew better. Alberta, after all, was intent upon rapidly allocating the forests, making it doubtful that it would greet companies with the toughest standards in the country. A close look at national and international pulp mill regulations in place at the time Daishowa made the decision to invest reveals their claims as self-serving and supports the position that the province's water pollution regulations played a role in stimulating Japanese interest in Alberta. When provincial politicians and civil servants were spending hundreds of thousands of dollars courting the "Shogun of Shizuoka" and other potential investors, Alberta practised a mill-specific approach to regulating the pulp and paper industry. Provincewide standards for the water pollutants produced by pulp mills simply did not exist. Instead, water pollution regulations were established on a mill-by-mill basis and pollution limits varied from one mill licence to the next. In this regulatory environment Daishowa could make a reasonable assumption—whatever effluent discharge standards the province would ask the company to meet, these standards would not be stricter than the discharge levels Alberta Environment had just approved for the modernization and expansion of Weldwood's Hinton kraft mill.

Were these limits the "toughest in Canada"? Were they stricter than Japanese regulations? Table 3, a cross-national comparison of kraft pulp mill effluent standards, outlines a number of important exceptions to Kitagawa's characterization of the Alberta regulatory environment, exceptions he recognized given his responsibilities for Daishowa Canada. For example, the pollution limits assigned to Weldwood's expanded Hinton kraft mill—a benchmark for the design of the Peace River kraft mill—were no stricter than the pollution standards applied to new kraft mills in British Columbia, a jurisdiction well-known to Daishowa. In fact, in regards to one type of pulp mill water pollution—total suspended solids (TSS)—the British Columbia standard for new kraft mills was 31 percent lower than the level Alberta had set for the Weldwood expansion. Moreover, the Procter and Gamble kraft mill near Grande Prairie had higher TSS and biological oxygen demand (BOD) limits than the general limits for new British Columbia mills. While some operating mills in British Columbia and other Canadian provinces discharged more water pollutants than the established Alberta mills, others were regulated more severely than Weldwood or Procter and Gamble. E. B. Eddy's Espanola, Ontario, operation, for example, was regulated much more severely than its Alberta counterparts. The same could be said for other potential North American sites for Japanese pulp mill expansion in the United States. In Japan, like Canada, the regulatory regime is mill-specific. There again certain mills faced much tougher water pollution regulations than those being asked of Weldwood's modernized, expanded facility. Daido Paper's nine hundred tonne bleached kraft operation could only discharge 51 percent of Weldwood's BOD limit and only 15 percent of the TSS limit set for the Alberta mill. In the light of this data the comments of both Fjordbotten and Kitagawa served only to create the illusion for their respective audiences that new pulp mills would pose few, if any, environmental risks. The prospect of Alberta Environment implementing the toughest standards in Canada was not self-evident—it depended upon the province adopting an aggressive posture in negotiations with its corporate suitors.

Table 3: Kraft Pulp Mill Effluent Standards, Various Jurisdictions, 1988[5]

Jurisdiction	BOD$_5$*—kg/tonne	TSS**—kg/tonne
British Columbia—new mills	7.5	10.0
MacMillan Bloedel (Harmac, B. C.)	30.0	17.5
Fletcher Challenge (Crofton, B. C.)	30.0	17.5
E. B. Eddy (Espanola, Ont.)	2.29	5.37
Kimberly-Clark (Terrace Bay, Ont.)	27.4	5.0
Procter and Gamble (Grande Prairie, Alberta)	9.4–11.3	13.9

Weldwood (Hinton, Alberta)
  −existing mill
  −expanded mill
	
	11.7
	7.0
		
		24.6
		14.5

Daishowa (Peace River, Alberta)
  −Daishowa's proposed criteria, 1987
  −1990 licence to operate
	
	7.0
	5.5
		
		14.5
		9.5

U. S. EPA	5.5	9.5
Buckeye Cellulose (Georgia)	2.65–5.3	2.9–5.8
Scott Paper (Maine)	5.9	12.5
Daido Paper (Japan)	3.6	2.2

* A standard measure of the biological oxygen demand (BOD) of pulp mill effluent. It is defined as "the number of pounds of dissolved oxygen required to stabilize, by biochemical action during an incubation period of five days at twenty degrees centigrade, the oxygen-demanding decomposible organic matter produced as waste from the production of one ton of pulp or paper" (Fisheries Act, Pulp and Paper Effluent Regulations, C.R.C. 1978, c. 830).

** TSS is the abbreviation for total suspended solids. It is defined by the federal Fisheries Act as "the filtered and dried residue present in the waste resulting from the processes involved in the operations of a mill" (Fisheries Act, Pulp and Paper Effluent Regulations, C.R.C. 1978, c. 830).

The Alberta regulatory environment offered other appealing features for Daishowa. Neither of the existing kraft mills in Alberta had placed limits upon the amounts of dioxins and furans, the chemical compounds of such great public worry, that could be discharged into the Wapiti and Athabasca rivers. Ken Kowalski, the province's environment minister, seemed untroubled about this situation. He was unconcerned over the amounts of dioxins and furans kraft pulp mills would discharge into the province's waters; he gave no indication that Alberta Environment would institute and enforce a limit on the amount of chlorinated organic compounds the mill could discharge into the Peace River. Kowalski seized upon scientific debates on the dioxin issue as evidence that the scientific community could not decide if this chlorine compound produced significant health risks. In the legislature he claimed that without a definitive conclusion, agreed to by all experts, he could not be sure whether further actions were needed to protect the environment. Daishowa, believing that the regulatory status quo was a stable one, would become very frustrated in the months ahead as the province changed its environmental standards in the face of public pressure and retroactively applied them to Daishowa.

"Show and Tell"

Alberta's apparently hospitable regulatory climate aside, Daishowa's proposal still faced the prospect of a provincial environmental assessment. The provincial government's environmental assessment process, outlined in section 8 of the Land Surface Conservation and Reclamation Act, gave the minister of the environment the authority to decide whether or not the sponsors of industrial or land use projects should prepare and submit an environmental impact assessment (EIA) report to Alberta Environment. The government's formal objective was to strike a balance between resource development and environmental quality. Realizing this balance depended heavily upon whether Alberta Environment would exercise the considerable discretionary authority contained in the legislation. This discretion—flexibility in the language of the province's EIA guidelines—produced a very ad hoc approach to environmental assessments. Assessment reports did not have to follow a prescribed method, actual information requirements were variable and subject to consultation with the sponsors, and the depth and rigour of assessments were unspecified. The Syncrude development had been one of the first, and clearly the most mammoth, resource project subjected to this EIA process. In Syncrude's case, it was nonsensical to talk of striking a balance between resource development and environmental quality—environmental quality was crushed by brute force and ignorance (as Petro-Canada executives described Syncrude's technology). Environment Canada's scathing critique of the environmental assessment report prepared by Syncrude in 1973 had been dismissed by William Yurko, the province's environment minister. Sounding more like a minister of industrial development than a minister of the environment, Yurko had argued that developing the tar sands was such an urgent priority it must proceed immediately. There was no time to gather basic knowledge about the Athabasca tar sands environment.

Could Albertans expect a more meaningful balance to be struck fourteen years later by Ken Kowalski? Hardly. Before running for the legislature Kowalski, a graduate of the University of Alberta and former high school teacher, had parlayed the political connections gained through his service as Deputy Premier Hugh Horner's executive assistant into the job of deputy minister of regional transportation services. First elected in 1979 as the MLA for the northern constituency of Barrhead, Kowalski entered the Getty cabinet as environment minister in 1986. His tenure in Alberta Environment was controversial, marked by his bitter criticisms of environmentalists, particularly those who opposed his department's plans to build a dam on the Oldman River—one of Alberta's last major free flowing rivers. He belittled his critics as marijuana smoking "social anarchists," an outlook that prompted a light-hearted, off-the-cuff verse from Sid Marty, the Alberta author, songwriter, and environmentalist:

He's got a party card.
He's got a gold card, too.
He's got political connections; gonna
mess with you.
Gonna bulldoze, dam, pave and cut, until
the devil comes to collect his butt.
Now who is Kowalski you might ask, and
why is he bent on the destructive task,
of slandering a powerless band of citizens
trying to protect the land.
He sounds like a redneck weird and bent,
yet he's minister of the environment . . . [6]

His generosity aside, Kowalski was an extremely self-assured minister, a man for whom personal opinion and objective truth appear synonymous. He claimed "a great deal of pride" in being characterized in the legislature as an autocratic minister.[7] Since Kowalski was prepared to use ongoing scientific debates as a reason for not considering the risks of dioxins and furans in provincial environmental assessment reviews, it was unlikely that someone who enjoyed being characterized as autocratic would use his discretion to ensure that the EIA process struck a more equitable balance between resource development and environmental quality. This balance became even more unlikely since Kowalski's discretion effectively was strengthened by a May 1986 federal-provincial agreement on environmental assessment negotiated by Fred Bradley, Kowalski's predecessor. One goal of the agreement was to ensure that environmental assessments would be conducted so as to reduce duplication and unnecessary regulation. Towards this end the two governments agreed to the principle that specific projects should only be subject to the environmental assessment procedures of the government enjoying primary constitutional jurisdiction. During the three-year life of the agreement eighteen projects were referred to Alberta for review. Daishowa's Peace River Pulp Mill was one of these projects.

Alberta Environment and Daishowa negotiated the script for the Peace River Pulp Mill EIA during the summer of 1987. Under the terms of provincial guidelines Daishowa would prepare an environmental assessment report for the consideration of Alberta Environment and other provincial departments. In early September Alberta Environment told Daishowa that, as part of this report, it must consult with local governments, groups, and downstream water users about the nature and the possible impact of the pulp mill project. Dutifully, Daishowa and its consultants met with eleven municipal councils, community organizations, and regional governments; public meetings were held in five communities in the Peace River region—Fort Vermillion, Paddle Prairie, Manning, Weberville, and Peace River. Those who attended these consultative sessions warmed to the promises of secure employment via economic diversification made by Daishowa's representatives. The Peace River region's economy, with agriculture, construction, and energy as its three pillars of employment, had faltered badly during the 1980s recession brought about by the collapse in commodity prices. Strong population immigration to the Peace country during the 1970s waned in the first half of the 1980s; the Peace region's September 1987 unemployment rate was 10.5 percent, twice as high as the unemployment rate most communities in the region boasted of in 1981.

Without a major injection of investment, economic growth was predicted to rise at an annual growth rate of only 1.5 percent between 1986 and 1990; without additional investment the region's population would probably remain stable, possibly decline. Against this background of economic stagnation Daishowa proposed new jobs with security and stability—commodities all too rarely found in "boom-bust" economies. As the Daishowa team moved up and down the highways of northern Alberta this was the elixir it promised to supply to residents of the Peace country. Kitagawa stressed to several audiences that "Daishowa pulp goes to Japan for paper production, therefore mill never shuts down due to market swings."[8] Tom Hamaoka also stressed this air of corporate invulnerability to market forces—Japanese demand for pulp had been so strong that Daishowa's Cariboo kraft mill had never been forced to shut down in fifteen years of operations.

This company offered more than job security and stability to the regional population—it also promised locals a substantial piece of the action. Daishowa, citing its experience in Quesnel, British Columbia, told its audiences that it regarded the local population as a stable, dependable supply of labour; the company would work with governments and schools in the Peace country to develop needed training programs; when people asked about whether Daishowa might build a paper mill in the future they were told that it was a possibility; when Métis from the Paddle Prairie Métis Settlement Area expressed interest in starting a chipping facility Daishowa offered to help lobby the provincial government for financial assistance.

The woodlands jobs that a Daishowa consultant suggested could go to the Paddle Prairie Métis would certainly be welcome. Resource development in northern Alberta had never been overly hospitable to Native participation. This inhospitality was underlined dramatically in testimony Father Camille Piché, an Oblate missionary in northern Canada for over twenty-five years, gave to the Alberta-Pacific Environmental Impact Assessment Review Board in November 1989. Father Piché spoke of the plight of the "Dene Tha'," a Slavey-Beaver phrase meaning ordinary or common people, living on the Assumption reservation, one hundred kilometres west of High Level. Portrayed as the poorest reserve in Alberta, the Dene Tha' had been marginalized by resource development. Assumption's unemployment rate was 85 percent; in 1988, over thirteen hundred crimes were recorded on the reserve; suicides and murders were common. The Assumption school, with over 260 students registered, graduated barely one Grade 12 student per year. The Canfor sawmill in High Level provided three hundred permanent jobs, none of which went to the Dene Tha'; apart from the occasional seasonal bush-clearing contract the Dene Tha' did not benefit from the woodlands jobs generated by the Canfor mill; no Dene Tha' were to be counted among the forty-eight full-time employees of the province's Footner Lake forest district. The place of the Dene Tha' in the established forest economy was captured well, if tragically, in the observation that when Canfor and the province built an interpretive forest trail as part of 1989's National Forest Week the only Dene Tha' to participate in this project were the young men in the minimum security jail who provided free labour. "The only thing the Dene Tha' have left," Father Piché added, "is the forest—we have taken everything else—the forest where they are still able to pursue a traditional lifestyle of hunting and trapping."[9]

There were limits, however, to what measures the corporation would take to assist such a marginalized element of Alberta society. Elmer Ghostkeeper of Paddle Prairie raised the issue of a Native hiring quota given the high level of unemployment in his community. Hamaoka's response was firm and to the point: "Daishowa's policy would be to hire the most qualified people available in the area and would not subject the project to any quotas."[10] Any assistance the company might offer the Paddle Prairie Métis to investigate the feasibility of a chipping operation was not synonymous with an offer to purchase chips— this question would be settled by the comparative costs of chip and log hauls. Daishowa, after all, owed primary allegiance to the profitability of its Japanese and Canadian operations. Hamaoka's remarks also identified the Achilles heel of any plan to hire large numbers of northerners generally, northern Natives in particular, to work in the pulp mill—the lack of the technological training and skills needed to work in Daishowa's very modern, automated mill.

Regional enthusiasm for the project was not diminished, and perhaps was nourished, by the confident replies the corporation's consultants offered to the few questions raised during its public consultation program about the environmental impact of the mill. These consultants, men with impressive academic credentials, offered opinions, adorned with the appropriate statistical regalia, that at times were so far-fetched that only the credulity of their lay audiences spared them from serious challenge. Those who were concerned with dioxins were reassured in various ways, some more ingenious than others. The company's dioxin expert, employed by a consulting firm with a longstanding record of contributions to the Progressive Conservative party, informed one meeting that there was no evidence to suggest that the Peace

River Pulp Mill would ever produce dioxins—a rather remarkable statement in light of the emerging consensus that the most significant source of dioxins in pulp mill effluents was the chlorine Daishowa proposed to use to bleach pulp white. A Métis audience was asked to believe that fish, if they did ingest dioxins, would eventually excrete this compound from their systems. The recent concern over dioxins was represented as simply a product of vastly improved measurement techniques—this ignored a number of scientific reports that suspected a link between dioxins and cancer. During the only public meeting held in Peace River, this line of argument was echoed by Michael Procter, the town's mayor, and by 1988 the chief financial officer of the Peace River Progressive Conservative Association. On no occasion was the veracity of this information questioned by the public audience, confirming once again the persuasiveness of professional credentials and corporate-financed expertise in settings where alternative sources of informed opinion are not to be found.

When the issue of the forests was raised—either in the context of reforestation or of alternative economic pursuits—Daishowa's officials did their best to reassure the public that they would serve as excellent stewards of the resource. If and when trappers were affected by the harvesting operations authorized by the Forest Management Agreement they would be dealt with individually by the company. Would the legacy of Daishowa be a Canadian equivalent of the deforestation of the Amazonian rainforest? Not at all, according to the company. In the first place the FMA required a reforestation plan. Also, aspen had earned its label of a "weed" from its tendency to regrow by itself, a natural regenerative process that could be maximized by thinning and cloning. For the most part though, Daishowa avoided dealing with the environmental impact of its proposed forestry operations in the EIA process. This impact would be addressed through the negotiation of the FMA—negotiations insulated and protected from public scrutiny.

From the company's perspective, the public consultation program was an important victory. Throughout this process Daishowa encountered only diffuse opposition—the minutes of its public meetings contain only scattered references to the potential for kraft mills to threaten human and/or environmental health. Most importantly, the company did not face a well-organized, well-informed opposition. The Friends of the Peace, an environmental group formed in response to this pulp mill project, did not emerge officially until June 1988, the month when Alberta Environment granted Daishowa a Permit to Construct and long after the curtains had been drawn on the company's public consultation exercise. When the group tried to raise questions about the environmental controls Daishowa planned to incorporate into the mill, the decision-making process was sometimes so advanced that the group was simply told that its interventions were too late. When the Friends of the Peace formally objected to Alberta Environment about the amount of dioxins the mill would dump into the Peace River and the failure of the company to consider the cumulative impact of these substances, the group was told that the time to raise those objections had passed. "It's part of the way the legal system is set up," said a departmental spokeswoman. "It's not appropriate to look at water quality when water quantity is the main issue."[11] In addition, the Friends of the North, an Edmonton-based environmental coalition which proved to be one of the most vociferous and persistent opponents of Daishowa and Alberta-Pacific, was not formed until March 1989. In the words of one member of this second environmental group: "It took nearly two years [after 1987] and numerous projects, under construction or completed, across most of northern Alberta until public awareness was aroused."[12]

The absence of a well-organized, well-informed opposition to Daishowa was certainly attributable in part to the allure of jobs and economic activity. However, the nature of the public consultation program also claims some of this responsibility. The brevity of the consultation exercise virtually assured insufficient time to organize a significant opposition to the mill proposal. John Sheehan, one of the founding members of the Friends of the Peace, remarked on the eve of the Daishowa mill's opening in September 1990 that: "We had a mill dropped on us without any opportunity to say whether we wanted it." Once the formal consultation period came to a close the company did not give environmental groups much chance to question the pulping or effluent technology choices the company had made. "At their last public meeting in November," Sheehan complained, "the company brought out seven experts but they only gave us two hours with them—that's not enough time to ask all the questions."[13]

This view on the opportunities to raise questions about the project runs counter to the picture drawn by Daishowa and its consultants. Near the end of its public consultations one consultant spoke of the company's extensive efforts to communicate with the interested public: "Daishowa has made a great effort to meet with as many groups as possible, however at some point there must be a limit—it is not feasible to meet with everyone."[14] While it certainly was not feasible to meet with everyone, Daishowa claimed that it had devoted three months to consulting the public. However, in reality this three months of consultation delivered little more than a handful of opportunities for public comment. Daishowa's own minutes of its public consultation programme reveal that only sixteen sessions were held with local governments, Métis groups, and the public—sessions spread over a mere six days. The brevity of the public consultation process was not the only feature of the assessment process which worked against meaningful public scrutiny of the proposal. In addition, the public received little advance notice of public meetings. Finally, neither the company nor the government offered the people of the Peace the range of information needed to assess thoughtfully the benefits and costs of this project. The company's public information brochure offered its readers a stylized drawing of the mill, a picture of a northern forest, a flow diagram of the pulping process, and three tables describing Daishowa's international operations, mill consumption and production statistics, and the project's projected economic impact—hardly the makings for serious analysis! Specifics regarding pollution, the anticipated FMA's size, length, and reforestation obligations, the stumpage fees the government would charge, and the impact of the project upon Native peoples, including the unresolved land claim of the Lubicon Cree, and traditional pursuits in the northern economy could not be found in the company's glossy brochure. Nor was the government, as the trustee of the resource, eager to offer the public the material needed to reach a more informed decision; public funding for groups to commission their own expert analyses was unavailable. It is no wonder those who questioned the value of the mill dismissed the EIA process as nothing more than a series of "show and tell" sessions.

Environmentalists criticized the Daishowa environmental assessment on other grounds as well. The company's assessment report ignored any mention of the impact this project would have upon Alberta's forests, except to say that the environmental impact of the forestry operations would be handled through the FMA the company hoped to negotiate with Forestry, Lands and Wildlife. John Younie, the New Democratic Party's environment critic, made the point when commenting upon the Alberta Newsprint Company paper mill proposal that environmental assessments that ignored the forests were unrealistic. Even the government's own expert review panel on forest management in Alberta agreed "with the public's concern that any EIA that covers only the impact of the pulp mill is inadequate and that the impact of forest management practices must also be reviewed."[15] Reading the company's assessment report one might conclude that pulp mills really did not have much of an impact upon forests at all. The willingness of Alberta Environment and Forestry, Lands and Wildlife to tolerate Daishowa's silence on this issue, a tolerance illustrated by their failure to request supplemental information in this regard, is astounding especially in light of the mill's voracious appetite for fibre. Timber for this facility would be drawn from an area of nearly 28,500 square kilometres. Every year the Peace River Pulp Mill would ingest 1.8 million cubic metres of wood. A better picture of the enormous amounts of fibre demanded by this mill might be provided by visualizing a Canadian Football League playing field as the mill's wood yard. To fill this wood yard with enough trees to feed the mill for a year trees would have to be piled to a height of 221 metres—the height of a 72 storey office building.

This neglect of the forests was symptomatic of several general gaps in the EIA process. Daishowa, drawing timber from thousands of square kilometres of Alberta, would join other pulp mills in Alberta and British Columbia in polluting the Peace River, a river that after running for nearly two thousand kilometres becomes a principal tributary of the Mackenzie, Canada's longest river. Yet, the EIA process made virtually no provisions to consider either the impact of this particular project or the cumulative impact of all the pulp mills on the Peace River upon the vast majority of downstream water users. While one public meeting was held in Fort Vermillion in recognition of the fact that this community drew its drinking water from the Peace, most of the company's environmental assessment commentary focussed upon an area falling within an eighty kilometre radius of the mill site.

Also, it was beyond the mandate of Alberta's EIA process to address the fundamental concerns Native peoples raised about the impact forestry projects would have upon existing treaty rights and outstanding land claims. According to the Alberta Natural Resources Act of 1930 the provincial government would only be obliged to respect a request from Ottawa to establish Indian reserves on "unoccupied Crown lands." According to the Alberta government's interpretation of this provision, once land was allocated to a competing land use or a surface lease was granted, the land in question ceased to be unoccupied. Natives in Alberta were suspicious that FMAs were just another device for undermining land claims and treaty rights. Chief Johnsen Sewepagaham of the Little Red River Cree, a band with approximately two thousand members and reserves on the Peace River between Fort Vermillion and Wood Buffalo National Park, worried that if FMAs constituted occupied land Natives would be barred from exercising their hunting and treaty rights. "If this position was adopted by the courts," Chief Sewepagaham warned, "it may prove disastrous for our people."[16] Moreover, as the Haida Nation found out during its battle to secure aboriginal title to South Moresby in British Columbia's Queen Charlotte Islands, forest tenure agreements constituted third-party interests in the land which had to be addressed in order to settle land claims—another complication to an already excruciatingly slow process.

To address the concerns raised by Chief Sewepagaham the province would have had to allow Natives a forum for examining the very development option the government was attached to so devoutly, namely, using northern forests to supply fibre for transnational pulp and paper giants. Time was needed for northern Native communities to learn about the size of plants such as the Peace River Pulp Mill and the scale of the forestry operations required to supply the plants with wood. This learning could not be produced by considering the forestry initiative on a piece-meal, mill-by-mill basis, the type of approach institutionalized in the province's EIA process. Rather, what was needed was, according to the Little Red River people and Father Piché, nothing less than an equivalent to the Berger Inquiry into the Mackenzie Valley Pipeline. This type of public inquiry would give northern Native communities opportunities to understand the economic and social change pulp mills would bring, to plan strategies to cope with adverse impacts upon the traditional economy, and to develop plans which would ensure that northern Natives benefited from this type of development. The province's blitzkrieg, its rush to commit the northern forests to pulp and paper development, did not offer these opportunities to Natives and others who were unconvinced that the forest strategy served the public interest well.

These sorts of criticisms help to make the argument that the province's forestry megaproject decision-making process was not designed to strike a balance between resource development and resource stewardship. It was naive, if not unfair, to expect the companies to broaden public hearings and invite opposition to their ventures. They could not be expected to submit their projects to a wide-ranging, critical examination. This was the government's responsibility and numerous factors prevented this from happening. First, striking a balance between development and stewardship required a holistic assessment of resource use options that did not fit the government's bureaucratic framework. Responsibility over forestry-related issues was divided primarily between Forestry, Lands and Wildlife and Alberta Environment. The environment department's responsibilities were confined to air and water quality issues. The trees themselves were the property of the forestry ministry and their disposition a matter reserved for its attention. The difficulties of coordination inherent in this administrative division of responsibility were aggravated by the fact that Forestry, Lands and Wildlife was a principal promoter of these ventures. Its outlook towards forest use differed little, if at all, from that of the forestry companies. Finally, the political enthusiasm for these projects was another brake upon widening the parameters of any project review.

Given the decision-making structures and the balance of political and bureaucratic opinion towards forestry development, it stands to reason that it was probably very difficult for Alberta Environment officials to push their environmental concerns aggressively. Nonetheless, they did criticize the Daishowa proposal. From Alberta Environment's perspective, the large size of the Peace River tempered departmental concerns about the mill's impact upon the river's oxygen content and colour—concerns that later would rise to bedevil Crestbrook Forest Industries' Alberta-Pacific project. Where the department had important concerns, however, was on the environmental subject causing the greatest amount of public anxiety—dioxins. The department approached this subject with a certain confidence that technological change offered the most promising path to balancing economic development and environmental integrity. Had Daishowa seriously considered incorporating technologies into the mill design which either would or might reduce the amounts of dioxin and its chlorinated organic cousins produced by the pulp bleaching process? More specifically, had the company considered the suitability and feasibility of two novel processes—extended delignification and chlorine dioxide substitution? Delignification is the point in the pulping process where wood chips, after being force-fed a cooking liquor made up of sodium hydroxide and sodium sulphate, are transferred to a pressure cooker where the chemical cocktail dissolves the lignin—the natural glue—that cements wood fibres together. This is where, to use the imagery of pulp mill builders, "the cellulosic fibers are liberated." Extended delignification, by prolonging the cooking time of the wood, reduces the amount of lignin in the pulp and, consequently, the amount of elemental chlorine or chlorine compounds needed to bleach the pulp. By substituting chlorine dioxide for some of the chlorine gas used in conventional bleaching the amount of chlorinated organics could be reduced as well.

For the company, Alberta Environment's concerns were viewed through the twin lenses of practicality and profitability. The company's avowed policy was to protect water quality with the "best practical technology." From Daishowa's perspective, best practical technology meant "employing modern control equipment capable of minimizing discharges over the short and long term, while ensuring that the capital and operating costs of this equipment will not unduly impair the economic viability of the mill."[17] Until these two technologies were proven elsewhere, both technically *and* economically, Daishowa did not want to implement them within their Peace River mill. While the mill's design made provisions for the future addition of an extended delignification system, Daishowa argued that this process was still an unproven technology—it was being used only in two Scandinavian mills and one North American mill. The feasibility of chlorine dioxide substitution was questionable also—it had never been applied to aspen. Daishowa did not want to embrace this technology without more information about how the all-important quality of bleached aspen pulp would be affected. Then there were the issues of the costs associated with incorporating and operating these systems. In Peace River the cost of chlorine dioxide was estimated to be 50 percent higher than the same amount of chlorine.

In the months following the public release of the initial mill design, Alberta Environment made some limited progress in nudging Daishowa towards building a cleaner mill. The company's Permit to Construct stipulated that the plant would have to provide for extended delignification and include the capability to optimize chlorine dioxide substitution—conditions little changed from what Daishowa offered initially. However, the pollution limits for BOD, TSS, and water colour outlined in this permit were somewhat stricter than those Daishowa proposed initially. Moreover, for the first time in any Canadian jurisdiction a regulatory limit was placed upon the amounts of chlorinated organics a mill could discharge into water—2.5 kg/ADT of Total Organo-Chlorine Compounds (TOCL).[18]

Alberta Environment, in its treatment of the Daishowa application to construct the Peace River mill, looked to technological change as the means of accommodating industrialization and environmental protection. In early December 1988, this preference for a technology-based approach to regulating the pulp and paper industry was formalized. Addressing the Environment Council of Alberta, environment minister Ian Reid, appointed to the environment portfolio in 1988, announced that new mills and mill expansions would be required to incorporate the "best available technology" into their design proposals; Alberta's rivers would be protected adequately by specifying the technologies that pulp and paper mills would have to employ. This commitment, coupled with spreading public concerns about the environmental consequences attending the rapid, wholesale commitment of the forests to pulp mill projects, placed provincial regulators and Daishowa in a quandary. If the best available technology condition was going to be applied to the Daishowa mill, the province would have to force the company to modify its mill design. It would have to ensure that all three "leading edge" technologies—extended delignification, oxygen delignification, and chlorine dioxide substitution—were in place when the mill began producing pulp in the summer of 1990. Although clearly reluctant to abandon its own schedule for the introduction of what were, from Daishowa's perspective, unproven technologies, and unhappy with this rewriting of environmental rules after the mill was already approved and under construction, the company nonetheless bowed to this demand. "Daishowa concluded," Hamaoka said, "that the public interest in environmental protection should dictate the earliest possible use of this pulping process."[19] The public interest identified by Hamaoka and the target of Alberta Environment's commitment to new kraft mill technologies was the public's concern about dioxins—the three technologies identified above were all designed to reduce dioxin formation in the pulping process. The effect of demanding their incorporation into the Peace River pulp mill was to reduce the allowable amount of AOX discharged from the mill to 1.4 kg/ADT, to less than one-half of the level specified previously in the Permit to Construct. These changes did not affect the amounts of BOD and TSS discharged into the Peace River.

Daishowa versus the Lubicon Lake Cree

The Little Red River Cree were certainly not the only Native band to demand that Native rights to the land should temper the province's headlong rush into forestry development. In Daishowa's case, the most prominent, the most troublesome, claimants of these rights were the Lubicon Lake Cree. The Lubicons, numbering some five hundred members, are centred in the territory around the community of Little Buffalo, approximately 105 kilometres east of the town of Peace River. Overlooked by federal Indian commissioners during their treaty negotiation foray into northern Alberta at the turn of the century, the Lubicon people's history since 1939 has been punctuated by efforts to negotiate a treaty with an unsympathetic federal government. While each passing decade has seen the circumstances of the Lubicon worsen, the greatest damage to the traditional economy and social fabric of these people accompanied the stampede of petroleum exploration and development firms into Lubicon territory after the 1979 oil price shock. Between 1979 and 1984, over four hundred wells were drilled within a fifteen mile radius of Little Buffalo. In a mere four years, more than eight times as many wells were drilled on territory claimed by the Lubicons than had been drilled altogether between 1950 and 1979. This frenzied search for oil, according to Fred Lennarson, the Lubicons' most prominent advisor, destroyed what previously had been a viable traditional hunting and trapping economy. All-weather roads criss-crossed the countryside; fires, some attributable to petroleum exploration, swept through the forests; the moose population—the backbone of the Native hunting economy— plummeted; oil company employees, obeying their employers, destroyed Lubicon traps and sabotaged the Native economy. It is little wonder that welfare rates among the Lubicon, like petroleum prices in 1979–80, skyrocketed. Welfare, as a percentage of the work force, rose from 10 to 90 percent between 1979–80 and 1983–84. The province did nothing to stem the occupation of Lubicon territory by the energy industry; in fact, government encouraged it. Forestry officials joined their counterparts from Municipal Affairs in putting pressure upon the residents of Little Buffalo to abandon their claim for a reserve.[20]

"Nobody's going to come and chop down our trees without a fight on our part."[21] With these defiant words Chief Bernard Ominayak, the generally soft-spoken but resolute chief of the Lubicon Cree, reacted angrily to news in February 1988 that the province had approved Daishowa's plans to build the Peace River Pulp Mill. The cause of Ominayak's anger was obvious. In dispensing the province's blessing, Premier Getty and Forestry minister Fjordbotten gave Daishowa timber harvesting and management rights to more than 29,000 square kilometres of the province, an area which encircled completely the 238 square kilometres the Lubicon proposed as the site for their reserve and encompassed the 10,400 square kilometres over which they claimed unextinguished aboriginal land rights. This announcement said a great deal about the strength of the province's commitments to industrial development, aboriginal interests, environmental integrity, and public participation in forestry decision making. The decision certainly was, in the premier's words, "indicative of our government's commitment to the forest industry sector of our economy and to our overall economic diversification strategy." At the same time, the announcement also confirmed the marginal standing of Native peoples when decisions were made about the future of Alberta's forests. Neither government nor industry approached the Lubicons about including territory over which they claimed unextinguished aboriginal land rights within Daishowa's FMA. Fjordbotten flatly dismissed the importance of Lubicon interests to provincial forest allocation policy. He told the legislature that the Lubicon issue was "a small area of concern. With all respect, Mr. Speaker, it was raised with them [Daishowa], and there was no alarmist approach in their concern being raised. I think the whole issue itself is being overplayed." Nick Taylor, the leader of the Alberta Liberal Party, asked the government why Alberta Environment, as part of the EIA process, did not demand that public hearings be held east of Peace River; he pointed out that this area, an area overlapping with traditional Lubicon territory, had been proposed by Daishowa as its single largest source of wood, supplying between 25 and 35 percent of the mill's requirements. For environment minister Kowalski, Peace River should have been convenient enough for the Lubicons; additional hearings in the Little Buffalo area were simply unnecessary. To be sure the Lubicons were not blameless; some of the responsibility for being left out of the consultative process must be borne by the Lubicon leadership. Kowalski was correct in noting that several public meetings had been held in November and the company's initial Environmental Assessment Report was distributed throughout the study region. Yet, criticisms of the Lubicons for not attending public hearings, such as those offered by Fjordbotten and Kowalski, missed a vital point mentioned earlier. Forest use, the most significant issue for Native peoples, was taboo within the EIA process. The setting for discussing forest use issues remained a private one, open only to senior forestry personnel and corporate managers. The Lubicon might be criticized for missing an opportunity to register their concerns in the public record but it must also be appreciated that, in Alberta, no venues existed for public examination of the forest use issues central to the Native agenda. When it came to FMAs, the temple doors were locked to the public.

This failure to consult fit well with the longstanding outlook of senior provincial forestry officials. These officials had collaborated in the province's efforts to erode the Lubicons' claim to a reserve at Little Buffalo. To Fred McDougall, there had never been any doubt that northern forests should be transformed into pulp and paper, a use which fit uneasily, if at all, with traditional Native economic pursuits. For him this goal had existed for decades and was clearly part of the public record; the *Atlas of Alberta*, published in 1969, confirmed this by detailing the vast Timber Development Areas later coveted by forest companies, as did the favourable reception a Peace River audience gave him in 1975 when he outlined a vision of forestry's future in northern Alberta.[22] The only issue was when these forests would be exploited by pulp and paper manufacturers; its resolution depended upon first identifying, then removing, legitimate and significant obstacles to this pattern of forest use. In this equation, Native peoples were neither significant nor did their interest in preserving a traditional hunting and trapping economy carry much legitimacy. The future of forestry development in Alberta, Forestry minister Fjordbotten reminded the legislature, was only limited by the need for infrastructure and transportation facilities.

The refusal to treat Native concerns with the same amount of legitimacy bestowed upon infrastructure concerns predisposed government to ignore Natives with outstanding land claims when it negotiated long-term resource management agreements and to convey wildly contradictory impressions of the Lubicon position. Fjordbotten disavowed any linkage between land claims and forestry projects; neither the Daishowa mill nor the minister's responsibility for managing the forests would have any impact at all upon the Lubicons. This was logical given the false premise Fjordbotten articulated, namely, that the only territorial question at issue in treaty negotiations was the size of a Lubicon reserve. Would it be as small as 65 square kilometres, as Alberta had offered in 1985, or as large as 238 square kilometres, as the Lubicons demanded? A senior forestry official made it clear to Ominayak that, for the time being, the province had excluded only 65 square kilometres of Lubicon claimed lands from Daishowa's FMA area. "During negotiations with Daishowa for the proposed Forest Management Agreement," C. B. Smith wrote, "the Department has taken into account your Band's claim. As identified on the enclosed map, 25.4 square miles near Lubicon Lake have been excluded from the proposed Forest Management Agreement area."[23] The consideration being shown by the Alberta Forest Service (AFS) and Fjordbotten's premise ignored the Lubicon claim that the band possessed unextinguished aboriginal land rights to over 10,400 square kilometres of territory, territory that overlapped the FMA area awarded to Daishowa and over which the Lubicon wanted a measure of control. These remarks, ones which minimized the amount of land claimed, were then joined by comments exaggerating Lubicon demands. The Lubicons demanded 10 percent of Alberta, sixty-six thousand square kilometres, according to Fjordbotten, more than six times the amount of territory over which the Lubicons wanted some measure of control in respect to environmental protection and wildlife management. Fjordbotten's inflated estimate—characterized by one Edmonton columnist as "downright foolish"—was, for the Lubicons, part of a deliberate campaign of disinformation designed to paint Lubicon territorial demands as unreasonable.

The premier's declaration that his government welcomed the plan to construct a bleached kraft pulp mill north of Peace River miscalculated quite badly the respective reservoirs of support in public opinion for forestry megaprojects and aboriginal rights as well as the worries the Lubicon issue would raise in the minds of Daishowa officials. Forestry minister Fjordbotten was sure that the promised employment gains from this project—630 mill and woodland jobs and 1,260 indirect jobs—would strike a receptive chord in the public and drown out any who questioned this allocation to a foreign-owned transnational of a provincial forest largely located on unceded aboriginal territory. The nearly two thousand jobs promised by a gigantic pulp mill complex could not be put on hold while governments and the Lubicon struggled to reach a land claims settlement. Such a logic did not persuade a "growing legion" of Lubicon supporters. Churches were especially prominent among the Lubicon defenders. Canada's Task Force on the Churches and Corporate Responsibility, Missionary Oblates, even Japan's National Christian Council, joined other religious and nonreligious groups in rallying behind the Lubicon position. When Daishowa's plans to log on unceded Lubicon territory would later become an explosive issue, the Canadian Council of Churches declared their support for the Lubicons' insistence that Daishowa stay out of this contested area. In the words of one spokesman for the council: "The churches of Canada are completely behind Chief Ominayak in this issue."[24] Even some of those who judged Ominayak harshly for adopting the risky, yet successful strategy of calling for a boycott of the 1988 Calgary Olympics—more pointedly the Glenbow Museum's plans to display a major exhibition of North American Native artifacts—objected to the province's cavalier treatment of the Lubicon land claim in the selection of the Daishowa FMA. The provincial government's campaign to discredit the Lubicons had had the opposite impact—support for their claim upon the land was growing.

Premier Getty, perhaps sensing that his team had fumbled the ball on this particular play, now intervened to the surprise of many commentators. Unlike Lougheed he seldom became involved personally in the business of individual departments, limiting his input to composing the government's playbook and leaving its execution to others. But, like Lougheed, Getty had been unsympathetic, even hostile, towards the Lubicons and any others who claimed aboriginal rights. This was not the profile of someone who would intervene at all, let alone in a conciliatory manner, when it came to this issue. Uncharacteristic as Getty's periodic interventions during 1988 may have been, his efforts to secure Ominayak's trust and to break the deadlock on the size of the Lubicon reserve were neither altruistic nor a sign of new-found faith in the justice of Lubicon grievances. Instead they arose from fear, fear that the Daishowa project, the flagship of the forest strategy, would be scuttled unless Alberta could deliver the political stability that the Forestry Industry Development Division had advertised to potential investors. Lubicon threats of "direct action," of taking action "on the ground," to prevent logging made Daishowa officials nervous and they urged the premier to settle this issue. The Daishowa project, as the flagship, had to be protected at all costs; the worries of Kitagawa and Hamaoka had to be soothed. Less than 250 square kilometres of boreal forest would soon become a penny ante bid in the high stakes game of attracting international forestry investment dollars being played by the Getty government.

Faced with vocal, well-organized support for the Lubicons and the prospects of placard-waving demonstrators parading outside its corporate offices, Daishowa opened a direct line of communication to the Lubicons. When Kitagawa journeyed to Edmonton in early March to urge Premier Getty to settle the dispute he also contacted Chief Ominayak and requested a meeting. At their meeting, held while pro-Lubicon supporters picketed in front of Daishowa's Vancouver offices, Daishowa portrayed itself as an innocent, well-intentioned, third party caught in the middle of the dispute between Ominayak's band and Canadian governments. Daishowa spun images of a company with a sincere interest in treating Native peoples fairly, of a company which had been advised poorly by the province when it came to the issue of consulting the Lubicons—a very plausible charge in light of the federal government's insistence that Alberta never even hinted that Daishowa's cutting rights would come in part from the disputed area. Since the company had already scheduled a meeting with representatives of Improvement District Number 17, a regional government encompassing Little Buffalo, it claimed the province told it that nothing more was required vis à vis the Lubicons, especially since any special effort on the part of Daishowa might jeopardize ongoing negotiations. Events in the month following the project's approval heightened the appreciation this Japanese company had for the essence of this Native grievance—an attitude the company stressed during its meeting with Chief Ominayak. Yet, the meeting between Kitagawa and Ominayak revealed the enormous gulf that separated their respective interpretations of the concrete territorial concessions that had to be made to satisfy this longstanding complaint. From the moment their March meeting concluded, Daishowa and the Lubicons wove very different interpretations of the understanding reached by the two parties. Did Daishowa, as the Lubicons asserted, agree to nothing less than a commitment to forego logging in the Lubicon traditional area until a settlement was reached? Or, as Daishowa maintained, did the company agree only to stay clear of whatever land would be designated as the Lubicon reserve and to consult with the chief on ways to minimize the injury logging in the remainder of the traditional area would inflict upon the hunting and trapping economy? Fred Lennarson insisted that the Lubicons never abandoned their intention "to retain wildlife management and environmental protection responsibilities" in the traditional territory once the site and size of a reserve had been agreed upon. Kitagawa was just as insistent that the only responsibilities of this nature that his company had to comply with would be detailed by the province in the terms of the FMA, not by the Lubicons.[25] Chief Ominayak joined the fray to stress the irrelevance of whatever wildlife and environmental provisions were included in a provincial FMA:

We never ceded our traditional area to the Federal Government in any legally or historically recognized way. The Federal Government didn't have the right to transfer our traditional area to the Provincial Government. Provincial Government jurisdiction simply doesn't apply and the terms and conditions of any business you might want to do in our traditional area will therefore have to be negotiated directly with us.[26]

With these radically different interpretations of the territorial and substantive limits of Lubicon and provincial control firmly entrenched in the minds of these protagonists, the stage was being set for future conflict and confrontation.

The only way to avoid such a confrontation, short of any party capitulating, lay in negotiating a comprehensive agreement that would address the issues associated with the reserve (its size, location, and membership), compensation for previous resource development, and Lubicon/provincial responsibilities over the vast bulk of the Lubicon traditional territory. Beginning with his decision to meet with Chief Ominayak in early March 1988, Premier Getty took a series of steps to reassure Daishowa, steps that effectively repudiated a key component of the province's longstanding Lubicon policy—the size of the area the province was prepared to transfer to Canada for establishing a reserve for the Lubicon Lake Band. The premier's March initiative—the development of a certain rapport with Chief Ominayak—won him kudos from the media, respect from Ominayak, and defused temporarily the challenge the Lubicons posed to petroleum and forestry development east of the Peace River. Getty promised to push Ottawa to resume negotiations; moreover, he proposed that a three-person tribunal mediate the dispute—a proposal Ominayak supported.

Despite these conciliatory gestures the situation soon deteriorated. Canada's magnanimous response to Getty's initiatives was to sue the province for 117 square kilometres of land for the Lubicon reserve. This lawsuit signalled Indian Affairs minister Bill McKnight's steadfast refusal to discuss compensation or the murkier issues associated with aboriginal title. For the Lubicon people the federal reaction to Alberta's overtures illustrated the folly of negotiating with an impassive, mean-spirited Canadian government. By the end of May the pendulum had swung once again towards the option of taking action, of asserting Native jurisdiction, on the ground. In early October the lawyers for the Lubicon people appeared in the Alberta Court of Appeal and declared that their clients were abandoning the Canadian legal system as a vehicle for pursuing their interests. Instead, on 15 October, the Lubicon Lake Cree would assert jurisdiction over the entirety of their traditional territory. The Lubicons would take over the oilfields. To gain access to Lubicon land, vehicles would have to clear band checkpoints; to work on Lubicon land, permits would have to be purchased from the band office. The band's strategy was clear: challenge provincial jurisdiction in the hope of forcing the Getty administration to push Canada to adopt a more accommodating position. Such brinkmanship angered the premier who demanded that Ominayak suspend the takeover of the oilfields for thirty days in order to breathe some life back into the negotiating option. Ominayak refused and on 15 October, as promised, the Lubicons erected checkpoints, barricades in the eyes of the provincial government and the oil companies, on all the main access roads into Lubicon territory. For five days the checkpoints stood and all petroleum production in the disputed area was halted. On the sixth day, the Royal Canadian Mounted Police moved in, the checkpoints were torn down, and twenty-seven people were arrested.

To his credit, after the RCMP crushed the effort to assert Native jurisdiction, Premier Getty did not use this episode as a pretext for slamming the door on negotiations. Instead, faced with continued if not growing public support for the Lubicons in the aftermath of the arrests, Getty returned to the tack he had steered previously—the search for the basis of a settlement. As the checkpoints were being torn down Getty telephoned Ominayak to urge the chief to return to the bargaining table. On 22 October the premier, the chief, and their advisors met in Grimshaw, a community of several thousand people just twenty-six kilometres southwest of Peace River that, in its early years, had served as the central community for a rich mixed farming district. There, the premier again showed surprising leadership and a willingness to abandon previously immovable provincial positions. By evening, the two leaders had reached the "Grimshaw Agreement." The premier was prepared to transfer 246 square kilometres of land—205 kilometres with mineral rights, 41 kilometres with surface rights only—to Canada for the band's reserve. While bowing to the Lubicon demand that this amount of territory be set aside for the reserve, the premier protected provincial jurisdiction and established industries in several ways. Generally speaking, the lands transferred would not include producing oil and gas properties; Canada would be responsible for compensating all third party interests; the issues of wildlife management and environmental protection—issues that received scant attention during all previous Lubicon-Alberta discussions—would be dealt with separately. The agreement also reflected well the perspective that dominated Getty's approach to the Lubicon issue over the previous seven months, a perspective where the issues associated with the reserve obscured all others.

Ominayak's defiant remarks about the willingness of the Lubicons to fight to prevent loggers from entering traditional Lubicon territories underscored an important early difference between the opposition of Natives and environmentalists to these projects. The Lubicons' interest in securing a land claim settlement led them to regard the forests as the most vital subject affected by Daishowa's arrival in Alberta. The mill, with its associated air and water pollution, was less important. This, in part, explains their decision not to participate in Daishowa's public consultation programme—a programme focussed predominantly upon the water and air pollution the mill would produce. When the Lubicons met with Daishowa Canada officials in March 1988, their spokesmen made it clear that they were not particularly concerned about the mill since it would not be constructed in the band's traditional territories. An untitled letter, dated 28 October, to the Lubicon mailing lists stated that:

Chief Ominayak acknowledged that the proposed pulp mill wasn't located in the traditional Lubicon area. If Daishowa was only proposing to harvest trees to support that mill from outside of the traditional Lubicon territory, the Chief said, there would be no problem. The problem would only arise, the Chief said, if Daishowa tried to harvest trees in the traditional Lubicon territory prior to settlement of Lubicon land rights and negotiation of an agreement with the Lubicon people regarding Lubicon environmental concerns.

The land claim, not pulp mill pollution, figured first and foremost in the Lubicons' campaign against Daishowa. While the forests eventually became a very important aspect of the environmentalists' critique, during the early stages of their opposition they focussed their energies upon the mill itself and the pollution it would produce. Dioxins and claims about the damage they would inflict upon the Peace River and those beings who relied upon its water and food were the flags environmentalists raised to encourage the public to join their fight against the mill. Given the speed with which the Daishowa project raced from the proposal to the construction stage, this difference in emphasis hampered the campaign against the mill. It effectively fragmented the opposition campaign with environmentalists directing their fury upon Alberta Environment while the Lubicons focussed upon Forestry, Lands and Wildlife. By the time the common ground between environmentalists and Natives was appreciated, as seen in several court actions launched by a preservationist coalition of environmental and Native groups, the mill was built and had received its operating licence.

Fire Bombs and Boycotts

On a bitterly cold November evening in 1990, two years and one month after the Grimshaw Summit, arsonists descended upon a logging camp run by Buchanan Lumber, a Daishowa subcontractor, fifty kilometres northeast of Little Buffalo and set fire to a trailer, a truck, and two skidders—machines which drag fallen trees to roadsides or clearings where they are delimbed before they are loaded onto trucks. On 4 December, Reinie Jobin, a resident of the Little Buffalo area although not himself a member of the Lubicon Band, was arrested by the RCMP outside the Red Earth Hotel; eight days later the RCMP announced that Jobin and twelve other men from the vicinity of Little

Buffalo, the so-called Lubicon 13, would be charged in connection with the arson. As was always the case when it came to the Lubicon dispute, whatever promise had been contained in a Lubicon-government agreement, here the Grimshaw Agreement, had been shattered. Why was the Buchanan Lumber logging camp attacked? Why couldn't the spirit of accommodation found in the Grimshaw Agreement be built upon?

In trying to understand why further confrontation, rather than a mutually acceptable settlement, developed in the months following Grimshaw we must look in several directions. The attitude of the federal government remained an important obstacle to settlement; Canada's "take-it-or-leave-it" offer of January 1989 did not satisfy any of the outstanding Lubicon demands, with the exception of the reserve area already conceded by Premier Getty. Yet, Canada alone was not to blame for the drift towards violent confrontation that occurred after Grimshaw. The general enthusiasm that welcomed the October Agreement on reserve size and location diverted attention from a huge unresolved issue. No single answer was forthcoming to the vital question: who controlled the access to the resources found in unceded Lubicon territory? For Daishowa and Alberta the territorial guarantee found in Grimshaw settled this issue once and for all. Within the boundaries described by this Agreement the Lubicon enjoyed total control over 205 square kilometres and a veto over development in the remainder of the reserve area. Daishowa, following its interpretation of the March 1988 meeting with Chief Ominayak, would not trespass upon this land. "No logging has taken place, nor will it, in the future reserve area," wrote Daishowa official James Morrison, "without authorization by the Lubicon Band. The Lubicon/Alberta Government agreement and the resulting FMA restrictions satisfy any assurances Daishowa gave the Lubicon Band in the spring of 1988."[27] But, the lands stretching beyond this reserve area should be open to exploitation and Daishowa would negotiate access to these forests only with the Forest Service. The company might consult with the Lubicons and others regarding its timber cutting plans, it would even create a Public Advisory Committee, but here the emphasis would fall upon the words "consult" and "advisory"—the wants of other resource users should not dictate how Daishowa exercised the management responsibilities the province would soon award it through an FMA.

This view of the world was accommodated easily within the provincial attorney general's position that Treaty 8 extinguished aboriginal claims, such as those the Lubicon were making to 10,400 square kilometres. It also was identical to the doctrine embraced by Forestry minister Fjordbotten, deputy minister McDougall, and the Alberta Forest Service. Fjordbotten was categorically opposed to any resource management scheme that departed from the status quo, a status quo distinguished by private consultations between the Alberta Forest Service and resource companies. The impatience and intolerance he showed towards the Lubicons was captured neatly in his claim that Albertans were really the victims in this dispute. "I, like many, feel it is inappropriate," Fjordbotten wrote, "for the Lubicon to hold Albertans ransom in their dispute with the federal government."[28] This allusion to a kidnapping, coming as it did on the eve of the attack upon the Buchanan logging camp, referred in the first instance to the longstanding Lubicon view that they had rights to share at least in managing the forests covering unceded territories. The Lubicon insisted upon reclaiming some responsibility for making wildlife management and environmental protection decisions in this area. According to Fred Lennarson, relinquishing the claim to these prerogatives, allowing the accelerated logging of the unceded lands Daishowa's fibre-hungry mill would demand, were nothing less than promises to destroy the remaining vestiges of traditional Lubicon society:

> experience made clear that once the trees were cut and gone there would be little hope that the Lubicon people would ever be compensated, there would no hope with regard to preserving even the remnants of a traditional way of life, [sic] there would be no hope with regard to Lubicon environmental concerns and the Lubicons would have lost what little leverage that they might still retain with regard to negotiating a settlement of Lubicon land rights.[29]

Lose the trees and the Lubicons' slide into violence, sickness, and despair would continue unchecked. Fjordbotten's ransom reference also took aim at Ominayak's 8 November declaration, a declaration reminiscent of the chief's statements from October 1988, that any timber cutting operation in unceded Lubicon territory which the Lubicons had not authorized would be stopped without warning. Loggers wishing to enter the forests would need Lubicon operating permits, licences, and leases; they would have to comply with whatever environmental protection and wildlife management standards the Band drafted.

Ominayak's strong language throughout the fall of 1990, culminating in the November declaration, closely followed the lessons of October 1988.

Through one week of confrontation, by making good on the threat to disrupt the income flows of oil and gas companies, the Lubicon accomplished more than they had during years of negotiations. Only by threatening or damaging corporate balance sheets and making corporations realize that the settlement of aboriginal claims was in their self-interest were the Lubicons able to force governments to modify their settlement offers. This aggressiveness might work again.

The first harvest from assuming this confrontational posture was reaped soon after a late September meeting between Ominayak and Norm and John Boucher, the owners of Boucher Brothers Lumber, a Daishowa logging sub-contractor. In early October, the Boucher brothers announced that they were abandoning their plans to log immediately outside the boundary of the proposed reserve area north east of Lubicon Lake. Newspaper reports also speculated, incorrectly, that Buchanan Lumber, a second Daishowa subcontractor, and Brewster Construction, a Daishowa subsidiary purchased in 1989, would abandon their plans to operate in the disputed territory during the 1990 season. After the attack on the Buchanan Lumber camp, although Brewster Construction continued to clear-cut spruce and aspen in an area they had been working since 1978, Daishowa shifted its search for timber outside the boundaries of the unceded territories. This concession from the company was reiterated in the 1991 harvesting plans. "It is our desire," Hamaoka explained when commenting upon his company's 1991 plans, "to confine the Peace River operations to the west side of the Peace River and our Brewster Construction operations will also demonstrate a sensitivity to this particular situation."[30]

The fires of tension engulfing the Lubicon situation also were stoked by the organizational culture and standard operating procedures of the Alberta Forest Service (AFS). For the AFS, the Lubicons were invisible; the Band's circumstances and interests inhabited a different dimension from that in which senior forestry officials travelled. The intent of the department to proceed with business-as-usual animated a variety of key events during this period. Only one month after the Grimshaw Agreement the AFS auctioned off two timber cutting quotas in unceded territory to Brewster Construction without consulting the Lubicon at all. As Reverend Bill Phipps of the Friends of the Lubicon said: "If you're in the process of negotiation you don't allow the sale of timber by one party without first consulting the other party. After all what does consultation mean?"[31] This was not the only time the department failed to consult the Band about the future of the forests; the Lubicons played no part in the negotiations over the terms of the FMA Daishowa and the province concluded in September 1989; the timber harvesting proposals for 1990/91, the proposals that sparked the firebombing of logging equipment, were approved by the department despite the fact that these plans called for at least three companies—Brewster Construction, Buchanan Lumber, and Boucher Brothers—to mount operations in disputed territory. Departmental explanations for these events were very bureaucratic and legalistic in their tone. The department had to safeguard its standard approach of regulating forest access. Cliff Smith, an assistant deputy minister in Forestry, Lands and Wildlife, pointed out when asked about the Brewster timber licence auction that "[i]t is possible for the right to be revoked but the integrity of the timber quota system could be at stake." Legalistic references were sprinkled liberally among Fjordbotten's remarks that he really had no choice but to let logging proceed, despite the threatened confrontation. "We have an obligation," he wrote, "to allow these companies to exercise their legal rights to access this wood."[32] Given the minister's discretion to modify the terms of these agreements and to assign alternative cutting sites for these companies, his protests that he was bound to see this specific pattern of timber cutting followed in 1990/91 carried little weight. Instead, it is certainly possible that Fjordbotten either did not take the Lubicons' threat seriously or perhaps even, as John McInnis, the New Democratic Party environment critic suggested, was quite content to see violence erupt during the 1990 logging season.

Daishowa, for its part, maintained before and after the firebombing that it was an innocent caught in a bilateral dispute between the Lubicons and the federal government. Tom Hamaoka, frustrated that the land claim still was unsettled and angered by the Lubicon strategy of using Daishowa's presence for leverage in their struggle, declared that: "Daishowa is here not to be a mediator; we're here to do business."[33] Yet, the company's frustration had already led it to lobby government. After the Lubicon issue first began to plague Daishowa's business plan the company raised its predicament and the need for a settlement with the federal government. Also, the company waged an aggressive public relations campaign to fight the image cultivated by the Lubicons and their supporters that Daishowa was a villain in this tale. The campaign reached its zenith during a public exchange of letters between Tom Hamaoka and Jan Reimer, Edmonton's mayor. The incident prompting this conflict was the decision by Edmonton Telephones (Ed Tel), the municipally-owned utility, to award its telephone directory contract to a printing firm that purchased paper from Daishowa America's Port Angeles, Washington, paper mill. The Lubicons and a variety of their supporters urged Mayor Reimer to use whatever power she could to force Ed Tel to reconsider its decision. Reimer's response, which effectively said that her hands were tied, also offered her personal sympathy for the Lubicon people. These last comments infuriated Hamaoka: "Daishowa has strived to become a good corporate citizen in your city and the Province." Not only, he argued, had his company been sensitive to aboriginal and environmental issues but Daishowa had "directly spent hundreds of millions of dollars in your city, both for construction and to support our ongoing operations." Reimer did not suffer these criticisms silently. Instead, she objected to the tone of economic intimidation in Hamaoka's letter and suggested that, if Daishowa was truly sensitive to aboriginal and environmental issues, it would not be taking wood from logging contractors operating in unceded Lubicon territory.[34] The Edmonton Chamber of Commerce and an overwhelming majority of city council, meanwhile, rushed to Hamaoka's side. A council resolution publicly chastized Reimer for voicing her opinion on issues outside the city's jurisdiction.

If nothing else, this conflict drew attention to the silence of the Edmonton business community when it came to the Lubicon issue. The very businesses that were so visible when it came to chasing Daishowa contracts vanished at the first hint of political controversy. "Where were they," one business columnist asked, "when Daishowa was getting beaten up in the press?"[35] More importantly, the Hamaoka-Reimer exchange is a key to understanding what was responsible, other than the possibility of further violence, for Daishowa's decision to avoid traditional Lubicon territory in its search for timber after the 1990 logging season. The harshness of Hamaoka's response to Reimer speaks well to the fear the mere whisper of the word "boycott" inspired in his company. Daishowa's constituencies, unlike Fjordbotten's or the Getty government's, were national and international. While the Peace River investment was made in order to secure fibre, obviously, the profitability of the Daishowa group of companies depended as well upon secure markets for its range of paper products. Hanging onto those markets had been threatened by the recession while retaining market share became even more important in light of the cash flow problems created by a skyrocketing corporate debt. During the 1980s, disenchanted with the unwillingness of governments to use their regulatory powers to protect the environment, the environmental movement discovered that the market, customarily regarded as the source of environmental problems, could be used as a weapon against polluters, against any industry it was battling. Boycotts had been used quite successfully against the Canadian sealing and fur industries. As was demonstrated during the Calgary Olympics, the Friends of the Lubicon were very capable of organizing successful boycotts. Laughed at at first by the Olympic Games' organizers, the boycott of the Glenbow Museum's "The Spirit Sings" exhibition was very successful. Not only did the Lubicons succeed in convincing a number of museums from around the world not to participate—a success which added legitimacy to their charges against Canada's governments and the oil industry—but they also gained important international and national publicity and support for the treaty fight.

The effectiveness of boycotts against forest companies was demonstrated in the summer of 1992 when Procter and Gamble sold all of its pulp and paper interests, including its just-modernized Grande Prairie pulp mill, to Weyerhaeuser Canada Company Limited. The price Weyerhaeuser paid for Procter and Gamble's Alberta and Georgia assets—six hundred million dollars—was not high, a sign that Procter and Gamble wanted out of the pulp business badly. Eric Jerrard, the former manager of public relations for the Grande Prairie mill, said:

> Boycotts had been organized by Greenpeace in Germany and some women's groups in the UK because of the Grande Prairie mill. The South Peace Environmental Association had gotten this information to them, David Suzuki had come down and agreed with it. It wasn't worth it for the company. They are a consumer based company, they need the support of the consumers, this mill was taking that away, so they decided to sell their interest in pulp companies. The company could respond to environmental calls by the consumers in other areas (packaging, etc.) but with the mill you can't get rid of all the pollution. It was just easier to sell.[36]

Daishowa would also feel the effects of a boycott strategy, this one organized by the Lubicons and their supporters. During the fall of 1991 letters of support for the Lubicon were written to Daishowa's Vancouver offices by environmental and aboriginal support groups from countries such as Germany, the United Kingdom, Australia, and Denmark. Some letters, such as the one from Pro Regenwald, a German organization concerned about the world's rainforests, warned that they would try to disrupt Daishowa's European markets unless the company withdrew from the disputed territory;[37] the Friends of the Lubicon in Toronto signalled their intention to approach government agencies demanding that they boycott Daishowa paper products; Ho-Lee-Chow, Knechtel's, the YWCA, Cultures Fresh Food Restaurants, *Now!* magazine, and the Body Shop either cancelled contracts with Daishowa or announced their intention to buy the company's paper products no longer; by July 1993 the Friends of the Lubicon claimed that at least twenty-six companies, representing over twenty-seven hundred retail outlets, had joined the boycott against Daishowa paper products. In December 1991 Hamaoka conceded that the boycott was having an impact. "It's gotten to the stage now," he admitted, "where, yes, we're feeling the economics. It's no longer good enough to have government support. The public has to also want [the mill]."[38] Worried about the prospects of a spreading protest the company stayed out of the disputed territory in the 1991–92 and 1992–93 logging seasons.

When Tom Hamaoka announced that his company would not log in the contested area during the winter of 1992–93 he tried to counter the image of the company that was being portrayed by those behind the boycott. Daishowa-Marubeni, the joint venture sought by Daishowa to alleviate its financial crisis, would not log in the area of concern to the Lubicons "to counter unfounded allegations and speculation that continues to arise concerning Daishowa's on-going operations and future plans . . . we believe that we have acted responsibly to help create a suitable environment for renewed discussions and negotiations between the principals in this complex dispute."[39] The seriousness with which the company regarded the boycott also was reflected in Daishowa-Marubeni's preparation of its own fact book on the Daishowa boycott for distribution to the company's customers. In addition to presenting its case for why the boycott was unjustified, Daishowa-Marubeni also offered to "provide any public/media information, legal advice, and spokespersons required to support any customer experiencing boycott pressure."[40]

Wood Buffalo et al.: The Courts As Last Resort

Daishowa's hopes that it could cultivate the image of a "good corporate citizen" were dashed when the company's complicity in the clearcutting of Wood Buffalo National Park was publicized in the fall of 1990. This national park, the world's second largest, had been carved out of Canada's Northwest Territories in 1922 to protect the wood bison. Designated as a World Heritage site by the United Nations in 1983, much of Wood Buffalo's history belies this tribute. At several points in this history the national park's integrity has been compromised; in the 1940s, loggers entered the park, ostensibly temporarily, in order to supply lumber for building the northern resource town of Uranium City. They never left. In 1982, this logging lease, now held by Canfor (Canadian Forest Products Limited), was renewed. When asked how the government could allow clearcutting in a national park, Environment Canada officials pointed towards public opinion. The assistant deputy minister responsible for parks suggested that the public was much less tolerant of clearcutting in the nineties than it had been in earlier decades. By 1990 the vistas of the scarred landscapes left in the wake of clearcutting seen on nightly news broadcasts reduced whatever public tolerance had existed previously for this style of forestry. Condemnations of this situation highlighted the near total absence of controls over logging practices in Wood Buffalo. Forest industry officials and forest department officials alike had recoiled at the environmentalists' charge that Canada was "Brazil of the North"—a country that destroyed forests without ensuring their perpetuation. Exaggerated as this charge generally might be, it fit the circumstances in Wood Buffalo perfectly. With few restrictions on its logging lease and no rules requiring the company to reforest and manage the forest as a renewable resource, Canfor logged just like the gold-seekers, cattle ranchers, and other destroyers of Amazonian rainforest. As a senior official of the Alberta Forest Service put it: "They're basically liquidating the forest up there as far as I can tell."[41] Daishowa's 1990 purchase of Canfor's High Level Sawmill Division and the sawmill's harvesting rights left Daishowa officials to deal with this public relations nightmare. While one might empathize with the sentiment expressed by Daishowa's senior official in Edmonton that racist overtones sometimes accompanied attacks on the company's Alberta operations, nonetheless, the company's behaviour ensured that garnering public sympathy would be very difficult.[42] When Daishowa purchased the High Level sawmill operation, it was agreed that Canfor would retain the legal title to the Wood Buffalo lease. This arrangement would forestall a ministerial review of the lease and eliminate any possibility that the federal government would cancel or seriously regulate the company's right to cut the largest stands of white spruce in Alberta. Ed Struzik, *The Edmonton Journal* reporter who broke the Wood Buffalo story, wrote that Canfor's senior vice-president of finance admitted that this omission was deliberate: "You don't look for trouble that way. . . . We didn't want the lease opened up. It doesn't make good business sense."[43] The company's image was also damaged by news that, unshackled by the harvesting area restrictions and reforestation obligations which usually attend timber cutting operations, Canfor, with Daishowa's blessing, planned to accelerate dramatically its timber cutting pace in the park. By nearly doubling the amount of wood taken from Wood Buffalo, all of the harvestable timber would likely disappear by 1995.

Impatient with the slow progress made in talks between Daishowa, Canfor, and the federal government over a possible buy-out of the Canfor timber lease and angered by the federal government's offer to allow Canfor to continue logging in the park for another two years, the Canadian Parks and Wilderness Society (CPAWS) turned to the courts. The Sierra Legal Defence Fund, on behalf of the CPAWS, challenged the legality of the Canfor lease. The federal government, spurred to take action because of the lawsuit, pleasantly surprised the CPAWS on the eve of going to trial by agreeing with the organization's claim that Canada had broken the law by letting Canfor log in Wood Buffalo. On 8 June 1992 the Federal Court of Canada heard the environmentalists argue that the lease violated the statutory duty of the federal government to maintain the parks in order "to leave them unimpaired for the enjoyment of future generations." Since Canfor did not intervene in the case the Federal Court could find the agreement invalid without actually trying the issues raised by the case.[44]

The decision by the CPAWS to turn to the courts to try to reverse public policy reflected a developing preference among environmental groups to "legalize" their political campaigns, to use litigation as a lever to further the preservationist principles they articulated. In Alberta, enthusiasm for the judicial option had been encouraged by the important, but limited, success the Canadian Wildlife Federation had realized in its campaign against the Rafferty-Alameda dam in southeastern Saskatchewan. The Federation argued successfully that this particular project had to undergo a federal environmental assessment as outlined in federal regulations. As the Federation would find out to its regret, however, securing a federal environmental assessment did not guarantee that environmentally suspect projects would be shelved; the procedural victory delivered by the Federal Court of Canada only temporarily halted dam construction. In regards to the Peace River pulp mill, the allure of court challenges for environmentalists also grew out of their own inability to organize either prior to the project's announcement or while this proposal was subjected to the company's abbreviated environmental assessment process. We have already noted the tardy formation of the Friends of the Peace and the Friends of the North. Plagued by a late start, these groups had little choice but to turn to the courts in the hope of reversing the course policy making had taken, especially after the federal government ignored their pleas to conduct a separate environmental assessment of the project.

In the stream of litigation levelled against Daishowa's Alberta operations, the victory of the CPAWS in the Wood Buffalo case was atypical; generally, the courts did not prove to be a very rewarding path to travel for those who opposed forestry megaprojects. Efforts to have the courts order a retrospective federal environmental assessment of the project, invalidate Daishowa's operating licence, and void the Daishowa FMA all failed. Such failures should be attributed largely to a misplaced faith that the judiciary would welcome the opportunity to assume an activist posture and challenge the norms of industrial society by interpreting issues that were shrouded in uncertainty in a fashion that would prohibit, delay, or place strict conditions upon forestry megaprojects. In the past, uncertainty generally had not been much of a barrier, barring an explicit statutory declaration, to projects promising economic growth. In the challenge to the Daishowa FMA, the Alberta Wilderness Association (AWA), the Sierra Club of Western Canada, the Peace River Environmental Society, and Peter Reese fought against this precedent and asked the courts to rule that provincial logging and reforestation practices could not guarantee the "perpetual sustained yield" of the forests called for by the FMA. Justice David McDonald acknowledged the uncertainty surrounding this promise; however, in his opinion the declared intent of the government and the company to manage the forests to realize this goal was sufficient to turn back the environmentalists' challenge.

The rush of environmentalists and Native groups to the province's courtrooms was a telling indication of just how disenchanted these constituencies were with traditional styles of representative government where politicians, held accountable to the public through the electoral process, make final decisions and bear the political responsibility for their actions. It is ironic, however, that this disenchantment led these groups to turn to an institution that, by its very design, holds what J. R. Mallory, a distinguished Canadian political scientist, called "a watching brief for the past." There was also an important element of desperation in the disenchantment of the environmentalists. They were so consumed with the need to defeat these projects that they advocated courses of action that, if successful, also may have frustrated the greater degree of public participation environmentalists called for. In several of the court challenges launched against Daishowa and Alberta-Pacific, these groups proposed alternatives that arguably furthered government by experts, not government by the people. Calls for a retrospective environmental assessment of Daishowa, while insisting upon public hearings, were inspired nonetheless by a faith that right-thinking technical experts would deliver decisions environmentalists could regard as just ones. So too, in one of the legal challenges to the Alberta-Pacific pulp mill, would environmentalists argue that licensing decisions should be entrusted to unaccountable administrators rather than to elected politicians— an alternative some certainly would regard as even less democratic than the situation about which environmentalists complained so bitterly.

The flood of litigation, a delight to a few select law firms, prompted an angry response from the province. In the wake of the decision sustaining the legality of the Daishowa FMA the Alberta government sought to recover $235,000 in court costs from the three environmental groups which contested the province's forestry management regime. Forestry minister Fjordbotten explained, "When the people take the government to court that's their responsibility to pick up the costs. . . . They say that might break the environmental groups. Well, I'm sorry, I'm not doing it in a vindictive way to get back at them."[45] Environmentalists thought otherwise; when Justice McDonald awarded costs of $77,000 to the government and Daishowa, members of the AWA and the Sierra Club reiterated their belief that the government was trying to punish the environmentalists for their opposition to the pulp mills and wanted to bankrupt them. For the AWA, this was not the first time when it appeared that the group's opposition to provincial policy prompted the government to punish the group. Previously, the AWA's increased reliance upon the media and legal system to challenge policies it disagreed with, particularly the Oldman River dam, coincided with a significant reduction in the grant the group received from the Recreation, Parks and Wildlife Foundation.[46] As this book went to press, the environmentalists, the provincial government, and Daishowa-Marubeni International appeared to be on the verge of concluding an agreement which would relieve the environmentalists' obligation to pay the court costs awarded by Justice McDonald. Although such an agreement obviously would remove a serious threat to the coffers of groups like the AWA and the Peace River Environmental Society, it would not strike down the precedent established by Justice McDonald's award. For environmental groups who in the future may consider using Alberta's courts to challenge public policy, the prospect of reimbursing their more well-heeled adversaries for court costs remains a very real danger of relying upon legal gambits.

In Mallory's classic study of the political conflicts sparked by the radical social credit initiatives introduced in Alberta during the Great Depression of the 1930s he wrote:

Political objectives, and the political theories which seek to give them universality, change in response to the most deeply felt needs of succeeding generations of men. But political institutions, including the framework of law by which men realize their social needs, are slow to change. The law is a conspicuous laggard in this respect and it is the existence of this lag which causes a political disequilibrium.[47]

Such a political disequilibrium, admittedly much less dramatic than that witnessed in Alberta during the Great Depression, emerged in the province once the provincial government began to pursue its forest strategy in earnest. The fibre syndrome, the ideological legacy of earlier decades, retained its firm grip upon the governing institutions of the province but challenges to its pre-eminence arose from an emerging preservationist coalition of Natives and environmentalists. The failure of the political institutions to incorporate the interests of these parties into policy making generally did not trouble either the governing Conservatives or Daishowa. Although Alberta Environment, the only government department to question the company's conclusions about acceptable environmental consequences, was able to draw upon this new public climate in order to secure concessions from the company, Forestry, Lands and Wildlife ensured that this reformist impulse would not enter the forests. The forests remained the preserve of the Forestry department, the chief apostle of the fibre syndrome.

For the Conservative government and Daishowa, the established legal framework was the epitome of acceptability and morality. For them, legality, public acceptability, and morality were interchangeable ideas. Taken to its extreme this attitude produced the spectacle of logging in a World Heritage site where Daishowa tried to deflect criticism and responsibility for this situation by citing the fact that Canfor, not Daishowa, had legal title to the logging lease. If the logging was legal, why wasn't it morally acceptable? Wasn't it unfair to criticize Daishowa since the timber it used at its High Level operations was obtained legally? Wood Buffalo was only the most extreme example of this insistence that all government and corporations should be expected to do to fulfill their obligations to the public was respect the letter of the law and agreements. When public consultation was required by law or government guidelines, as was the case for environmental assessments of major industrial projects, the amount of consultation offered by the company or demanded by government was minimal; when public consultation lacked a statutory basis, as in the case of negotiating Forest Management Agreements, it simply did not take place. If environmental groups were late to oppose the specifics of the mill's design they were told that the appropriate legal moment to register their objections had come and gone. When Natives claimed that historical grievances must be satisfied before further resource extraction could take place, they initially were dismissed because their demands questioned the legitimacy of the province's legal framework. The province had legal obligations to the companies which had to be respected; accommodating Lubicon interests by finding alternative supplies of timber for logging contractors made department officials uneasy because it questioned established practices. Only when the company felt threatened by the prospect of a boycott of its products and felt the need to stay out of the contested area was the government willing to offer Daishowa timber from areas outside of the Lubicons' area of concern.

1 . Andrew Nikiforuk and Ed Struzik, "Letters," *Report on Business Magazine* (February 1990), 9.
2 . Akira Nakamura, "Environmentalism and the Growth Machine: The System of Political Economy and 'Kogai' Control in Japan," *Governance*, 5 (1992), 192–93.
3 . LeRoy Fjordbotten, "Letters," *Report on Business Magazine* (February 1990), 9.
4 . H. A. Simons Ltd. and Pacific Liaicon Ltd., *Environmental Assessment Report Addendum: Public Consultation Program Documentation* (December 1987).
5 . Alberta Environment, "Comparison of Effluent Standards for Pulp Mills," 30 September 1988, mimeo.
6 . Mike Lamb, "A Man in His Element," *Calgary Herald*, 29 May 1988.
7 . Alberta, Legislative Assembly, *Alberta Hansard*, 19 April 1988, 543.
8 . *Environmental Assessment Report Addendum: Public Consultation Program Documentation* (December 1987).
9 . The Alberta-Pacific Environment Impact Assessment Review Board, *Public Hearing Proceedings, Fort Chipewyan, November 9, 1989*, Volume II, 1461.
10 . Pacific Liaicon Ltd., *Alberta Project Minutes of Meeting, Paddle Prairie, 4 November 1987*, 23.
11 . Kerri Gnass, "Objections to Daishowa 'not appropriate'," *High Prairie Mirror,* 27 July 1988.
12 . Dave Parker, "Efones and the Great Forest Sell-Off," *Environment Network News*, No. 13 (January/February 1991), 27.
13 . Jack Danylchuk, "Daishowa Mill Opens on Schedule but in Dispute," *The Edmonton Journal*, 22 September 1990.

14 . Pacific Liaicon Ltd., *Alberta Project Minutes of Meeting, Peace River, 5 November 1987*, 27.

15 . The panel went on to say: "However, we believe that, rather than an EIA, what is needed is a dynamic forest management review and monitoring system, including public involvement, that ensures forest management practices are environmentally and economically sound. It should be a continuous and co-operative process, incorporating review, assessment, information, regulation, and enforcement." Alberta, Expert Review Panel on Forest Management, *Forest Management in Alberta: Report of the Expert Review Panel* (Edmonton: 1990), 18.

16 . The Alberta-Pacific Environment Impact Assessment Review Board, *Public Hearing Proceedings, Fort Chipewyan, November 9, 1989*, Volume II, 1445.

17 . H. A. Simons Ltd. and Pacific Liaicon Ltd., *Environmental Assessment Report (1987)*, 1–13.

18 . In future Alberta would regulate chlorinated organics by establishing AOX discharge levels. AOX, adsorbable organic halides, refers to the presence of chlorinated organic compounds in pulp mill effluent. Specifically, it refers to halogenated organic compounds that are adsorbable by activated carbon. An AOX equivalent of the TOCL ratio of 2.5 kg/ADT found in Daishowa's Permit to Construct is 3.25 kg/ADT. By comparison the AOX kg/ADT levels set by Ontario (1991), British Columbia (1991), and Sweden (1989) were 2.5, 2.5, and 2.0. In Japan a voluntary standard of 1.5 kg/ADT was to be "imposed" by the Japan Paper Association in 1993.

19 . "Klein says a tonne of chlorines into the Peace River is a historic achievement," *The Mirror—Northern Report*, August 1989.

20 . John Goddard, *Last Stand of the Lubicon Cree* (Vancouver: Douglas & McIntyre, 1991), especially Chapter 8, "The Master Strategy," 74–85.

21 . Neil Waugh and Mindelle Jacobs, "Firm Gets 'Lubicon Land'," *Edmonton Sun*, 9 February 1988.

22 . Fred McDougall, interview with author, 21 May 1991.

23 . C. B. Smith, assistant deputy minister, Alberta Forest Service. Letter to Chief Bernard Ominayak, 12 February 1988, 2.

24 . Hugh Paxton, "The Warpath to Tokyo," *Japan Times Weekly*, 12 October 1991.

25 . These differences are contained in correspondence between Lennarson and Kitagawa. See F. M. Lennarson, letter to Koichi Kitagawa, 14 March 1988. K. Kitigawa, senior vice president & general manager, Daishowa Canada Co. Ltd., letter to THE MIMIR CORPORATION, attention F. M. Lennarson, 25 March 1988.

26 . Chief Bernard Ominayak, Lubicon Lake Band, letter to K. Kitagawa, senior vice president & general manager, Daishowa Canada Co. Ltd., 2 April 1988.

27 . James P. Morrison, general manager, Daishowa Canada Co. Ltd., Edmonton Office, letter to Mr. David Hallman, Taskforce on the Churches and Corporate Responsibility, 8 January 1991.

28 . LeRoy Fjordbotten, letter to A. S. Andrucson, 19 November 1990.

29 . Memo to File from FL, 25 September 1990 re 24 September 1990 Meeting with Brewster Construction, mimeo.

30 . Transcript of CBC Radio News Broadcast, Wednesday 9 October 1991; see also Erin Ellis, "Daishowa Plans Not to Log Land Claimed by Lubicons," *The Edmonton Journal*, 13 October 1991.

31 . Bryan Brochu, "Timber Sale Compromises Lubicon Negotiation Position," *Alberta Native News*, February 1989.

32 . LeRoy Fjordbotten, letter to A. S. Andrucson, 19 November 1990.

33 . Transcript of ITV News Broadcast, 9 October 1991.

34 . These positions were outlined in a series of letters. See Tom Hamaoka, vice president & general manager, Daishowa Canada Co. Ltd., letter to Her Worship, Jan Reimer, 23 September 1991; Jan Reimer, mayor, letter to Tom Hamaoka, vice president & general manager, Daishowa Canada Co. Ltd., 1 October 1991.

35 . Rod Ziegler, "Daishowa Doesn't Deserve to be Goat in Lubicon Land Dispute," *The Edmonton Journal*, 10 October 1991.

36 . Eric Jerrard, interview with Kathleen Stokes, Grande Prairie, 31 August 1992.

37 . Angelika Zirngibl, letter to Tom Hamaoka, vice president, Daishowa Canada Company Ltd., 28 August 1991.

38 . John Goddard, "Daishowa Boycott Defends Lubicon Land," in *Save our Boreal Forests: The Mystery and The Heritage* (Western Canada Wilderness Committee Alberta Branch Educational Report), 11 (Fall 1992), 1.

39 . Daishowa Canada Co. Ltd., News Release, 25 November 1992.

40 . Daishowa-Marubeni, "Fact Book—Daishowa Boycott" (no date).

41 . Ed Struzik, "'Carmanah North' in Peril," *Edmonton Journal*, 16 December 1990.

42 . James Morrison, the general manager of Daishowa's Edmonton office said: "Articles about Daishowa have Japanese owned, and Procter and Gamble doesn't have American owned followed by its name. We have been surprised by the degree of racism." James Morrison, interview with author, Edmonton, 9 May 1992.

43 . Ed Struzik, "Canfor Says It Kept Lease to Avoid Scrutiny of Logging in Park," *The Edmonton Journal*, 23 October 1990.

44 . Canadian Parks and Wilderness Society v. Wood Buffalo National Park et al., 55 F.T.R., 286.

45 . Richard Helm, "Environmentalists Handed Gov't Legal Bill," 14 May 1992.

46 . Ray Rasmussen of the CPAWS felt that the cut in the AWA's provincial funding might be explained in this way. See Dr. R. V. Rasmussen, "Public Participation and Environmental Decision Making in Alberta," in Alberta Society of Provincial Biologists and Canadian Society of Environmental Biologists, Alberta Chapter, *Seeking Consensus: the Public's Role in Environmental Decision Making* (Edmonton: 1988), 49.

47 . J. R. Mallory, *Social Credit and the Federal Power in Canada* (Toronto: University of Toronto Press, 1954), 196.

CHAPTER 5

Alberta-Pacific:
the Political Economy of Growth

WHEN A HORSE SHITS, A HUNDRED SPARROWS FEED.

—*PROVERB*

IT IS CLEAR TO US THAT, LIKE THE METIS, THE KEY TO TRUE SELF-
DETERMINATION FOR INDIAN PEOPLE IS SELF-SUFFICIENCY THROUGH
THE DEVELOPMENT OF A SECURE ECONOMIC BASE. WE CANNOT FORGET
THE OIL AND GAS BOOM OF THE SEVENTIES, AND HOW LITTLE WE
BENEFITED FROM IT. INDIAN AND METIS PEOPLE WERE SUPPOSED TO
PARTICIPATE IN THAT BOOM, BUT WE DIDN'T BECAUSE WE WEREN'T
READY AND WE DIDN'T INSIST THAT WAYS BE FOUND TO ENSURE WE
WERE READY TO TAKE ADVANTAGE OF THOSE OPPORTUNITIES. . . . WE
CANNOT LET THAT HAPPEN TO US IN THE FORESTRY BOOM OF THE
NINETIES.

—*JOINT METIS ASSOCIATION OF ALBERTA AND INDIAN ASSOCIATION OF ALBERTA*
SUBMISSION TO THE ALBERTA-PACIFIC ENVIRONMENTAL IMPACT ASSESSMENT REVIEW
BOARD HEARINGS, 30 NOVEMBER 1989.

 Stuart Lang, visionary, president of Crestbrook Forest In-
dustries of Cranbrook, BC, and the Mitsubishi Corpora-
tion's main man in the western Canadian forestry industry,[1]
is offended by our rude suggestion that the $1.3 billion Al-
berta-Pacific (ALPAC) pulp mill project near Athabasca in
northeast Alberta is "big." Lang, a man who thought "big" in Latin America
for years, is known to his critics and supporters alike as the guiding genius
behind the Athabasca mill, the jewel in the crown of the Getty forestry policy.
"Big" has been hard to sell in much of Alberta since the end of the oil boom,
and big pulp mills with their disturbing clearcuts, toxic effluents, and air pollutants are not popular with an increasingly green public opinion, especially in

the urbanized areas of the province. Forty years ago, such impacts were barely noticed, let alone debated, because they were seen as the necessary price of economic progress; that generation, in both the capitalist and socialist world, had an unshakeable faith in the capacity of science and technology (including military technology) to manipulate nature and bring about a society in which, as Ronald Reagan used to say in the old television commercials, "progress is our most important product." The politicians and civil servants who set out under Don Getty's marching orders to industrialize the northern boreal forests by building huge pulp and paper mills on the Peace and Athabasca rivers were unreconstructed liberal optimists who retained a fifties faith in the unmitigated blessings of growth and state-of-the-art technology: a faith that, at least in the post-Chernobyl European-North American world, was shared by fewer and fewer true believers. If the Alberta planners were prejudiced in favour of growth through resource extraction, it was partly because their generation had imbibed Keynesian beliefs in the need to create employment and in the possibility of using the powers of government to shape the economy and society; they believed in the positive state and regarded the more extreme environmentalists as publicity-seeking urban romantics who—like the nineteenth century anarchists derided in the novels of Dostoevsky—would if necessary throw whole communities out of work in order to impose their will on everyone else. (But if this was true of a few, it was clearly not a fair characterization of those who saw the forestry and pulp mill strategy as potentially disastrous for the northern ecology and believed that some of the promill supporters were totally indifferent to the effects of multiple pulp mills on the great rivers of the North.) In any event, Alberta's economic development planners saw new technologies as the answer to virtually all of the problems raised by the critics of the Getty government's forestry and pulp mill strategy. Thus, the deputy minister of economic development and trade, reacting to our suggestion that Alberta was using up common property resources such as water and air in order to harvest and process its forests, answered with a striking statement of faith in the powers of technology:

If you'd asked me that question back in the Seventies, I'd have said, "My goodness, we've got some real problems." Now I'm sitting here in the Nineties, and we've corrected all these problems—or they're being corrected. As an example, the Hinton [pulp] mill. I'll bet you've driven by that mill ten times lately and you haven't smelled one thing. Remember the old days? When you were 30 miles away and you'd smell it? It's clean now. . . . We've had the strictest regulations in the world; technology and stricter regulations have allowed us to get 100 times better. We used to be talking of parts per million, now we're talking parts per billion. So I don't see why technology can't allow it. . . . The Athabasca river will be cleaner after ALPAC is built than it was five years ago.[2]

Putting to one side the ritualistic assertion that Alberta's regulations are the strictest "in the world"—they are not—there is obviously a measure of truth in this statement, although we would argue that what has driven the clean-up has been less the possibility of technological improvements than the unrelenting political pressures from environmental groups and the public. In many situations, including Hinton's once notorious pulp mill, new technologies have clearly mitigated some of the worst environmental impacts; we saw in chapter 2, for instance, that mechanical pulp mills such as Millar Western's at Whitecourt are able to produce pulp without the use of chlorine bleach, while the same firm's mill at Meadow Lake, Saskatchewan, uses a closed-loop process that involves no discharge of effluents into nearby water systems whatsoever. There is, then, some opportunity for technological progress, after all. Having granted the role of technical change, however, the economic planner's view that "we've corrected all these problems" is so far from being accepted by environmentalists and many other Canadians that we can call it a cultural curiosity, an artifact from a bygone era.

If the faith in technological progress has waned and environmentalism grown in Alberta, it is partly because a bitter lesson was learned by Albertans from the recession of the early 1980s when the cancellation of a few massive energy projects brought the province's oil-dependent economy to a virtual standstill. Although many Albertans had supported the construction of oil sands plants, petrochemical ventures, and new pipelines in the growth economy of the 1970s, the new skepticism is that resource megaprojects such as ALPAC are too susceptible to cost overruns, too vulnerable to shifts in international prices, and too hard on ecological systems to go ahead without expensive government backstopping. The whole dominant extractive economy that has sustained Alberta's growth since the late 1940s is seen by some critics as outmoded and too precariously linked to the fate of a few big resource projects. Yet, as we noted in an earlier chapter, the provincial government headed by Don Getty did not agree with the skeptics on the issue of megaprojects. Premier Getty, whose view of economic development was uncomplicated and based on Alberta's past successes with large projects, might well have agreed (he is a great lover of race horses) with the sense of the earthy proverb that opens this chapter. For those on Getty's side of the debate, megaprojects are necessary because of the spinoff economic activities they create for the "hundred sparrows"—that is, local business; and multinational enterprise, the "horse," is the indispensable agent of development in a resource periphery such as Alberta.

On the other side of the question, it is argued that these massive, technologically-driven projects create relatively few jobs, and that those jobs that are created are usually beyond the reach of local people because of their lack of training, skills, and other resources. Thus, a locally-owned sawmill or other wood products operation might employ, for example, sixty to seventy-five individuals (including Natives); yet few of these would qualify to work in a modern pulp mill or even—because of the high cost of, or the skills needed to operate, mechanical harvesting equipment—in the forests supplying the mill. Allocating the timber resources in favour of the more capital intensive and modernized projects may be, then, a way of creating new unemployment in the region. "Where are all the people?" is a common question from visitors to a newly modernized pulp mill such as Weldwood's at Hinton. The answer is that many of them have gone, made redundant by smart machines. The mill is being run by a handful of people sitting in a quiet, air-conditioned computer control room, a high-tech setting that seems to have no physical connection to the massive, noisy, and smelly machines producing the pulp. While we are not opposed to technical change, it is important to note that such change has negative as well as positive effects. Computer-based technologies are not neutral. Even the jobs of those few hundred highly-skilled persons who end up working in complex modern pulp mills like Daishowa or ALPAC are themselves vulnerable to capitalist competition, with its relentless pressure to drive costs down through the introduction of new labour-saving technologies. It is therefore at least worth debating whether government policy should explicitly favour and attempt to accelerate the use of the most technologically-intensive harvesting and pulping processes with subsidies and the allocation of land and resources to the transnationals.

At an early point in the process, ALPAC's Stuart Lang publicly extolled the proposed Alberta-Pacific project as one of the largest kraft pulp mills in the world—which was true enough—but such statements actually galvanized and enlarged the environmental movement in Alberta, concentrating the public's attention on the state of the province's great northern rivers and ALPAC's massive Forest Management Area (about 10 percent of Alberta's land surface, around 1 percent of Canada's), extended by the Getty government in virtual perpetuity to this Japanese-controlled corporate venture. In a letter to forestry deputy minister Fred McDougall, written in July 1988, Lang's own Crestbrook firm, whose controlling shareholders are the great Japanese trading company Mitsubishi Corporation and the Honshu Paper Company, also of Japan, had described their proposed fifteen hundred-tonnes-per-day mill as of "world-scale size with low unit costs of production in order to withstand the varying market conditions which are a well known characteristic of the pulp and paper industry. It will be the largest single-line kraft pulp mill in the world, and another 'first' for the Province of Alberta."[3] But that was not necessarily to say that ALPAC was "big," Lang told us. He himself had grown up in Newfoundland, and in those days there were pulp mills in that province that dwarfed any modern Canadian forestry megaproject. A short, stocky individual who speaks in rapid-fire monologues, Lang is a promoter who admits to no doubts about his visionary concepts. He is an eloquent defender of Japanese foreign investment in North America, and he played a central role in persuading the Alberta government to choose the Mitsubishi-controlled ALPAC venture instead of several alternative proposals. But Lang was patronizing, even dismissive, of his critics in the environmental movement—a serious error in the case of ALPAC—and he clearly oversold the Athabasca pulp mill to both the government and his Japanese corporate sponsors.

Stuart Lang landed at Crestbrook in 1979 following his involvement in the grandiose "Ludwig affair" in South America. A chemical engineer from Bowater Newfoundland, at Cornerbrook, Lang had moved to Mexico as resident engineer for Tuxtepec Corporation, and then for sixteen years was a vice-president of Olinkraft's Brazilian operations. Then, in the later 1970s, Lang was in the Amazon as a vice-president for production of Jari Forest Products where he was involved in the start-up of the Jari river pulp complex in Brazil. This fantastic scheme which Stuart Lang helped bring to life was the dream of Daniel Ludwig, an extraordinarily rich German-American industrialist and shipping magnate who wanted to go into the pulp business in Brazil's Amazon and make a fortune in the rainforest, and who hired Lang to help bring it about. In the event, no fortunes were made—one at least was lost—but the story itself, though true, was extravagant enough to have come from a Hollywood script.

Those who have seen the film *Fitzcarraldo* will know that in the 1890s an Irishman, known as "Fitzcarrald" to the Peruvians living in the upper reaches of the Amazon, hatched a wild scheme that made him a fortune in the rubber trade. In order to reach lands never before exploited by the rubber barons, Fitzcarrald dismantled a large riverboat and used hundreds of Indians to carry the parts of his craft in a lengthy portage between tributaries of the Amazon. After their incredible trek, Fitzcarrald reassembled, launched, and used his riverboat to penetrate and exploit virgin rubber-producing territories.

About eighty years later, a latter-day-Fitzcarrald, billionaire Daniel Ludwig, sought in similar fashion to turn a fortune in the Brazilian Amazon from the creation of vast tree plantations and a pulp-exporting empire at Jari River, a tributary which joins the Amazon near its mouth. First, Ludwig sought the perfect tree, one that offered good fibre, grew quickly, resisted disease and pests, and could be used to make pulp and solid wood products. He settled on Gmelina arborea, a tree native to Burma and India, and his company—Jari Forestal e Agropecuaria Ltda.—planted over two hundred thousand acres of it and Caribbean pine in plantations near the Jari River. Ludwig then sought out the support of the Brazilian state, which in 1974 had set out a national plan to make Brazil a major pulp exporter; to bring the Jari River venture a step closer to completion, Brazil's National Bank for Economic Development guaranteed a $200 million foreign loan to Jari Forestal so that Ludwig could build a huge 250,000-metric-tonne-per-year bleached kraft pulp mill on the shores of the remote Jari River, a mere fifteen hundred miles from civilization and thousands more from its major markets. Like Alberta a decade later, Brazil justified its subsidization of this unlikely resource venture on the grounds that, according to industry projections, prices would be high as market pulp would very soon be in short supply. The projections stoked the euphoria of the credulous politicians who generously backed the Jari River project, but they were of course quite wrong. By the early 1980s, the world market for pulp was in glut, not shortage, and prices were slumping.

Rather than attempt to build a new pulp mill at Jari River, Ludwig unveiled a grandiose scheme worthy of the Irishman, Fitzcarrald. Having first borrowed $250 million from the Japanese Import-Export Bank, Ludwig commissioned a Japanese engineering firm to build a $200 million pulp mill in sections in Japan; and then used tugboats to tow it 15,500 miles across the ocean to Brazil. The pulp mill was then towed up the Amazon River to the Jari River where it was assembled and, in the glutted markets of the early 1980s, went broke and was finally bought up by the Brazilian government. What Ludwig called "the biggest crap game of my career" was over; he was reported to have lost one billion dollars on the Jari River scheme.[4] Two years before Ludwig himself backed out, Stuart Lang—whose role in this whole affair is not clear—departed the Amazon for the presidency of Crestbrook in British Columbia. For some reason this episode is still cited by some of Don Getty's forestry planners as evidence that Stuart Lang was a "visionary" who could build the world's largest pulp mill in a remote location and somehow make money.

ALPAC is the largest of the new and expanded pulp mills and newsprint mills constructed in Alberta under the Getty forestry initiative. From the standpoint of those who measure progress in terms of the latest and best technology, ALPAC is state-of-the-art technical progress. The big bleached kraft pulp mill is located on high ground on the south bank of the Athabasca River about fifty kilometres downstream of the town of Athabasca, and roughly equidistant between Athabasca and Lac La Biche. The immense hinterland from which the mill will derive its fibre supply is an area of sixty-one thousand square kilometres of provincial Crown lands covering most of the northeast of the province, an area larger than New Brunswick. ALPAC will take 90 percent of its wood requirements from these public lands, the remainder from privately-owned forests from farmers, Native settlements, and others. Capable of producing up to fifteen hundred air dried tonnes a day of pulp from a mixture of 77 percent hardwood (mostly aspen) and 23 percent softwood (mostly spruce) and employing about eleven hundred permanent staff at the mill and in the woodlands, ALPAC received the province's initial go-ahead in late 1988, but it was delayed for many months due to controversy and environmental hearings (subjects of the next chapter), and the $1.3 billion mill was not up and getting into production until the fall of 1993. Is ALPAC the opening wedge in the wider industrialization of the northeast of Alberta? As will be seen below, in its negotiations with the ALPAC joint venturers the Getty cabinet wanted to secure "full utilization" of the resource and the development of secondary manufacturing from pulp production, and it sought to maximize so-called Alberta industrial benefits by getting Alberta supplier companies into the project. As with Daishowa-Marubeni at Peace River, the Alberta government approved ALPAC on the understanding that the pulp mill would, market conditions permitting, eventually integrate forward into the manufacture of fine paper, and its Forest Management Agreement of 30 August 1991 describes Alberta-Pacific as "a

joint venture for the purpose of a single two phased pulp and paper mill project."
But the joint venturers' obligation to go into paper production in Alberta is
conditional upon a world-class paper mill (with a minimum capital cost of two
hundred million dollars and an annual production capacity of one hundred
thousand to two hundred thousand finished metric tonnes of fine paper) receiving a positive economic feasibility study from the companies themselves,
and it is not clear that this will be forthcoming from the multinationals since,
notwithstanding the views of the provincial government, the location economics
of producing fine papers do not favour areas such as Alberta.[5] Left exclusively
to market forces, the decisions as to where to locate modern paper mills would
not lead the industry to Peace River or Athabasca.

It is important to note that ALPAC emerged as a by-product of Alberta's
diversification strategy: the concept for the project came as much from the
state as from the forestry transnationals, and it exists, in large part, because of
costly government concessions to Japanese capital—concessions that went well
beyond what had been offered to Daishowa during earlier negotiations over
the Peace River pulp mill. Mitsubishi, Honshu Paper, and the Alberta government first held discussions in Japan when Premier Getty's forestry initiative
had been set out by Al Brennan and other officials to the leading Japanese
paper companies during a swing through East Asia. Taiwan, Korea, and Japan
were the principal targets of this and subsequent missions. The evidence suggests that the Albertans were convinced that the Japanese were literally invin-
cible on the playing fields of trade, investment, and technological development. America was in irreversible decline and protectionist in policy; Japan
was on the rise and made no mistakes: thus, Alberta's problem was simply to
get Japan's attention. Brennan's team had prepared an investor-friendly video
called "Room to Grow," which opens on the docks somewhere in Japan. A
Japanese executive spots a newly-arrived shipment of wood products. Where,
he asks an assistant, did that wood come from? "Alberta," replies the assistant.
"Ah, Alberta. Berry good."

In Japan the Albertans talked to Oji Paper, Daishowa, Honshu Paper, and
two of the great trading companies, Marubeni Corporation (a partner with
Daishowa in British Columbia pulp projects) and Mitsubishi Corporation, one
of the world's largest and most diversified international companies. Oji, Japan's biggest paper producer, did not bite; but the other four subsequently
became involved in major capital projects in northern Alberta: Daishowa and
Marubeni in the northwest; Mitsubishi and Honshu in the ALPAC venture in

the northeast. Although Honshu and some other Japanese companies have a passive stake in the ALPAC complex, for all intents and purposes ALPAC is mostly a venture of Mitsubishi Corporation, and we shall have this central fact in mind as we analyze the project. Among other things, Mitsubishi has been a banker, investor, guarantor, supplier of technology, and sole marketing outlet for ALPAC; it also provided guarantees to cover any overruns caused by changing environmental standards and made other commitments to make the project's financing possible. Mitsubishi's involvement with ALPAC seems to have been part of a strategy of expanding its overall business operations in North America in the late 1980s while it was cash-rich and currency conditions were favourable. It was also assisting Crestbrook to find a more attractive fibre supply in the aspen forests of northeast Alberta. Unlike, say, Daishowa, Mitsubishi—a trading company—is not in business to produce pulp worldwide and use it in an integrated system to make paper; but it does buy and trade pulp among many commodities, and pulp and paper account for part of the giant firm's sales and profits. Mitsubishi brings enormous financial resources, marketing knowledge, and technological know-how to any venture in which it is involved, and its entry (via Crestbrook) into Alberta's forestry sweepstakes gave the Getty government's policy immense credibility. The essence of the deal that began to emerge from the Japanese side was this: in return for government support that would lower the political and financial risks of investing in the joint venture and long-term supply arangements, Mitsubishi would undertake to arrange the financing for the group and to purchase and market worldwide the entire output of the big pulp mill.

The key decisions were made in Japan. But at about the same time in 1987, Stuart Lang met Al Brennan, head of Alberta's new Forest Industry Development Division, for breakfast in Calgary; there the two expatriate Newfoundlanders chatted about Lang's ambitions for Crestbrook Forest Industries and its two great Japanese transnational owners. Notwithstanding the size of its backers, Crestbrook was still a very small player in the Canadian forest industry—far too small and regional to take on some of the big projects it wanted. As of 1988, according to a Price Waterhouse survey, Crestbrook was the eighteenth largest publicly-traded forest products company as measured by sales revenues and was much smaller than any of the ten largest privately held firms in the sector. From its origins as Cranbrook Sash and Door in 1898, Crestbrook's operations were centred in the East Kootenay region in southeastern British Columbia. In August 1966, Crestbrook signed a joint venture agreement with Honshu Paper and Mitsubishi Corporation under which the two Japanese transnationals agreed to finance the construction of a four hundred-tonnes-per-day bleached kraft pulp mill at Skookumchuck, near the town of Cranbrook. In return for this financing, the Japanese acquired effective control of Crestbrook and its production; through a pulp sales agreement, Crestbrook was required to sell at a discount to Honshu and Mitsubishi all of the mill's output of market pulp over twenty years. Having a guaranteed outlet for its entire production is of obvious benefit to the mill and Alberta, but Crestbrook gave up all control over the price paid for its pulp. In what appears to be a fairly standard arrangement in transfer pricing by international resource producers, the pulp sales agreement discounted Crestbrook's production by a few million dollars per year; a similar agreement, which guarantees to purchase all of ALPAC's daily fifteen hundred tonnes of output for an agreed discount, has been negotiated by the mill's owners, and this could become a mechanism for transferring profits out of Alberta. Crestbrook's own pulp sales arrangement, covering the marketing at its Skookumchuck mill, has been the subject of a Revenue Canada, Taxation, investigation and of court actions. Relying on pricing information obtained from a confidential survey, in 1989 Revenue Canada reassessed Crestbrook's taxes for 1984, 1985, and 1986, arguing that the sales agreement had been used to discount prices excessively and to move profits out of Canada. It was alleged that Crestbrook owed the Crown an additional $4.9 million, but at the time of writing the assessment is still under appeal.[6] Transfer pricing is used by many multinationals in many jurisdictions to shift taxable income to different entities within the same firm, but it can be very difficult to monitor and to prevent. It is worth noting that Mitsubishi Corporation has been accused of using its role as sole purchaser of forestry products in jurisdictions such as Papua New Guinea to engage in extensive transfer pricing and secretly to transfer profits offshore.[7] Yet, to repeat, the agreement is also viewed by Alberta government officials as a major advantage to the province because it guarantees a market for the mill's output and stability for the region. There is a tradeoff here that arises from the initial decision to do business with transnationals such as Mitsubishi, for they bring costs as well as advantages even in their pricing strategies.

When Stuart Lang and Al Brennan met in Calgary, Lang mentioned the possibility of Crestbrook building a small paper mill in southern Alberta. But his heart belonged to a much larger vision (perhaps he missed Brazil; the Athabasca was not the Amazon, but it would do). What he really wanted to do was to build a "big" pulp mill in northeast Alberta—the biggest single-line pulp mill in the world, as he later described it—but he admitted that one of his Japanese backers, Honshu Paper, was reluctant to become involved in Alberta. Mitsubishi, on the other hand, was looking to expand in North America and was supportive of Crestbrook's "mission statement": its mission as stated in its annual reports was now "to achieve the status of a world-scale, integrated forest products company in North America, with continuous operations in forestry, pulp and paper products manufacturing in several political and economic jurisdictions." The statement nicely concealed Crestbrook's very modest profitability and lack of experience in building and operating large projects. But Alberta's forestry planners, seeing Japan and Mitsubishi between the lines, could hardly have been more impressed.

Crestbrook's interest in expanding beyond British Columbia was based on several factors. The company's access to new timber resources was being threatened on several fronts. British Columbia was, according to Stuart Lang, using all of its available fibre and this would constrain Crestbrook's ambition to expand. Moreover, the trees that were available were becoming more and more expensive to cut, as the British Columbia government had increased its stumpage fees, or royalties, after the initial victory by American lumber producers in the Canada-United States softwood lumber dispute. From 1987 to 1988, Crestbrook's stumpage costs rose by 80 percent, from $5.2 million to $9.5. million, leading Lang to blame the Crown's royalties for dragging down the company's financial performance. He claimed that its wood costs in Alberta—where the company was gaining access principally to hardwood resources with very low stumpage fees—were 40 percent lower than they were in British Columbia (twenty dollars versus thirty-five dollars per cubic metre), and "regulators" in British Columbia were largely responsible.[8] And then there were British Columbia's environmentalists. Environmental groups had already succeeded in removing portions of the forestry land use base in the neighbouring West Kootenays. The Valhalla Conservation Society's successful campaign to create Valhalla Provincial Park, a wilderness park overlooking the western shores of Slocan Lake, reduced the annual allowable cut of forest companies operating in this area. Their vocal presence at tree farm licence hearings prompted Lang to call the hearings "a zoo and a disgrace to intelligent civilization."[9] In an open letter to his employees, written in the summer of 1991, he lamented that: "Our provincial resource base is under threat from several sources including provincial government actions, Native land claims and extreme preservationists whose hidden agenda is an end to the forest industry in British Columbia. Put simply, loss of timber means the industry and Crestbrook have to reduce operations. A sharp loss could mean the end of our Company."[10] And finally, there was British Columbia's infamous labour climate. While the company enjoyed reasonably good relations with the Pulp, Paper and Woodworkers of Canada, in 1986 Crestbrook had been hit with an eighteen-week shutdown by the International Woodworkers of America, the worst strike in the company's history. Lang tended to blame the wage demands of the trade unions for those difficulties that could not be attributed to the provincial "regulators" or the environmentalists; with so many other groups conspiring to destroy the forestry industry, there was little left over for which to blame management. A visionary, he dreamed of moving Crestbrook and its Japanese backers to free-enterprise Alberta where, relative to British Columbia, the pastures—but not the environmentalists—were greener and the hardwood forests much cheaper. The Alberta-Pacific project in the Athabasca region of northeast Alberta was his ticket.

Bypassed by the Boom

The Athabasca/Lac La Biche region is one of Alberta's poorest: even during the years of the oil boom, by which it was mostly bypassed, the Athabasca area suffered from a lack of economic growth. A largely rural, thinly populated region of dense forest and numerous lakes—it has less than 1 percent of Alberta's population—the Athabasca area lacks the energy resource wealth and the productive agricultural lands that have blessed many other parts of the province. Its agricultural potential is constrained by its short growing season and moderate to severe limitations on soils quality for the growing of crops. Its principal resource is its aspen forests, which until recently were regarded as "weeds" by potential developers. The primary occupational categories include farming and construction which employ nearly half the work force. Educational and per capita income levels are well below provincial levels: as of the mid-1980s, 24 percent of the population had less than grade nine schooling, and school enrolments declined steadily after 1971. Of the thirty-one counties in the province of Alberta, the county of Athabasca ranked as number thirty-one in fiscal capacity as of 1989. No natural features such as a national park exist in or near the Athabasca region and, aside from the historic Athabasca River transportation routes to the north, there are few obvious points of interest that would attract large numbers of tourists. The river's low flows during the winter months make it a poor receptor of industrial effluents, a factor that ought to have discouraged its industrial development via tar sands plants, pulp mills, and so on. The major highways to and from key destinations (for example, Edmonton to Fort McMurray) do not even require travel directly through the region, and this too has been a factor in Athabasca's slow decline. The area does boast a large number of lakes, a few of which are populated by summer cottages and cabins, but there is a lack of infrastructure to support a significant tourist sector based on these. Some of the Native communities in the area— for example, Calling Lake—suffer from very high levels of unemployment, poverty, and social ills: hence, they have become pockets of high welfare dependency. The small, attractive town of Athabasca itself, formerly Athabasca Landing, has had a precarious existence through most of this century. Not only is it bypassed by the major north-south highways: the close proximity of Edmonton, a major metropolitan centre, causes a serious leakage of retail and service trade revenue from the town and other communities of the region.[11] The town of Athabasca struggled for decades to keep its population above two thousand, many of its young people choosing to migrate to the larger population centres, and saw its tax base wither to the point where very few public investments could be made. The recession of the early 1980s hit the region very hard, notwithstanding the province's fortuitous decision to relocate Athabasca University, a distance-learning institution, from Edmonton to the town of Athabasca. In sum, prior to the controversy over the $1.3 billion Alberta-Pacific project in the late 1980s, the region of Athabasca/Lac La Biche was depressed relative to much of Alberta and there was a keen interest among local business and politicians in attracting new capital investment to the area. Crestbrook and its partners would have little difficulty in finding support and building a prodevelopment coalition in such circumstances.

Facing economic stagnation and demographic decline, in 1985 the Athabasca county's Regional Economic Development Committee—led by the then reeve of the county, Bill Kostiw—had authorized the Finnish-based economic consulting group, EKONO, to study the region's resources and to develop strategies to improve the economy by creating more jobs and industry. The report was thorough, realistic, and relatively optimistic about Athabasca's longer-term prospects. It proposed no single cure for the region's developmental ills. Interestingly, although the idea of locating a large pulp mill or some other big project in the region had been circulating for some years, EKONO's lengthy report on the Athabasca region argued against a "megaproject" economic strategy. Given the province's and the region's history of boom-and-bust cycles and the need for diversity as well as stability, the focus of development should be pluralistic:

> The needs of Athabasca Region are many and diverse. Conceptually, they can be viewed in baseball terms, as a need for a string of "base hits" rather than for a "home run." Both approaches will result in runs scored, but in the case of Athabasca Region, the cumulative effect of several interrelated development initiatives appears to have a much better chance for success than looking for a single economic "grand slam."[12]

EKONO's alternative to the "grand slam" emphasis on a single large project was to propose the diversification of the regional economy via the gradual development of retail trade, tourism, value-added forest products manufacturing (furniture manufacturing was discussed under this heading), industrial development, and peat production. EKONO argued that in order to diversify, the Athabasca region had to generate a better supply of venture capital, adequate infrastructure, some growth in its tax base to finance public investments, and better information about the community's goals and resources. But the report was only a beginning: having outlined some of the constraints to development and then identified some possible areas for new investment and growth, EKONO had in no sense resolved the difficulties involved in getting the private sector to invest in these areas, let alone in specific ventures or companies; the report changed nothing, created no jobs, built no new roads, generated no wealth. In the long run, with effort and luck the Athabasca region's economy might improve if EKONO's advice were followed; in the short run, the report offered a strategy but no panacea, no instant relief from the problems of poverty, stagnation, and unemployment. For those living and working in the region and who had been bypassed by Alberta's booms, this consulting report was in no sense a real alternative to what, a couple of years hence, Crestbrook and Mitsubishi and Honshu Paper and other multinationals in the Alberta-Pacific project were able to offer Athabasca/Lac La Biche: the world's largest single-line pulp mill, more than a billion dollars in investment, more than a thousand permanent jobs, new infrastructure and public investments, a better tax base, and so forth, through the development of the region's forestry resources. Even if ALPAC was based on the "grand slam" approach and was nothing more than a scaled-up resource-extractive project with little manufacturing added, it was bound to have political appeal in a producing region that had never garnered its share of the spoils from Alberta's boom periods. Significantly, Bill Kostiw, the man who had as reeve of Athabasca county commissioned the EKONO report, also played an important role in getting the ALPAC project and its tax benefits located in the county. This is not to say that the inhabitants of Athabasca/Lac La Biche were—or are—indifferent to the environmental critiques of the huge project, but it is plain that the promise of material benefits and growth was very persuasive to those living in the area who (rightly or naively) thought they could benefit economically and saw no alternative routes to prosperity. Arguably, ALPAC won the hearts and minds of the people of the region by default—that is, it won because there *was* no existing alternative that offered economic growth and hope, and because the environmental opponents of the project failed to deliver such alternatives to create growth. The political realities were such that, in the absence of realistic economic alternatives, efforts by the critics to derail ALPAC would generate great resentment in the region and support for the project, even among those who might have opposed it initially on other grounds.

Benefits: Corporate and Albertan

Crestbrook's ALPAC project was selected by the Getty government in December 1988 after months of strenuous behind-the-scenes lobbying by its backers and other major forest companies for the exclusive rights to harvest the Lac La Biche forest, a huge expanse of northeast Alberta. There were half a dozen proposals under consideration, including a chemithermomechanical project favoured by some environmentalists and the New Democrat MLA for Athabasca/Lac La Biche, but the cabinet's short list came down to two transnationals: Alberta-Pacific and the American forestry giant, Weyerhaeuser (one of whose lobbyists was Calgary corporate lawyer and former premier Peter Lougheed). Although it had the best site and the strongest backing among local politicians and business, not everyone in the Alberta government was impressed by Crestbrook's credentials, and Weyerhaeuser's proposal also had influential supporters—for instance, Fred McDougall, the deputy minister of the forestry department, was skeptical about the Crestbrook project and favoured Weyerhaeuser (indeed, McDougall left the Alberta government to head up Weyerhaeuser's Alberta operations shortly after the cabinet's decision in favour of ALPAC). But ALPAC was selected, we believe, because it was the biggest proposal offering the best package of industrial benefits to Alberta business, because it offered guaranteed marketing arrangements that would allow the pulp mill to sell its pulp output during market downturns, an important factor for politicians worried about the instability of northern communities, and because ALPAC's proposal had been carefully tailored to meet the political and economic priorities of the Getty cabinet, especially on the issue of Alberta industrial benefits. In a more general sense, the choice of ALPAC also reflected the growing takeover in the late 1980s of Japanese transnational capital in North American industries traditionally under United States dominance. At this point, the Japanese were cash-rich and looking for security of fibre supply rather than short-term profits, and were thus able to take a longer and more accommodating view of what the Alberta government required than did their United States rivals; relative to the Americans, they had held, moreover, a more explicitly "political" view of overseas investments in forestry at least since the publication of MITI's administrative guidance of the early 1980s. By operating through risk-spreading joint ventures involving both Japanese paper producers and trading companies as investors, and by entering into partnerships with resource-owning governments, the transnationals could stabilize their long-term production agreements and secure their supplies of fibre from politically safe areas such as northern Alberta. In the case of ALPAC, the Japanese would accommodate Alberta's interests in economic diversification and "Alberta benefits" in return for the payment for infrastructure, financial participation and—most important—guaranteed long-term access to hardwood fibre. Until the project's vulnerability to environmentalist attacks was exposed, ALPAC seemed to be a textbook example of the MITI model of stable overseas investment.

The ALPAC joint venture came together in 1988; its ownership is based on a web of risk-sharing agreements among Japanese-controlled entities. Crestbrook—itself controlled by Mitsubishi/Honshu—holds a 40 percent interest in the ALPAC joint venture; 35 percent is held by MC Forest Investment, which itself is 85.72 percent-owned by Mitsubishi and 14.28 percent-owned by Hokuetsu Paper Mills; and the remaining 25 percent is held by Kanzaki Paper Canada. Mitsubishi is the dominant interest in the group. The cost and risk of financing the $1.3 billion project are, we believe, extremely attractive to these Japanese-owned corporate interests, though much less attractive to the Alberta government and to taxpayers. From the outset, Alberta agreed to fund the provision of all the transportation infrastructure for the ALPAC project, a commitment whose final cost amounted to seventy-five million dollars. In addition, Crestbrook initially requested $150 million in government financing in the pulp mill either as direct equity investment or in the form of a debenture subordinated to private-sector loans. Why? Alberta had not given such concessions to Daishowa, and these very big and wealthy companies were certainly in no need of direct financing from government. In the first place, such financing would deepen the state's direct involvement in the project, eliminate the fiction of its neutrality as between proponents and critics, and give it a stronger political interest in its success: if ALPAC went under, so too would the government's direct financial stake in the project. Second, government financial participation would make bank financing easier to obtain and limit the companies' risks to this particular project in case of a failure.

ALPAC appears to have had no difficulty in obtaining Alberta's financial aid for the pulp mill. The Alberta government did not take an equity position in the project, but it eventually agreed to invest $275 million in subordinated debentures in the joint venturers in ALPAC—that is, in Crestbrook, MC Forest Investment, and Kanzaki. The debentures are held by the Alberta Heritage Savings Trust Fund, and they are subordinated to the banks' syndicated mortgage loan of $720 million, which means that the banks will be paid in full before the province receives a cent on its loans. This direct financial involvement by the province permitted the commercial financing of the project on a "limited recourse" basis, which in effect means that the investing multinational corporations are risking nothing more than what they have invested as equity in ALPAC—around $310 million. In case of a default, the banks and the province would have no recourse against the other corporate assets of the multinationals. For the equity holders the financing agreement appears to be very attractive, and this is primarily because of Alberta's willingness to accept large risks and deferred revenues. Thus, Crestbrook obtains the ownership and profits of 40 percent of the $1.3 billion project and its daily output of fifteen hundred tonnes of pulp for just $124 million in equity.[13] Alberta, with its $350 million investment in ALPAC's roads, rail spur, other infrastructure and subordinated loans, obtains none of the equity or the profits and only very low stumpage fees; but the taxpayer does end up socializing much of the risk of the private investment of the multinationals. It is the same strategy that Alberta's "free enterprise" government used in attracting multibillion dollar investments to oil megaprojects in the 1970s, and it is also one that Mitsubishi and its allies from Japan have used in differing industries around the world. The argument that such deals are inevitable is weakened, however, by the fact that Daishowa was willing to proceed just a year earlier without the government's financial participation in the mill and without taxpayers assuming such risks. Daishowa had demonstrated it was the secure supply of fibre, not concessions on capital, that had brought the Japanese to Alberta. ALPAC received a good deal more than it really required. A better government would have prevented such an outcome.

As for access to the resource, the Japanese owners of ALPAC secured their exclusive long-term control over a very large supply of low-cost hardwood timber via the renewable twenty-year FMA that they concluded with the Alberta government in August 1991. This was the *sine qua non* for ALPAC's investment. Tenure over the timber supply was a far more important and "bankable" asset to the transnationals than any financial concessions received from Alberta: without security of tenure over the fibre supply, longer term investments would not be made and the banks would not loan capital. ALPAC's FMA is lengthy and legalistic and cannot be fully analyzed here, but its main features can be briefly related to the strategies of the government and the companies. A general, if subjective, observation is that the FMA seems to be rather generous to the Japanese joint venturers in ALPAC, particularly when we consider that many of the ministerial powers that can hypothetically be used to require the companies to meet their obligations to Alberta are unlikely to be tested. The forestry companies will derive their fibre supply from an immense area of approximately 6.1 million hectares or 61,000 square kilometres of Crown lands in northeast Alberta, as well as from privately owned lands to the south of the FMA. Perhaps half of this area can be regarded as holding productive forests. With few exceptions and qualifications, the FMA gives the ALPAC companies the management rights within the entire area for establishing, growing, and harvesting deciduous and coniferous trees on a perpetual sustained yield basis for a period of twenty years, renewable every twenty years subject to satisfactory performance and mutual agreement. ALPAC receives exclusive management rights over virtually all the aspen hardwood supplies in the FMA, and shares the rights to the various softwood species—spruce, jackpine, and so on—with the existing quota-holders, most of whom will end up as suppliers to the mill. In return, ALPAC's joint venturers are obliged, in the words of the FMA, "to progressively reforest at their own expense all land cut over by the Joint Venture Parties under this Agreement." To supply the pulp mill's fibre requirements,

ALPAC receives under the FMA what is by any standard a very large annual allowable cut (AAC) of approximately 2.94 million cubic metres, of which 2.44 million cubic metres is hardwood and 500,000 cubic metres is softwood. (The companies intend to cut up to 2.5 million cubic metres a year.) Under the 1991 FMA, the companies were to pay stumpage charges of $2.09 per cubic metre for coniferous species, and $0.40 per cubic metre for deciduous species; but the stumpage fees are revised each year on the basis of bleached kraft pulp prices in the United States market, and since 1991 prices have been falling. (Data compiled by the Canadian Pulp and Paper Association in 1989 revealed that Alberta's stumpage fees were among the lowest in Canada, and well below those charged by British Columbia, Ontario, and Quebec. Only Saskatchewan and Manitoba charged less per cubic metre for softwood pulp.)[14]

Throughout this study we have noted that in order to diversify its oil-dependent economic base, Alberta wanted to achieve a fuller utilization of its forestry resources, to increase employment in the forestry sector, to develop the north, and to assist the growing secondary manufacturing component of its hardwood forest industry. A vast potential was thought to exist for the use of Alberta's aspen resources, especially in pulp, panelboards, lumber, and specialty forest products. These were the aims that lay behind the generous financial concessions and forestry management powers that were negotiated with Mitsubishi and its partners. ALPAC was a central element—perhaps *the* central element—in the strategy of using the forestry sector to achieve broader economic goals: it was by far the largest of the pulp and newsprint mills with the largest employment potential, it was under close public scrutiny, and ALPAC also came late enough for the government to begin to implement policies which it had not had in place when some of the earlier projects were under construction. The preamble to ALPAC's FMA states the forestry minister's desire "to provide for the fullest possible economic utilization of timber from the forest management area and stable employment in local communities by maximizing the value of the timber resource base while maintaining a forest environment of high quality," and under section 7(b) the minister is empowered to act unilaterally, and without compensating the joint venturers, if the underutilization of the resource is significant. The ALPAC companies are further obliged under section 39 of their FMA to "satisfy the Minister of Economic Development throughout the term of this Agreement with respect to the use, wherever practicable of Alberta engineering and other professional services, and Alberta tradesman and other construction personnel, equipment, materials and supplies from Alberta." And, as noted earlier, the government's desire for a second stage of value-added development is strongly reflected in the FMA:

> AND WHEREAS the Joint Venture Parties have agreed to construct and operate a bleached kraft pulp mill within the vicinity of Grassland, Alberta, with an initial rated capacity of 1500 air dry metric tonnes per day and conditioned on establishing the economic feasibility of a paper mill, a world class paper mill adjacent thereto, capable of manufacturing fine paper (excluding newsprint) with a minimum capital cost of Two Hundred Million ($200,000,000) Dollars, (based on 1988 constant dollar equivalents) and an initial rated capacity of between 100,000 and 200,000 finished metric tonnes of fine paper annually. . . .

ALPAC was to be the catalyst for industrialization beyond pulp production. From December 1988, when Alberta-Pacific received its first approval, the Alberta government was enthusiastic about the secondary manufacturing that could be added to the big project. One official with the department of economic development spoke ebulliently of adding three billion dollars to the primary investments in pulp mills, with the creation of another twenty thousand jobs: "With the range of quality of pulp we will have, you can do everything from cigarette papers to Xerox paper to high-gloss magazine papers to box cartons—the whole range. The investment could equal that in the primary production facilities."[15] This was mostly a delusion. Adding value to primary resource extraction, a policy that had been a near obsession of Peter Lougheed's governments in the 1970s, could be achieved by establishing and linking supplier industries with the pulp mill; but the Getty administration was in addition determined to get beyond pulp production and export and to use its bargaining leverage—its financial support and control of the access to the resource—to establish a forward-linked "world-scale" fine paper industry in Alberta. There are many precedents for such a policy in Canadian economic history—Ontario's old "manufacturing condition" preventing the export of unprocessed logs to the United States is perhaps the best known—but the Getty cabinet evidently found a precedent for their own strategy in the creation of a natural gas-based petrochemical industry in Alberta in the late 1970s.

To our knowledge, however, at no point did Crestbrook and its partners commit to the construction of a fine paper mill. In his initial negotiating position of July 1988, Stuart Lang went some distance to meet the province's Alberta-first development goals: ALPAC, wherever possible, would use Alberta expertise, companies, goods, services, and materials, and would "transfer technology, expertise and know-how that is essential for the expansion, growth and on-going operation of a successfully operated forest products complex." Crestbrook stated that it would "bring the most advanced state-of-the-art manufacturing technology to the project" and provide a pulp sales agreement "which will be a commitment to take the product output thus ensuring industrial viability." There would be eleven hundred permanent jobs created in the forests and the pulp mill, and (this was Crestbrook's estimate) some eight hundred other indirect and induced jobs in the local area, plus another eight hundred jobs elsewhere in Alberta, and the investment of more than one billion dollars would stimulate growth, notably in Edmonton and Calgary, in the service sector, equipment supply, consulting, transportation, utilities, retail distribution, and so on. Alberta companies such as Stanley Associates Engineering were being brought into joint ventures with bigger forestry-related firms, such as H. A. Simons, on ALPAC's design and construction. Crestbrook's plan to obtain about 10 percent of its yearly roundwood harvest of 2.5 million cubic metres on private lands would generate some five million dollars of income for local farmers, Native settlements and wood-lot owners (and, not coincidentally, create a stronger base of support for ALPAC). Another goal was to develop a softwood chip supply by systematic expansion of the independent sawmill sector, though whether it would long remain "independent" after being linked to ALPAC's system of production was not discussed:

> As part of its program, CFI [Crestbrook] also proposes. . . a program to develop the capability of independent sawmillers and other small operators in the area. CFI does not intend to own or operate any sawmilling or panelboard facilities in the area; however, we wish to encourage wood product operators to improve and expand existing operations and develop new solid wood converting facilities. This program is key to CFI's proposal. It is the means by which CFI can help economic and community development in the area and, at the same time, assist itself by developing a long term sustained supply of softwood residuals.[16]

In these and other ways Crestbrook and its partners sought to link their proposal to the industrial strategy priorities of the Getty government. This certainly played a major role in the government's choice of Crestbrook. On the issue of linked "Alberta benefits" to supplier industries and on employment, Crestbrook's application was reportedly superior to all others. Yet there was no commitment to build a fine paper mill, and certainly none to do so as quickly as the government wished it done: Crestbrook said that aspen kraft pulp "has the potential to become one of the most highly valued furnishes for printing papers over the next decade, perhaps equivalent to plantation eucalyptus pulps from Iberia and Brazil." But it would agree only to study the feasibility of further investment in value-added paper manufacturing and to report to the government two years following start-up of the kraft mill.[17]

The paper mill controversy aside, the government's heavy stress on Alberta industrial benefits was in conflict with the timing of this and the other pulp mill projects. It all happened too quickly for many of these benefits to materialize. Alberta's forestry department under LeRoy Fjordbotten was in the business of encouraging a great timber giveaway in the late 1980s, and in the haste of the process, we think, much of the potential economic rent and other benefits from the resource development was lost. The losses include the benefits from the opportunities foregone by denying so much of the resource to others—independent sawmillers, Native settlements, other developers— and imposing a single vision and plan for development on such a vast area. From motives that are not altogether clear, the cabinet placed a big premium on speed in the allocation of the resources and the timing of forestry projects. Whether the driving force was the four-year electoral cycle or Premier Getty's own desire for fast results on unemployment or (perhaps most likely) the forestry planners' insistence that big capital investments be secured while international pulp prices were still high, the government's haste was imprudent. Indeed, the Getty cabinet approved construction of five new pulp and newsprint mills and the expansion of two existing kraft mills and allocated virtually the entire boreal forestry resource from early 1986 to December 1988—less than two years. All of these large mills are located on the Athabasca and Peace river systems, and the Alberta government had no knowledge as to the likely environmental impact of these multiple developments on these systems. The impacts on the boreal forest were not known. In addition, the rapid sequencing of these big projects was bound to affect the amount of Alberta content that could be squeezed into, for instance, the contracting, engineering, supplies, equipment, and so on. Alberta had no pulp industry suppliers, no pulp industry expertise in general, when the process began in 1986: thus, inevitably, a large amount of the labour and machinery used in the early projects had to be brought in from outside. Moreover, the Alberta benefits policy is a voluntary one—it does not exist in legislation—and the province relies heavily upon corporate goodwill, particularly where contracts are not procured via bidding. The quarterly procurement reports in which the companies give details on who their suppliers are, and how much of their materials and equipment originates in Alberta, Canada, or foreign countries, are not available for public review. It is relatively easy for a supplier based in, say, British Columbia or the United States to set up a distribution office in Alberta, and then to have a piece of equipment given a high Alberta content rating. We were told that on the major pulp mill projects, construction work was close to 100 percent Albertan, engineering and consulting was about 50 percent Albertan, and equipment and materials were approximately 25 percent in Alberta content; but these figures could not be confirmed. On construction of the later forestry projects such as ALPAC, Alberta content appears to have been quite high, except on equipment and materials. The low percentages recorded in the latter categories, and especially in the development of some of the more advanced technologies, would suggest that the industrial benefits from the pulp mills have been short-term, with only small long-term gains (for example, the development of a trio of sodium chlorate plants and a magnesium sulphite plant to supply the new pulp mills) that fulfill the aim of diversification. A policy of gradualism rather than haste might have allowed for a longer-run economic diversification and for more time to analyze and mitigate the worst of the environmental effects of the pulp mills. In any event, the government's industrial benefits program was not consistent with the timber rush induced by Getty and Fjordbotten, and what was achieved was more a program of short-term economic stimulus via big capital projects than longer-term diversification.

Supporting the Mill

Alberta-Pacific was the largest and most expensive of the big forestry projects, and the Getty government evidently expected it to receive widespread support and prompt approval from regulatory bodies. The government's envoys to Asia had at least implicitly pledged this to the Japanese transnationals, and there was little in the province's postwar history of resource development that would lead the government or anyone else to expect much opposition to the project. Unlike in British Columbia or the American Pacific Northwest, in Alberta (as one forestry executive was heard to remark) the politician' pulp companies on both cheeks and gave them grants. Nonetheless, ALPAC, far from being a popular venture, was very nearly derailed by its opponents: as we will show in the following chapter, in 1989–90 ALPAC became the focus and emblem of a very effective, well-organized environmental opposition to the entire forestry and pulp mill strategy. ALPAC, indeed, transformed environmentalism in Alberta. To the horror of the cabinet and the disgust of ALPAC's joint venturers—Stuart Lang complained that he was being forced "to lower" himself to the level of public hearings—the big Athabasca/Lac La Biche pulp mill altered the political debate in Alberta between resource developers and preservationists. The experience of ALPAC forced a reluctant provincial government to change the regulatory framework for natural resource projects in order to avert further controversies. ALPAC changed Alberta's politics.

Let us conclude this chapter with a sketch of some of those who fought for ALPAC. What were their reasons? Why did they fight the environmentalists? The promill supporters—a very loosely-organized group of interests and individuals that lobbied on ALPAC's behalf after the project ran into serious opposition in 1989—were of course motivated by the desire for jobs, industry, a better tax base, better roads, and better prospects for their families (or, simply, by material interests). They argued for these things at the public hearings on the project, and most of them emphatically stated their support for a good environment as well as for economic growth. But they were an angry, resentful group as well, and this is perhaps less easily accounted for by the pull of material factors. Inhabitants of the Athabasca/Lac La Biche area and of other northeast communities, they watched with dismay the coalition opposed to ALPAC form and grow, and they became politically moved by a strong sense of regionalism or local self-determination and by a rural dislike of urban intruders, and especially of "interference" by middle-class environmentalists, scientists, and other academics in what they saw as their affairs. Class and urban-rural divisions were at work here. It might be said that ALPAC pushed the mill's backers into a revolt against the domination of the city and its ideas over their lives. Certainly the forestry issue was pushing the Getty Conservatives away from the cities. Forestry minister Fjordbotten, himself a rancher from the south, was bewildered and angered by the public furore he and his policies attracted in the cities, particularly in Calgary, in the late 1980s. Did Calgary's middle-class lifestyle not derive from the same dominant resource extractive economy that ALPAC represented? Although some of the major business associations backed the pulp mills, the absence of urban support was puzzling, Fjordbotten

and his colleagues thought, because Edmonton and Calgary were major economic beneficiaries of projects like ALPAC and Daishowa (Edmonton's share of
ALPAC's construction expenditures was reported to have been six hundred million dollars). The tensions between the rural north and the bigger cities were
symbolized in the very public hostilities between Daishowa and the social democratic mayor of Edmonton, Jan Reimer, over the latter's support for the Lubicon
Indians in their conflict with the Japanese forestry firm. The urban-rural split
over forestry development versus wilderness preservation was not, of course, a
phenomenon confined to Alberta: the growth of urban environmentalism in
Europe, North America, and Japan has been linked to this same issue.

It is rather too easy to dismiss the rural or conservative side in this debate.
The environmentalists were "politically correct," but not always wise in their
assaults on the proposed project and the need for economic growth for the
region. The critics of ALPAC had chosen to "concentrate on the science," on air
and water rather than people and poverty and unemployment; and that offended the mill's supporters who wanted to raise the social conditions in the
region. Rural people disliked the know-all arrogance of the academic environmentalists. Both sides had scientists. Whose knowledge, whose science, should
prevail? The backers of the mill saw that, in the city media's eyes, ALPAC's science was by definition tainted by self-interest; were the critics, then, free of
bias and self-interest? They saw the scientific critique of the project as nar-
rowly professional, jargon-ridden, and indifferent to the chronic social problems of the region. "Clean air and pure water mean little to people living in
futility," an exasperated Métis leader told the ALPAC environmental hearings.
That was not meant to imply indifference to clean air and pure water, but to
raise the social issue to an equal footing. To some, the scientific critique also
implied that those who lived in the region—some of their families had lived
there for thousands of years—were ignorant about the environment, ignorant
of the river, the forest, and the animals. Were they not a part of the environment? This mistrust of science made it difficult for the critics to forge any
alliances with Native communities, which had their own views of environmental issues. Francois Cardinal, a Calling Lake trapper and a disillusioned
supporter of ALPAC, underlined the Natives' skepticism of the environmentalists and the scientific critique: "The environmentalists are outside people who
never came here, never asked us what Native people know, what's going to
happen; we know what's going to happen to animals, the land. Friends of the
Athabasca, Friends of the North never came, they rely on books, science, we

rely on experience. . . . but they ignore us, they believe they are smarter than Native persons. But they have no common sense."[18] The critics raised few economic alternatives, and even the Natives rejected the idea of a return to the traditional economy; that had died in the fifties with the coming of the oil industry and welfare. Mike Cardinal, a Cree from Calling Lake, and after 1989 the Conservative MLA for Athabasca/Lac La Biche (and then minister of family and social services) played a central role in organizing political support for alpac; he did so in part because he saw that forestry was the only alternative to welfare and 80–90 percent Native unemployment or leaving the region. There was, he told us mildly, "a lack of understanding in urban areas" over the true choices in the north-east of Alberta.[19] And Bill Kostiw, another key organizer for the pro-ALPAC coalition, even remarked: "We feel that working in a controlled environment of the pulp mill is as good or better than sending our youth to the smog and pollution of the cities."[20]

The pro-ALPAC supporters believed the urban media to be irretrievably biased against the mill. Up to twelve hundred of the supporters publicly demonstrated for the mill in June of 1989, and they bitterly complained that the media ignored the demonstration in favour of ALPAC's opponents. The pro-mill group, concentrated as it mainly was in the region of Athabasca/Lac La Biche, saw few realistic job-creating alternatives to ALPAC—"eco-tourism," whatever its realistic opportunities, was perceived as an elitist idea of the critics and had little local support; the pro-ALPAC bloc described the opponents of the project as sincere but profoundly naive individuals who would not have to suffer the consequences if the pulp mill did not go ahead: "they would be happy to leave this area in a depressed economic state so that it can remain natural in case they decide one day to venture off the highway for a visit," one intervenor bitterly remarked to the Alberta-Pacific Environmental Impact Assessment Review Board.[21] People were leaving the region because of the economy, and supporters of the mill saw it as a lure to bring them home. The Community Association of Calling Lake, a mostly Cree community of several hundred people living near the mill site, hoped that ALPAC "will motivate our young people to stay in school and to advance their education. At this point in time there is no perceived need for them to complete even basic schooling. Most of the local employment possibilities are so few, and of such a low calibre, that no higher education is required. Those community members who wish to make careers for themselves, or who simply want a more secure lifestyle, have to leave and move to larger centres. This has had, and is having, negative effects on both family and community life and on our cultural development." Yet all the truckers who worked for the mill would have to own their own equipment—a huge financial hurdle for most—and ALPAC's stated policy of hiring only those who had completed grade 12 education would "effectively eliminate the vast majority of the employable people in Calling Lake."[22] The Natives at Calling Lake who supported the mill back in 1988 had been told, said Francois Cardinal: "All will work; even the horses." Of course, it didn't work out like that.

1 . Crestbrook Forest Industries Ltd. announced in March 1994 that Stuart Lang would be replaced as president and chief operating officer of the company as of 5 May 1994; Lang was to be made "Vice Chairman, a newly created executive position in the Company." Lang had been president and CEO for fifteen years when he was replaced.

2 . Interview with Al McDonald, 12 August 1992.

3 . Crestbrook Forest Industries, letter of July 29 1988 to F.W. McDougall, deputy minister of Renewable Resources, Government of Alberta.

4 . Information on the Ludwig affair and Lang's role is from: *Financial Post*, 29 September, 1979, 30; *Pulp and Paper*, March 1979; *Chemical Week*, 3 August, 1977; and *The Economist*, 9 July 1983.

5 . Government of Alberta, Forests Act, Forest Management Agreement of 30 August 1991 between Her Majesty the Queen in right of Alberta and Crestbrook Forest Industries Ltd. et al. See especially p. 1 and Appendix "F."

6 . Transfer pricing is used by many multinationals in many jurisdictions to shift taxable income to different entities within the same firm, but it can be very difficult to monitor and to prevent. On Revenue Canada Taxation's case against Crestbrook, see Crestbrook Forest Industries Ltd., *Prospectus* for a share offering on or about 12 November 1991, 25; *The Globe and Mail*, 29 February 1992, B5.

7 . An example of such charges is by George Marshall, London Rainforest Action Group, "The Activities of Mitsubishi in Papua New Guinea," 9 November 1992.

8 . See *Financial Post*, 18 May 1988, 22; *Kootenay Advertiser*, 27 March 1989, 4; *Cranbrook Daily Townsman*, 22 March 1989.

9 . See *Kootenay Advertiser*, 27 March 1989, 4.

10 . Crestbrook Forest Industries, *The CFI Log*, Summer 1991, 5.

11 . EKONO Consultants Ltd., *Economic Development and Resource Utilization Study*, Regional Economic Development Committee, Athabasca, Alberta, 1985.

12 . Ibid., IV–3.

13 . On the financing, see Crestbrook's *Prospectus*, cited in footnote 6, and the Alberta Heritage Savings Trust Fund, *Annual Report*, 1991–92, 51, footnote b.

14 . See *The Edmonton Journal*, 16 July 1989.

15 . There are many such statements; this quotation is taken from *The Edmonton Journal*, 23 December 1988.

16 . "Crestbrook's Proposed Forest Development Program For North-East Alberta," attached to Stuart Lang's letter to F.W. McDougall, deputy minister of Renewable Resources, 29 July 1988.

17 . Ibid.

18 . Interview with Francois Cardinal, Calling Lake, 26 May 1993.

19 . Interview with Mike Cardinal, Edmonton, 23 October 1991.

20 . At V.19, Proceedings, 2602.

21 . Tim Juhlin, 3 November 1989. ALPAC EIA Review Board, Proceedings, V. 6-7, 978.

22 . Six Calling Lake Community Association Members, 2 December 1989. EIA Review Board Public Hearing Filed Document 0-78, 6 pages.

CHAPTER 6

Alberta-Pacific:
The Environmentalists Fight Back

MY PHILOSOPHY IS THAT PEOPLE ARE ALWAYS THE BOSS. TOO OFTEN,
THE GOVERNMENT SAYS, "THIS IS WHAT WE THINK THEY NEED" AND
DEVELOPS IT. THEN THE GOVERNMENT GETS INTO TROUBLE WHEN
THEY TRY TO DELIVER IT. THE GOVERNMENT OUGHT NEVER TO GIVE
TO PEOPLE WHAT THEY THINK THEY NEED, BUT WHAT THEY HONESTLY
DESIRE. IT HAS TO RESPOND TO THE LEGITIMATE NEEDS, WANTS AND
DESIRES OF THE PEOPLE.

RALPH KLEIN, MINISTER OF THE ENVIRONMENT,

CALGARY HERALD SUNDAY MAGAZINE, 31 DECEMBER 1989

SOME OF THE PEOPLE FROM HERE [ATHABASCA] MET WITH SOME
ALBERTA ENVIRONMENT PEOPLE AND THEY SAID: "AIR AND WATER ARE
MILL STOPPERS—PEOPLE AREN'T." SO WE CONCENTRATED ON THE
SCIENCE.

WILLIAM FULLER, FRIENDS OF THE ATHABASCA, 28 MAY 1992

 Spring is glorious in the boreal forest. Picturesque forma-
tions of geese, ducks, and other waterfowl fly northward to
breeding destinations in northern Alberta and Canada's
northern territories. Below them, the forest and lakes teem
with new life. Woodpeckers and many other forest nesting
birds search out new homes in the dead standing trees and snags which some
foresters take to signify an unhealthy forest. Loons, rulers of Canada's large
northern lakes, return to fill the cool evenings with their haunting calls. Mos-
quitoes and black flies, the unpopular residents of this ecosystem, have yet to
make their appearance felt. By late May, for nearly seventeen hours a day,
sunlight bathes this mosaic of forest, lakes, rivers, peatland fens, and bogs. In
poorly-drained peatlands, stunted black spruce and American larch trees stand

over Labrador tea, fly-eating Pitcher plants, and thick, spongy sphagnum mosses. Drier sites are dominated by mixedwood stands of budding aspen and white spruce, the species coveted by pulp and paper makers. During a late spring visit to Bill Fuller, professor emeritus of zoology from the University of Alberta, now retired on an acreage some twenty-four kilometres southwest of the Alberta-Pacific pulp mill, it was impossible to ignore these aesthetic reasons for his adamant, outspoken opposition to the "world's largest single-line pulp mill." As we talked about the wildlife which regularly visited his garden and the Friends of the Athabasca, the environmental group he belonged to, the medleys of finches, chickadees, and other songbirds of the boreal forest filled his cedar log lined living room. On that afternoon, the Fuller acreage resembled a naturalist's paradise. How could someone fortunate enough to retire to this magnificent setting stand idly by while plans were hatched to build a gigantic pulp mill on his doorstep?

Four years before our interview, more than the melodies of songbirds and the hammering of pileated woodpeckers filled the air in the boreal forest. Rumours that the Athabasca–Lac La Biche area would host one or more forestry megaprojects also rustled through the aspen forests in "the Land of the Whispering Hills." Some, as we have seen already, were excited by these rumours. The Town of Athabasca, Athabasca County Council, the Athabasca Chamber of Commerce, and the Athabasca Regional Economic Development Association were enthusiasts for industrial development and had lobbied the Getty government and Conservative members of Parliament to get the mill. For this constituency the lure of jobs, population growth, new infrastructure, and a larger industrial tax base from which to finance public investments eventually tilted the balance in favour of pulp mill development. For some of these pulp mill boosters, to the extent they entertained thoughts about the environmental consequences of development, they did so solely in terms of the mill's location. Build the mill well downstream and downwind of Athabasca and they would be satisfied. More cavalier attitudes towards pulp mill pollution also could be found. One local sawmill owner and pulp mill supporter expressed his feelings this way: "A lot of people worry about the river. I don't. The river has never given me anything—never even caught a fish out of it."[1]

Others, Fuller among them, were troubled by the rumours of development. Events during the summer of 1988 demonstrated that increasing numbers of Athabasca area residents indeed *were* concerned about the river's health and the environmental consequences of pulp mill operations. Some seized upon a local newspaper's announcement in late July, that pulp mill development was imminent, to question the wisdom of putting a bleached kraft mill anywhere on the Athabasca. While the local business community intensified its efforts to market the Athabasca area as the most suitable candidate for a mill, other residents began to organize opposition to a bleached kraft mill. The nucleus of this emerging opposition was composed to a considerable extent of faculty and staff from Athabasca University, a provincial distance learning postsecondary institution established in Edmonton in 1972 and moved to Athabasca in 1984. "There's no question," offered Fuller, "that a lot of the leadership came from the university."[2] Letters and articles from Fuller, Mike and Jane Gismondi, Robert Holmberg, Barry Johnstone, and Louis Schmittroth appeared in the Athabasca area newspapers throughout August and raised concerns about the rush to turn the boreal forest into pulp and paper. Near the end of August— the month when McDougall wanted to announce a decision—this opposition began to organize in earnest. Here the leadership of Barry Johnstone and Louis Schmittroth was pivotal. Barry Johnstone was a sociologist at the university who would later be forced to leave his position—a departure attributed variously to either his failure to fulfill contract commitments or to his intense opposition to Alberta-Pacific. Louis Schmittroth, who first came to Athabasca to raise sheep before working at the university, later used his computing modeling skills to critique the claims Alberta-Pacific would make about the impact its mill would have upon oxygen levels in the river. A 25 August public meeting—organized by Johnstone and Schmittroth and attended by more than two hundred people—marked the conception of the Friends of the Athabasca (FOTA). Guest speakers from several organizations spoke about the environmental effects of pulp mills, the alternative paths economic development could take in the region, and demanded that the public play a more prominent role in environmental decision-making. By the end of the evening an overwhelming majority of the audience favoured public hearings and an environmental impact assessment as ways to scrutinize any proposed development.

Johnstone and Schmittroth did not allow the momentum of this meeting to slip away. The founders of the Friends of the Athabasca acted out of a certain sense of urgency, fueled in part by the suspicion that, in the case of Daishowa, Peace River environmentalists had organized too late to stop the project. By mid-September the group had decided to register the Friends under the terms of the Alberta Societies Act and adopted a mission statement. FOTA dedicated itself to safeguarding the environment in the Athabasca watershed, to the practice of sustainable development, and to public participation in economic development and environmental decision-making. FOTA's appearance and its call for public participation in decision making clearly alarmed some local pulp mill promoters. Jim Woodward, the county manager, called upon County Council to reiterate its faith in the pulp mill option, in light of "negative meetings" held by "a minority group to try and scare people off of the idea. . . ."[3]

Woodward's characterization of FOTA's position was simply a caricature of the early perspective the Friends adopted on the relationship between economic growth and environmental protection. During the phony war conducted before the December 1988 announcement that Crestbrook's bid had been accepted in principle, the Friends did not demand that local and provincial politicians entirely abandon their dreams of pulp mill-led development in the Athabasca region. Rather, they focussed their campaign against bleached kraft mills and the chlorinated organics—especially dioxins and furans—they produced. While Crestbrook and Weyerhaeuser promoted their plans for huge bleached kraft operations to government officials behind-the-scenes, the Friends made very public arguments in favour of smaller, chemithermomechanical pulp (CTMP) mills. In September, for example, the Friends met with Leo Piquette, the local New Democratic Party MLA, and Northern Forest Industries Limited—Piquette's preferred forestry company. Although by this time the Northern bid was not being considered seriously by the government, its proposed CTMP mill appealed to the Friends. Since organochlorines are not produced by CTMP mills, the Northern project was regarded as less harmful to the environment. This concern about organochlorines and a preference for CTMP mills were consistent themes in the lobbying efforts of the Friends of the Athabasca during the phony war of 1988. Up until the Alberta-Pacific project was announced in December, debate centred on the issue of dioxins and furans. In September, Schmittroth used a FOTA resolution to try to persuade Ian Reid, the minister of the environment, to oppose kraft mill development. The FOTA resolution urged the government to refuse to license any mill using a chlorine-based pulping process unless the zero-discharge of organochlorines could be guaranteed.[4] Instead, the Friends urged Alberta "to encourage" CTMP mills as part of a multiple-use approach to forest management. The same message was delivered to Athabasca Town Council. In November, a delegation from the Friends urged council to qualify its unconditional support for any type of pulp mill. Council flatly refused their request that the town only offer its support to a CTMP mill. Greater success awaited the group in its efforts to increase the public's involvement in the environmental assessment process.

A variety of circumstances contributed to the emergence of the type of forestry-centred environmental critiques offered by groups such as the FOTA. Samuel Hays, the American historian, has argued that many environmental struggles in the United States since 1945 have been struggles over community protection, battles by local community organizations to protect their quality of life from gigantic intrusions associated with large-scale, technologically-sophisticated projects. This theme was linked intimately with another—protecting human health from the toxic byproducts of industrial production. Both themes are important to understanding the early focus of the FOTA. The interest in promoting CTMP mills as an alternative to bleached kraft operations reflected the group's preference for smaller scale industrial development. The health risks associated with bleached kraft pulp mills became an important catalyst for organizing its environmental opposition to the government's forestry strategy. While it would be a mistake to claim that FOTA was motivated solely by the health issue, nonetheless human health was much more central to the agenda of this newly minted northern Alberta group than it was to the earlier generations of environmental organizations.

According to Crestbrook and pulp and paper industry journals, these environmental concerns, whether focussed upon human health or the ecosystem, were unwarranted. The company had "always been particularly aware of its environmental responsibilities."[5] Crestbrook's one and only kraft pulp mill, located at Skookumchuck, British Columbia, thirty-five kilometres north of Cranbrook in the heart of the East Kootenays, was cited as proof of the company's dedication to reducing or eliminating the air and water pollution produced by the 580 ADT/day mill. The company boasted that it used "sophisticated measures" to protect the environment. On clearcutting, the issue giving the worst nightmares to British Columbia forestry executives, the company used "before and after" photography to defend their logging and reforestation practices. Photographs of fresh clearcuts were presented alongside pictures taken years later of the same scene to illustrate the company's commitment to treating the forests as a renewable resource. "We don't," Stuart Lang told the company's 1991 annual general meeting, "willy-nilly cut, pillage and plunder."

A very different story was told by Natives and environmentalists from the East Kootenays. Their impressions of Crestbrook's environmental record were much bleaker. When they appeared before the Environmental Impact Assessment Review Board created to evaluate the Alberta-Pacific proposal, they portrayed Crestbrook as a company that simply could not be trusted when it came to protecting the environment.[6] To them, the company was sneaky, a corporation that hid information from the public or distorted information to portray the company in a wildly flattering light. They urged Albertans to force Alberta-Pacific, Crestbrook's joint venture and a company whose senior managers cut their teeth in the Skookumchuck mill, to sign very specific, unambiguous, legally-enforceable commitments on environmental protection issues. On too many occasions, Crestbrook kept damaging information hidden from public review, used misleading information to reassure the public, and reneged on verbal promises to modify its logging practices. During the Environmental Impact Assessment hearings, these groups highlighted over a dozen incidents which they felt sustained their charge that Crestbrook was a violator, not a protector, of the environment. Clearcuts without buffers to protect mountain streams, chronic violations of air quality standards, and the contamination of ground water to the point where drinking water at the mill had to be delivered by truck were among the examples used by these British Columbia environmentalists to tarnish the glowing environmental reputation Crestbrook tried to create.

Given the state of warfare between environmentalists and the British Columbia forest industry, this unflattering assessment of Crestbrook's environmental performance comes as no surprise. For each rhetorical barrage launched by industry, environmentalists may be sure to retaliate with one of their own. For the disinterested observer, suspicious of the motives of both sides of this debate, these rhetorical assaults may be frustrating. They obscure the basic point that our attitudes towards how the forests should be used depend to an important degree upon where we sit. Unemployed construction workers in the Athabasca area likely regard the trade-off between jobs and forest preservation raised in Alberta's version of this debate in a very different light than tenured university professors or Native trappers. Consequently, some caution is advised when interpreting either the rosy pictures offered by the forest companies or the damning appraisals served up by environmental groups.

Certainly, the evidence environmentalists have gathered on the operations of Mitsubishi and Honshu Paper outside of British Columbia is anything but flattering. These Japanese multinationals do not compromise corporate profitability for the sake of environmental preservation. Where governments

are lax, where they allow companies to evade pollution regulations and reforestation obligations, these companies are reported to behave accordingly. They
literally mine the forests. In South America, Mitsubishi has a 49.5 percent
interest in Eido do Brasil Madeiras S. A., one of the largest plywood mills in
the Amazon estuary. The same environmentalists who credit this company for
some pioneering work in reforestation nonetheless doubt whether Eido's efforts are intensive enough to sustain its operations over the long term. Moreover, Eido's willingness to look the other way and buy logs from independent
contractors who ignore the minimum timber size limits stipulated in forest
harvesting regulations sustains the environmentalists' worries that this plywood mill's hunger for tropical timber may cripple the forest's powers of self-
renewal. In the temperate forests of Chile, Mitsubishi's forest management
practices have also been called into question. Its affiliates have been criticized
for converting the native beech forests into wood chips and eucalyptus plantations.[7]

To date, however, the strongest condemnations of Mitsubishi have aimed
at the company's role in exploiting the tropical rainforests of Southeast Asia,
particularly Malaysia. Throughout the 1980s, Japan's appetite for Malaysian
timber grew. By the twilight of the decade, the Malaysian states of Sarawak
and Sabah, located on the northern coast of the island of Borneo, supplied
approximately 90 percent of all the tropical logs imported by Japan. Between
1980 and 1990 Japan's imports of tropical logs from Sarawak tripled, propel-
ling its timber production to a record level. In a country where government
did not insist that companies practice sustained-yield forest management,
Mitsubishi joined other Japanese firms in stripping the countryside of its rainforests at an alarming rate. By 1989, three million hectares of Sarawak's primary forests, nearly one-quarter of all the land in the state, had been logged. If
logging continued at this furious pace, some predicted that all of Sarawak's
primary forests would be gone by the year 2004.[8] Mitsubishi, as a *sogososha* or
general trading house, is involved directly in all stages of the Malaysian tropical timber trade. The company owns 60 percent of Daiya Malaysia Sdn. Bhd.,
a company which logs, transports, and sells timber in Sarawak. Other affilia-
tions extend Mitsubishi's role in timber production. It possesses a ninety thousand hectare logging concession and is a partner in two plywood mills on the
Malyasian peninsula. In combination with an affiliated company, Meiwa Trading (66.8 percent owned by member companies of the Mitsubishi *keiretsu*, or
corporate grouping), Mitsubishi Corporation ranked among the ten largest
Japanese importers of Malaysian tropical logs and sawnwood in 1990.

Japan's position as the world's leading importer of tropical timber and the rapid depletion of tropical rainforests in countries such as Malaysia were the catalysts for the launch of a "Ban Japan from the Rainforest Campaign" by a worldwide network of environmental groups in 1989. Because of Mitsubishi's high profile in the Japanese and international economies, the company became a primary target of the environmental movement. Mitsubishi's responses to these attacks, the latest attack being the "Boycott Mitsubishi" campaign spearheaded by the Rainforest Action Network, appear more symbolic than substantive. Mitsibushi has created an Environmental Affairs Department, announced a gradual reduction of Malaysian timber imports, initiated a rainforest reforestation experiment in Sarawak, and entered, for a brief time, Japanese classrooms. These initiatives have not impressed the company's environmental opponents. The Netherlands' chapter of Friends of the Earth argues that Mitsubishi simply replaced Malaysian supplies of logs and sawnwood with plywood from Indonesia and that the high cost of trying to reforest a fifty hectare plot in Sarawak proves that companies will never even attempt to reforest the millions of hectares of rainforest they have logged.[9] Mitsubishi's tendency to shrug off criticisms of its tropical rainforest operations was underlined by its rather preposterous efforts to sway the opinion of Japanese schoolchildren. In late 1990, the comic book "For Gaia" was distributed in Japanese schools. Mr. Hino, the comic's hero, is troubled by the environmentalists' accusations that Mitsubishi is guilty of deforestation and travels to southeast Asia to investigate these charges. To his relief, his aerial survey of Southeast Asian nations reveals that the forests have suffered little from logging. The shifting cultivation practiced by indigenous peoples, not commercial forestry, is blamed for deforestation. In 1992, the Japanese Ministry of Education ordered the removal of "For Gaia" from all schools "because," according to the ministry, "the book is public relations material for just one company."[10]

A more academic assessment of the operations of Honshu Paper, the other Japanese principal in Crestbrook, suggests that this firm too has despoiled tropical rainforests. Like Hitachi, Fuji, Kawasaki, and Isuzu, firms whose names are much more recognizable to most North Americans, Honshu is a member of the Dai-ichi Kangyo *keiretsu*. In the rainforests of Papua New Guinea (PNG), Honshu operates one of the few tropical forest woodchip clearcutting operations in the world. Its interest in PNG dates from the late 1960s when shrinking domestic chip supplies, American log export restrictions, and fierce competition between Japanese pulp and paper producers prompted the industry to search in earnest for new sources of woodchips to feed its expansion. According to an agreement reached in 1971, JANT (Japan and New Guinea Timber Company Limited), a Honshu subsidiary, received the rights to remove all pulpwood from a lowland rainforest in northeastern PNG for a twenty-year period. In exchange for these rights, JANT built the woodchipping plant, port facilities, and logging roads needed to deliver PNG's trees to Honshu's Japanese mills. Other potential industrial benefits the company dangled before an eager government never materialized. A promised plywood mill was never built—a slumping veneer market, JANT's debt, and the financial woes besetting Japanese plywood mills were all blamed for JANT's refusal to honour this commitment. Nor, according to an account of pulpwood logging in PNG, was it very likely that JANT ever kept its promise to study the feasibility of building a pulp mill at the port of Madang.

Important forest management promises also were not kept. JANT did not fulfill its promise to reforest the natural forests it clearcut. Again, industry economics were blamed in part. The last half of the 1970s saw Japanese pulp and paper producers suffer through one of the worst downturns in their industry's history. For Honshu, earnings stagnated, then declined, over this period. Its mediocre financial performance dampened the company's enthusiasm for its plans for plantation reforestation, especially if the government would give the company more natural forests to clearcut. The government of PNG was certainly not blameless in this regard. It shared responsibility for the failure of the promised reforestation initiatives to materialize. One of the attractions of PNG to Honshu had been the promise that the company would be able to secure long-term land tenure, tenure the government was subsequently unable to provide. This failure, in turn, accelerated the clearcutting of the remaining stands of natural forests. In 1986, Lamb reported that "it appeared that most of the accessible forest would be completely logged out within a few years." As time passed, JANT's forestry practices, practices that PNG did little, if anything, to change, treated the forests more and more as a nonrenewable resource:

Rather disturbingly, however, it seemed that many of the logging standards established in earlier years had been abandoned. The logging coupes were much larger than before and tended to form long continuous swathes. No buffer strips were being left along streamsides and no particular care was being taken to keep logging debris out of the streams. In fact, some of the earlier streamside buffer strips had been revisited and logged. The overwhelming impression was that provincial authorities had ceased to police environmental safeguards and that JANT had abandoned its former standards.[11]

As forestry practices deteriorated, the potential of this rainforest to recover dimmed.

Our appraisal of the commitment of Crestbrook and its owners to environmental protection, similarly, does not improve when we examine other potentially more sympathetic sources of information. The company's responses to British Columbia environmental regulations stand out in this respect, particularly the lengthy history surrounding the province's efforts to force Crestbrook to reduce the discolouring effect of the pulp mill's effluent upon the Kootenay River. The milky blue-green colour of the Kootenay north of Skookumchuck betrays the river's origins in the glaciers of the Canadian Rockies. The picture presented by this river as it carves its way southward through the Rocky Mountain Trench, the Rockies to the east—the Purcells to the west, is breathtaking and vital to the marketing of the East Kootenays as a tourist destination. The aesthetic importance of the Kootenay led the province in October 1971 to order Crestbrook to take steps by August 1975 to reduce the colour of the effluent the mill discharged into the river. Crestbrook stalled. Using whatever administrative procedures were available to it, the company fought the government and delayed the implementation of a colour control system for ten years. First, the company asked that the concerns over discolouration should be set aside until such time as the mill expanded. Government refused. Next, after government asked the company to submit a pollution reduction plan "as soon as possible," the company replied that, because of the company's financial condition, it could not address the colour issue until 1983. Again, government refused to grant this extension and ordered the company to implement its pollution control strategy by no later than 31 October 1981. Crestbrook stalled again. It appealed to the Pollution Control Board that the colour limit set by regulators was "impractical." When the board rejected this appeal Crestbrook turned to the provincial cabinet. Ignored by Social Credit politicians, the company finally obeyed the original order and implemented pollution control measures but, on principle, refused to withdraw the appeal to cabinet.[12] Crestbrook was pugnacious in this battle over the environmental performance of its Skookumchuck mill, more concerned with protecting its bottom line than in protecting the environment. A pollution control system the company liked to brag about in the late 1980s as proof of its commitment to environmental protection only resulted from the tenacity of regulators, not from any environmental foresight on Crestbrook's part. If the company had had its way, the Kootenay River would probably still be waiting for the company to take action. Judging by the international record of Honshu and Mitsubishi in British Columbia and elsewhere, Alberta's regulators would need healthy measures of vigilance and persistence in order to ensure that Alberta-Pacific respected environmental and reforestation regulations.

Alberta Environment and the Technological Fix

Unbeknownst to the Friends of the Athabasca, officials in Alberta Environment shared some of their concerns about the environmental consequences of additional pulp mills on the Athabasca River. In April 1988, months before the rumours about Crestbrook's intent became public, departmental officials met with Crestbrook and raised concerns about the impact that another kraft mill could have on the Athabasca River. Their worries were more multifaceted than the early positions taken by the FOTA. Alberta Environment was concerned about more than just the discharge of organochlorines into the river—the department also worried about the cumulative impact of existing and proposed mills upon the Athabasca River's ability to sustain life. The number of pulp mills planning to dump effluent into the Athabasca threatened to reduce the amount of oxygen in stretches of the river to dangerously low levels: death by suffocation likely would be the fate of a wide range of aquatic life in these portions of the river. To address these concerns Crestbrook commissioned Stanley Associates Engineering Limited of Edmonton (a firm with a strong commercial interest in the mill proceeding) to prepare an initial aquatic environmental evaluation for the environmental protection services branch. Stanley's conclusion? Under certain conditions five mills could operate on the Athabasca without violating the province's dissolved oxygen guidelines.[13]

Alberta Environment greeted this claim skeptically. Officials questioned the accuracy of several key assumptions of the Stanley report. The Water Quality Control Branch, while commending Crestbrook for submitting this initial evaluation, warned in one memorandum that Crestbrook's kraft mill might compromise the quality of Fort McMurray's drinking water. In its opinion, Stanley's assumptions were designed to place Crestbrook's project in a favourable light. Even if these assumptions were accurate, however, they left "no room for error, lower flows, or other BOD inputs." Moreover, dioxins—the object of greatest public fear—were not addressed at all in Stanley's assessment. Finally, while the incremental impact on the Athabasca's water quality of the mill Crestbrook proposed would be less than that of Weldwood's Hinton mill, an official from the branch worried nonetheless about the cumulative impact of all these mills on the river: "[I]n combination with other proposed mills it will very probably result in non-compliance for a number of parameters including oxygen."[14] In layman's terms, there was a strong likelihood that aquatic life in portions of the Athabasca would be harmed, if not wiped out altogether, by additional pulp mills on the river.

Other divisions in Alberta Environment also questioned the environmental soundness of more pulp mills on the Athabasca. The department's planning division also worried that the assimilative capacity of the Athabasca might be exceeded if Crestbrook's project proceeded. The division's acting director consequently recommended that "the department should consider a moratorium on approving new pulp mills with major effluents until such time as the planning study we are coordinating for the [Athabasca] basin is completed." At the very least he thought the project should be delayed until the department's dissolved oxygen models had been developed to assess the impact of future pulp mill operations on water quality downstream of Athabasca. He also recommended that the department "should insist that the mill use oxygen bleaching technology" to eliminate the concern about organochlorines and improve the quality of the mill's effluent.[15]

The director of the Standards and Approvals Division also had serious reservations about the Stanley report—it simply did not "satisfy our needs." Before an additional kraft mill could be considered on the Athabasca no fewer than eleven process and waste water components would have to be incorporated into Crestbrook's mill design. These concerns—for example, the suggestion that CFI should be asked to reduce the amount of organochlorines produced to 1.5 kg/tonne—promised to place a very heavy, perhaps unbearable, burden upon Crestbrook.

Two approaches to evaluating Crestbrook's development proposal animated these initial departmental assessments. The first adopted a technological focus in order to accommodate the company's ambitions, reflecting a belief that technology would ride to the rescue. By incorporating the "best available technology" into its mill design and installing sufficient waste water storage capacity to store effluent over the winter months, Crestbrook might satisfy Alberta

Environment's concerns regarding organochlorines and dissolved oxygen levels in the Athabasca. The second approach focussed more upon the ecosystem than technology. It was less accommodating and could have had much more drastic consequences for the idea of building a gigantic bleached kraft pulp mill on the Athabasca. It would have delayed considering any project on the river until a more adequate information base had been established. Crestbrook and other corporate suitors would have to wait until the department had better insights into the impact of pulp mill pollution upon the Athabasca River's ability to support life.

Throughout the summer and fall of 1988 Alberta Environment's approach to Crestbrook softened. The department assumed a more accommodating profile. Technology would be the means to ensure an harmonious marriage between pulp mill development and environmental protection. Would Crestbrook redesign its original proposal in order to soothe the department's concerns about the pollutants in the proposed mill's effluent? By late fall the company proposed to modify the mill's design criteria to reduce the estimated amounts of chlorinated organics by half and other pollutants significantly as well. These changes to the mill's design criteria, however, did not satisfy Alberta Environment officials. In line with the predisposition to follow the technology beacon, they requested additional reductions where reductions were technologically feasible. On this basis, Alberta Environment sought even lower ratios of total suspended solids. In regards to chlorinated organics—the chemical family to which dioxins and furans belong—the department wanted total elimination of these pollutants from the mill's effluent. However, since the technology did not exist to enable a bleached kraft mill to attain this objective the department did not push the issue.[16]

In early December the department formally adopted and endorsed this technology-based approach to regulating the pulp and paper industry. Addressing the Environment Council of Alberta, environment minister Ian Reid announced that new mills and mill expansions would be required to incorporate the "best available technology" into their design proposals. He promised that Alberta's rivers would be protected adequately by specifying the technologies that pulp and paper mills would have to employ. The Permit to Construct and the Licence to Operate would remain the key provincial regulatory instruments. In the short run the distinction between established and new or proposed mills meant that the official discharge standards would vary from one facility to the next. The discharge limits allowed an older facility, such as

Weldwood's Hinton mill, were far too lenient to be granted to new pulp mills that could incorporate more modern technologies into their project design. Later, environmental assessment hearings highlighted a significant flaw in this approach to environmental regulation. To some extent, the technology-based alternative assumed that river systems such as the Athabasca had an infinite capacity to receive pollutants. It ignored the possibility that, at some point, even with the "best available technology," the cumulative impact of pollution would destroy aquatic life. Reliance upon technology alone, given the number of mills proposed for the Athabasca River system, could not guarantee quality water.

Environmental Impact Assessment: Just a Formality?

In early December the phony war ended dramatically. In a one week period, Premier Getty announced five forestry projects. These projects included a $365 million expansion of the Procter and Gamble kraft mill in Grande Prairie (this expansion never went ahead), a $182 million CTMP pulp mill that Alberta Energy proposed to build at Slave Lake, a $35 million wood processing plant in Manning, and a $16 million sawmill in Lac La Biche. The crowning jewel of this list was announced on 13 December in Athabasca. Premier Getty, joined by his forestry and environment ministers, local politicians, and even the NDP MLA for Athabasca-Lac La Biche, announced his government's approval-in-principle for Crestbrook's $1.3 billion Alberta-Pacific pulp mill venture. Final approval would have to await, first, Alberta-Pacific's successful completion of the environmental impact assessment (EIA) process called for by the province's Land Surface and Reclamation Act and, second, the negotiation of a satisfactory Forest Management Agreement. But some left the premier's Athabasca press conference with the impression that these steps were little more than formalities and offered no chance to derail the government's intent to bring "the world's largest single-line pulp mill" to northeastern Alberta. When Peter Opryshko, the son of original homesteaders in this area, dared to question the wisdom of this decision, Getty crushed him. "You know," the premier said, "I don't have time for complainers like you"—a remark more characteristic of someone serving categorical approval, not approval-in-principle, to his guests.[17]

Crestbrook certainly did not regard the EIA process as anything other than a formality. The company did not anticipate that the environmental assessment of its project would take long—in late October the company's project schedule set aside only two months for an EIA. This cavalier attitude towards environmental assessment reflected more than simple corporate arrogance. Its roots were firmly fixed in the province's long-standing tendency to give only cosmetic consideration to the environmental impacts of major resource projects. Years ago, this tendency could be seen during the enthusiastic promotion of proposals to extract petroleum from the Athabasca tar sands. In the forestry sector, the silence with which the Lougheed government greeted a major report on the environmental effects of forestry operations completed in 1979 by the Environment Council of Alberta demonstrated well that, in this sector too, environmental considerations resided only on the periphery of the decision-making process. The EIA process formalized this marginalization. The EIA called for by the Land Surface Conservation and Reclamation Act obliged the sponsor of a major resource use project to evaluate the environmental impact of the project and specify how damage to the environment would be mitigated. Once a company completed an environmental impact statement it would present it to the public for review, usually through company-sponsored open houses or public meetings in communities adjacent to the project. Ostensibly, the public's comments and concerns would be addressed by the sponsor before the EIA statement would be forwarded to the government. Alberta Environment then would lead an interdepartmental review to evaluate the content of the assessment. In the event this review identified information deficiencies, project sponsors were required to prepare supplemental information. Projects would only be approved once these information requirements had been satisfied.

Many aspects of this process angered environmental groups. Its public review provisions were regarded as little more than a sham. Company-sponsored open houses—"show and tell sessions" in the words of environmentalists—were poor substitutes for vigorous, independent public hearings. Opposition groups also complained that they were generally given insufficient time to respond to environmental assessment statements and that, as public interest groups, they did not have the funds required to retain the experts needed to examine a company's proposal. This decision-making setting clearly favoured corporate and governmental actors. The remedy for this situation proposed by the FOTA illustrated the group's basic mistrust of conventional political debate. Their preferred replacement for the conventional environmental assessment process was a hearing format modeled after the province's Energy Resources Conservation Board. The quasi-judicial nature of ERCB hearings appealed to the FOTA as a promising approach to conflict resolution. An independent board composed only of environmental experts should be charged with the task of making decisions in respect to the competing claims of environmentalists and the corporation.[18]

The government seemed to show some sympathy to these objections. The February 1989 Throne Speech promised an opportunity to comment and participate for those who were interested in the Alberta-Pacific project. In a letter sent to various local politicians and Native leaders, but not to environmental groups, environment minister Reid stated that Alberta-Pacific required "a project specific review process to accommodate public concerns for environmental protection." He promised that local governments would play an important role in this review and, to that end, guaranteed that local communities would have at least three members on the EIA Review Board. Furthermore, local community leaders were invited to nominate individuals for the board. The government's initial response to charges that the assessment process precluded effective public participation took the shape then of a project-specific five person citizens' review board. For Alberta-Pacific, this innovative review panel was only a symbolic gesture; they did not regard it as a serious obstacle. When Crestbrook met with officials from Alberta Environment's Standards and Approvals Division on 28 April it still intended to secure all necessary environmental approvals and begin construction in July.

While the proposed citizens' review board modified the province's assessment process, it did not satisfy the Friends of the Athabasca. One prominent member of the FOTA saw this board as merely a mouthpiece for those who supported the mill. "Its members," wrote Bill Fuller, "will be drawn from local communities on the advice of local politicians, who universally favour the mill without regard to its environmental effects. That is not the kind of 'independence' that is required."[19] Moreover, by populating the review board with local citizens this format did not meet the FOTA's desire to secure an independent scientific analysis of the company's proposals and claims.

When Ian Reid went down to defeat in the March 1989 election, Premier Getty turned the reins of the environment ministry and Alberta-Pacific's environmental assessment, over to a newcomer to the provincial legislature, Ralph Klein, the extremely popular former mayor of Calgary. During his previous nine years in municipal politics Klein, by throwing the doors of city hall open to the public and community groups, had burned a populist brand into the door of the mayor's office. Consulting with Calgarians was his forte and he restored a feeling among citizens that the mayor's office belonged to them, not to the oil companies and real estate developers. While he was Calgary's mayor, Klein drew upon the experience gained through his eleven years as a city hall television reporter and used the media skillfully to project a homespun, man-of-the-people image. Eating hotdogs for lunch on the steps of city hall, hoisting a few pints with his beer-drinking buddies at the St. Louis Hotel, fishing for the Bow River's famous rainbow trout were all images he used to develop this theme. As mayor, Klein led a charmed life. His heavy drinking, behaviour that would have ruined most politicians, endeared Klein to Calgarians.[20] Even public outbursts which revealed a decidedly more ugly side of his brand of populist politics did not damage his popular appeal. In 1982, at the peak of the energy boom, Klein referred to eastern Canadians who journeyed to Alberta to look for work in the province's oilfields as "creeps and bums" and, like a marshal on the frontiers of the American west, warned them to stay out of town. They were not welcome in Calgary. Those Calgarians who objected to Klein's lack of charity not only forgave him, they helped send him back to successive terms as mayor with mammoth victories. In 1986, he received 92 percent of the votes—an unheard of percentage. This charisma and electoral popularity transformed Klein, "the cheery politician who prefers to be called Ralph," into a highly sought-after political commodity in the late 1980s. Despite the fact that Klein did not have deep roots in the Progressive Conservative party—he was rumoured to want the leadership of the provincial Liberals—senior Tories courted him with promises of a cabinet position and the role of Getty's southern Alberta lieutenant. Klein could not resist these overtures and ran for the Progressive Conservatives in the constituency of Calgary-Elbow in the March 1989 election.

After a narrow provincial victory by the standards of his mayoralty triumphs—Klein won his riding by only 823 votes—political pundits wondered what style of politics Klein would bring to the environment ministry and how he would be received by his cabinet colleagues. Would he pack his populism in his bags when he moved to Edmonton? Would his new colleagues, at least several of whom questioned the strength of this newborn Tory's commitment to the party, give him the freedom needed to play the populist? In the early days it appeared that Klein the populist had indeed come to Edmonton and environmentalists were encouraged by his approach. Unlike his predecessor, he reached out to environmentalists. Whereas Reid would not even talk to some groups over the telephone, Klein met them personally to hear their concerns. After meeting with the Friends of the North, Klein asked Alberta-Pacific to delay the open house discussions of the company's proposal in order to give the mill's opponents time to swallow and digest its six hundred page environmental assessment report. More significantly, Klein seemed prepared to accept and respond to criticisms of the province's environmental assessment process. He would modify the process if it would increase public input; he pledged limited amounts of funding to groups who wished to appear before the Alberta-Pacific Environmental Impact Assessment Review Board. Also, in an interview with *The Edmonton Journal*, Klein staked out a surprisingly tough position on the Alberta-Pacific project given the premier's enthusiasm for the initiative: "If, in fact, it's going to show a danger to the drinking water in Fort McMurray and that there is the possibility of people's lives or health being threatened, then it ought not to be built."[21] A month later in the legislature, Klein rose to the opposition's bait and reiterated that, yes, he would stand up for the environment, even if that meant direct conflict with his premier. If an environmental assessment of the Alberta-Pacific mill showed a threat to the environment, he would go against Getty.

Talk in politics is cheap. Within weeks of Klein's tough talk it became clear that the environment minister did not have the clout, even if he had the heart, to deliver on his promises. Many helmsmen wanted to steer the Alberta-Pacific Environmental Assessment. They held, however, wildly varying ideas of what course this assessment should follow. Some sought an expert and exhaustive assessment. Federal agencies, the Government of the Northwest Territories, and environmental groups leaned in this direction. We already have noted the environmentalists' preference for a scientist-dominated review process. The Government of the NWT, as a downstream user of water flowing through the Peace-Athabasca systems, was very concerned about the impact which pulp mill effluents would have upon the water quality of its rivers and streams. Ottawa's interest in expanding the scope of the assessment was more surprising. Three years earlier, in 1986, Canada and Alberta had signed a federal-provincial agreement concerning environmental impact assessments. In order to avoid duplication, projects which touched both federal and provincial responsibilities only would be reviewed by the government enjoying primary constitutional authority. When it came to pulp and paper, the province claimed this authority and Ottawa agreed, standing on the sidelines as the province reviewed Daishowa and the other pulp and paper projects. Suddenly, on the eve of examining the Alberta-Pacific project, Ottawa became much more assertive and demanded to participate directly in the proceedings. This dramatic change of heart was prompted by a judgment from the Federal Court of Canada. In April 1989 the Court accepted the Canadian Wildlife Federation's argument that federal environmental regulations required Ottawa to review the controversial Rafferty-Alameda dam in southeastern Saskatchewan. This judgment implied that the federal government had to conduct an Environmental Assessment Review Process (EARP) whenever a development proposal affected federal responsibilities. The Federal Court ruling called into question the premise of the 1986 Canada-Alberta arrangement which invited governments to delegate environmental assessment responsibilities. In light of the legal uncertainty stirred up by the Federal Court decision, the 1986 agreement was not renewed after it expired in May 1989. If Alberta wanted to avoid a separate federal environmental assessment of the Alberta-Pacific proposal, the province had to invite Ottawa to participate and devise a hearing format which would approximate more demanding federal requirements.

Ottawa's intervention pushed Klein to broaden the scope of an inquiry into the Alberta-Pacific mill. Others preferred a limited investigation, overseen by locals. The first indication from Alberta Environment that a unique review board would be set up to examine the pulp mill noted that the board would be "made up primarily of citizens in affected communities." Forestry minister LeRoy Fjordbotten and his deputy minister, Fred McDougall, fought to limit the scope of the looming environmental assessment. Klein's musings that he would give the ALPAC review board the autonomy to set its own terms of reference were far too accommodating and directionless for Fjordbotten and McDougall's tastes. Fjordbotten had been surprised at the opposition the projects generated, and the last thing he wanted was a high-profile public pulpit that pulp mill opponents could use to criticize Forestry's timber allocation, timber cutting, and reforestation decisions. He was particularly concerned that the federal government would use its Fisheries Act to try to force the province to conduct public environmental assessments of its forest management agreements.[22] Faithful to a long-standing recipe for political success in Alberta politics, Fjordbotten used the constitution to rationalize his insistence that forestry practices must be exempted from a federal-provincial environmental assessment. Forests were a provincial resource and Ottawa had no business telling the provinces what to do with their trees. If Fjordbotten needed any other justification for trying to insulate forestry management from public scrutiny, he found it in the existence of studies from the 1970s on the environmental effects of forestry operations. The fact that the government had ignored major recommendations from the Environment Council of Alberta's 1979 report was apparently of no consequence. His position was clear-cut. The environmental impacts of the timber cutting aspects of the project should be handled through Forestry, Lands and Wildlife's timber management planning process—a notoriously inaccessible process to environmentalists.

The First Alberta-Pacific Environmental Review: What About the Trees?

In July of 1989 the Alberta-Pacific Environmental Impact Assessment review board was created, the product of an agreement between Canada and Alberta and the host for many of the conflicting demands that had appeared during the previous three months. The composition of the Review Board reflected Environment Canada's concerns that the federal government should nominate members. Two of the review board's eight members would be federal appointments while the chair would be appointed jointly by Ottawa and Alberta. Four of the members would be appointed by Klein's department and one member would be appointed by the Government of the Northwest Territories. Alberta's appointments were faithful to the logic of its earlier citizens' review board proposal—all of Klein's appointments were local citizens and none of them had any special scientific or environmental expertise. Expert scientific advice came through the federal appointments. Two environmental scientists—Bill Ross and David Schindler—were nominated by the federal minister of the environment. Schindler's appointment was regarded as a coup by environmentalists familiar with his scientific reputation. The FOTA's Bill Fuller, who had served as a member of a federal environmental assessment review panel examining the bison of Wood Buffalo National Park, was approached by Bob Connolly, the chair of the Bison Review Panel and a senior official in the Canada's Environmental Assessment Review Office, about possible candidates for the federal positions on the ALPAC review board. When Schindler's name was suggested, Fuller agreed wholeheartedly.[23]

The clash between those with expansionary and limiting agendas for the Alberta-Pacific inquiry left its marks upon the review board's terms of reference. Those who wanted the board to have a sweeping mandate received some satisfaction in Klein's instructions to the board that it consider the cumulative effects of all pulp mill discharges into the Peace-Athabasca river system. How-ever, these terms of reference also offered the first concrete signs of Klein's unwillingness or inability to stand up for his philosophy that "people are al-ways the boss." His commitment to listening to public opinion was beginning to crack under the reality that the Alberta-Pacific project was a linchpin of the government's diversification strategy, a linchpin that more senior ministers such as Fjordbotten were not going to allow him to tinker with. The reality of Klein's situation was that although he sat at the cabinet table he remained an outsider, nothing more than a junior minister in a government where it was an article of faith that economic development, even if it was subsidized heavily by government, took precedence over environmental protection. By giving de-tailed instructions to the review board, Klein backtracked on his earlier under-takings that he would allow it to establish its own terms of reference. He aban-doned the declaration he made in earlier discussions of the citizen's review panel, a declaration that he would give the review panel "the opportunity to conduct public hearings or to complete the process in any way, shape, or form it sees fit."[24] Moreover, Fjordbotten could claim nearly total victory in his ef-forts to ensure that environmental questions about forest management would not be aired in public. The principle that trees were the preserve of Forestry, Lands and Wildlife was preserved by Fjordbotten; Klein's terms of reference prevented the board from examining the environmental effects of most of the timber-cutting operations needed to feed the mill. The only forestry practices that could be considered were those affecting the lands enclosed by Indian reserves, an area of federal responsibility. Excluding any discussion of the terms of the Alberta-Pacific Forest Management Agreement, an FMA covering an area the size of New Brunswick, from the review board's mandate infuri-ated the Native peoples and environmentalists who participated in the subse-quent public hearings. Virtually every environmental group appearing before the EIA review board echoed the sentiment offered by a representative of the province's own Environment Council that excluding most of the timber har-vesting from the board's mandate was "ecologically unacceptable."

On 30 October 1989 the federal-provincial review board met in Fort McMurray to hold its first public hearing into the Alberta-Pacific proposal. By the time the hearings concluded in mid-December a total of twenty-seven meetings had been held in eleven communities. The response of the public to this opportunity to offer input into the policy making process was overwhelm-ing and generally hostile to the project; 750 written briefs were submitted and

250 presentations were made to the review board during seven weeks of hearings. Most of these submissions were opposed to the mill. Day after day the review board heard criticisms of the project. As the hearings neared their conclusion in mid-December, Stuart Lang had had enough. At a Cranbrook business luncheon Lang lashed out at environmentalists and the notion that his company's proposal should face any type of public hearing process. According to Crestbrook's president, the delay caused by the public hearings had already increased the cost of the Alberta-Pacific project by $166 million, a high price to pay for the "shouting, singing, and showmanship" that had taken place at the hearings. "I feel uncomfortable that we've had to lower ourselves to the public hearing process," Lang said. "I think the criticism is a disgrace."[25]

Within the limited agenda Klein gave the review board, the pulp mill's effluent discharge into the Athabasca River emerged as the most controversial issue. While intervenors criticized the company's socioeconomic assessment—"a glib analysis of community impacts" was the FOTA's judgment—the sulphur dioxide emissions to the atmosphere, the site of the mill, and the province's financial assistance to the project, the dominant theme in most interventions was the river. What damage would the water quality and fisheries of the Athabasca suffer from the daily dumping of tonnes of pollutants into its waters? What health risks awaited humans and other animals who relied upon the Athabasca for water and food? In raising these questions environmentalists relied heavily upon science. Scientific findings, after all, had been crucial to the gains made by environmentalists in the 1970s and 1980s. In the ALPAC case, the inadequacy of scientific information was seized upon by most environmental groups. Whatever the issue, environmentalists pointed to the questionable quality of ALPAC's science, the insufficiency of the information available to decision-makers or doubts regarding the predictive models used to estimate the Athabasca River's pollution tolerance. In the extreme this position led to calls for the company to prove that, in the long run, its mill would not harm the environment—what Greenpeace called a "guilty until proven innocent" perspective—an exercise utterly alien to corporate and government planners. Somewhat less dramatically, this view demanded a moratorium on the ALPAC project until basic data on wildlife habitat and the Athabasca River had been gathered. A popular perspective among environmental groups, this demand for additional information was also articulated by federal and provincial government departments. Scientists from the federal departments of Environment and Fisheries and Oceans were especially critical of the information deficiencies in the ALPAC EIA review. Until these deficiencies were corrected governments should not consider recommending approval of the ALPAC development. The thrust of this strategy played to the predispositions of at least one member of the review board, Dr. David Schindler, who in the mid–1970s had criticized an emerging breed of scientist, impact statement specialists, individuals who "write large reports containing reams of uninterpreted and incomplete descriptive data, and in some cases, construct 'predictive' models irrespective of the quality of the data base."[26] In addition to pointing to the inadequacies in the data base needed to judge the impact of alpac, the federal departments were very concerned about the cumulative impact of existing and proposed pulp mills upon the Peace-Athabasca rivers and Wood Buffalo National Park. So concerned were they about the dissolved oxygen levels in this river system that they urged Alberta to reconsider its approval of Alberta Energy's CTMP mill under construction on the Lesser Slave River, a tributary to the Athabasca.

Well-organized, well-financed aboriginal governments, such as the Athabasca Tribal Corporation, also ably played the scientific expert gambit demanded by the review board format. They pitted their experts—"white people with Indian hearts" in the words of the Bigstone Cree nation—against ALPAC's experts and more than held their own in the dueling scientist game. If review board members and politicians insisted upon scientific information, then Native peoples would find the experts needed to give it to them. Native concerns about the health of the Peace-Athabasca system were delivered in state-of-the-art terminology. Like the experts commissioned by environmentalists, the approaches of Native experts seemed to come right out of dialogue which could have been written for Mr. Data, the android who stars in the futuristic television series, "Star Trek: The Next Generation." "Mr. Data," Captain Picard might ask, "how can we detect the incidence and origin of dioxins and furans in the sediments of the Athabasca Delta?" "No problem, Captain," Data would reply, "I will simply use the computer's 'Nebulizing Ion Induced Coupled Plasma analysis techniques.' You will have your answer shortly."[27]

Although polluting the Athabasca River dominated the public hearings, environmentalists launched other attacks upon the Alberta-Pacific project. Air pollution, global warming, recycling, endangered species, ecological reserves, timber harvesting, the mill's local socioeconomic impacts, and the company's decision to build the mill in the heart of the small farming community of Prosperity were all raised during the public hearings. Since Klein forbid the review board from considering the mill's financial feasibility, markets, or other nonenvironmental aspects of the project, few groups dared to enter the forbidden territory inhabited by economic assumptions. A few, however, did tread very lightly upon this forbidden terrain. The Athabasca Tribal Corporation took aim at the terms of reference which outlawed economic and forest management considerations. Michael Percy, a University of Alberta economist retained by the Tribal Corporation, pointed out how the government's failure to use some form of market mechanism to allocate timber made it impossible to determine what economic returns, if any, Albertans would receive from this resource. The Mother Earth Healing Society, a society whose environmental outlook was rooted in traditional Native spiritual values, also questioned the economic assumptions underlying the headlong rush into pulp production. How could government believe and accept so eagerly the rosy pulp-demand scenarios pulp companies presented? The Alberta Wilderness Association aimed one salvo at the subsidies the state was pouring upon pulp companies. Each direct job created in the pulp sector cost provincial taxpayers $340,000 in subsidies. The economic elements in the AWA's presentation—it also demanded a cost-benefit analysis of the project—grew out of the appreciation, as Vivian Pharis put it, "that our politicians only think economics, so you have to go after that argument to get anywhere with them."[28] "Thinking economics," however, means many things. While Pharis presumed that Conservative politicians worshipped a market logic, this was not the economic altar where provincial Conservatives congregated. Instead, they worshipped economic growth and grew impatient with market conditions that slowed the pace of development. The market starved diversification. Nor, more bluntly, did a faith in markets deliver contracts to construction companies, consulting engineers, and other constituencies whom the provincial Progressive Conservatives counted among their faithful. Fjordbotten put little trust in what the market logic at the heart of cost-benefit analyses offered the prospects for development in northern Alberta:

But as far as doing a full-blown cost benefit economic analysis, frankly I don't think it would win. Prior to becoming the forestry minister I was part of the forestry committee and we were doing hearings on the Berland area—all that ended up with those public hearings and all of the cost/benefit analysis was a sawmill at Grande Cache that has had difficulty being viable.[29]

The lesson Fjordbotten took from this earlier experience was that market economics was the bane of industrial development in northern Alberta. When the Friends of the North pushed Fjordbotten on the cost-benefit analysis issue one member of the group was dumbfounded when the minister replied: "If God had wanted cost benefit analysis, he could not have built the world in seven days."[30] To talk market economics, albeit in whispers, as several of the environmental opponents of Alberta-Pacific tried to do, was to speak a language Conservative promoters of pulp mills in the North simply did not understand. They were in a hurry and paying too much attention to the market would only slow them down.

The provincial government's refusal to allow the review board to examine the environmental effects of most of the timber cutting needed to feed the mill muffled the criticisms of many of the aboriginal people who journeyed to community halls throughout northeastern Alberta to oppose this pulp mill project. These were people who, although concerned about water pollution, had a much more intimate relationship with the forests because the forest was the centre of their bush economy. Some were suspicious of environmentalists, blaming their antifur campaigns for low fur prices. Practitioners of a traditional way of life rejected the Native MLA Mike Cardinal's view that the bush economy did not have a future and that forestry projects such as ALPAC offered the best paths towards a better life. Some of their presentations argued that, even if they took Cardinal's counsel and welcomed the pulp companies, the computerization of mill operations would prove to be an insurmountable obstacle for many of them. The mechanization of harvesting reduced job opportunities for Natives since it favoured those with capital and few Natives could raise the $450,000 needed to purchase a new feller-buncher, an essential piece of equipment in today's mechanized harvesting system. According to this Native perspective, pulp mills did not promise a better life; they were the opening bars of a dirge:

The land won't come back as quickly as these experts say. We have lived with this land for many generations. We know its cycles. We know it won't be the same after they take away the trees. This destruction weighs heavily on us, like a war. There is no war but we are being destroyed. You don't need a war to destoy [sic] a Native person, just take away the bush, just take away the trees. That will destroy us. The money will be all that is left.[31]

Louis Cardinal, a member of the Bigstone Cree Nation, typified these Albertans.

Cardinal had lived his entire life in the small village of Peerless Lake some 240 kilometres north of Athabasca and spent most of his fifty-five years working on traplines. The bush was his life and a lifetime of experience gave him a great deal of knowledge about the cycles and habits of wildlife. When he asked a researcher who was doing a land use survey for the Bigstone Cree, "Do they [government] know that we live here?" he seemed generally perplexed that government would support a project that would disrupt his traditional way of life without first asking Native people how it would affect their lives. For people such as Louis Cardinal, the bush economy was not simply a relic from the Native past; it was dynamic, valuable, and worth encouraging. Resource planning studies support this view. The Bigstone Band sponsored testimony showing that, in northeastern British Columbia, the bush economy generated more than half the gross income of the Kaska Dena people. Removing old growth timber in the ALPAC FMA area, in the opinion of a resource planner retained by the band, would devastate moose and furbearing populations and with them, whatever promises the bush economy offered. Although the review board sympathized with the circumstances faced by those who wanted to pursue a traditional lifestyle, its terms of reference blocked it from doing more than simply urging the government and ALPAC to incorporate Native concerns into the forest planning process.

As the review board concluded its hearings it seemed that the hard-hitting scientific critique employed by environmentalists might pay dividends to those who opposed the project. This was certainly the impression Klein created. Since the review board had traveled extensively and heard a great deal of evidence, Klein argued that the politics of the situation demanded that the government respect whatever recommendation the board would make. "I think it would be political folly, " Klein said, "not to abide by the recommendations."[32] From the perspective of Forestry, Lands and Wildlife, Klein's willingness to accept the board's recommendation was dangerous. It threatened ALPAC's future and, more generally, the government's economic development motif. Klein was taken seriously by Fjordbotten because public opinion, particularly in Edmonton and Calgary, seemed to support taking a tough stand against Alberta-Pacific.[33] In light of Klein's public statements, it appeared that environmentalists had cause for celebration when the review board reported at the beginning of March 1990. The politics of resource exploitation had seldom seen the sort of recommendation the review board delivered to Klein—the Alberta-Pacific pulp mill "should not be approved at this time." Board members worried about

the impact more pulp mill pollution would have upon the amounts of chlorinated organics and dissolved oxygen found in the Athabasca. Instead of blessing
the Alberta-Pacific mill, the review board recommended further scientific studies into the Athabasca and Peace river systems "to determine if the Alberta-
Pacific proposed mill could proceed without serious hazard to life in the river
and for downstream users."[34] In the board's eyes, the environmentalists had
won the day.

Moving the Goalposts—
the Second Alberta-Pacific Review

Briefly, it appeared as if the scientific critiques offered by environmentalists
and environmental departments alike had succeeded. In Athabasca, Klein announced that the government would abide by the recommendation that the
project should be delayed until additional research was gathered on the state
of the Athabasca River. Premier Getty, standing alongside Klein, seemed to
echo the environment minister's message. The hearings had been "very unique
and important" and the premier assured Albertans that environmentally un-
sound projects would not be allowed to proceed in their province. When Getty
was asked if it was possible to find a compromise that would accommodate
environmental protection and Alberta-Pacific's wish to proceed quickly he said:
"Not a compromise on the environment. No."[35] The premier's words won
him praise. The media's reaction to Getty's statements was reminiscent of its
reaction to his efforts to reach out to Chief Ominayak. Compliments filled the
pages of the daily newspapers. Some suggested that the government's response
signaled "a new era in provincial politics"; others described the response as "a
courageous move"; even a business columnist could be counted among those
who felt that the board offered sound advice. Only Mike Cardinal, the Native
Conservative MLA for Athabasca-Lac La Biche and a loyal ALPAC booster, came
out strongly against the review board's findings—particularly the section on
Native concerns—and worried that the call for studies would lead ALPAC to
abandon the project.

Yet, even as those who opposed the mill congratulated each other, the
pro-pulp mill lobby in the government prepared its counterattack. Under its
influence the provincial government would soon walk away from any commitment to the ALPAC moratorium. The moratorium proposal jeopardized all of
the government's commitments to the Japanese interests behind ALPAC, and a

failure of this massive project would discourage all subsequent investors. Fjordbotten had made this latter point as he sat and waited for the release of the Alberta-Pacific review board report: "I think it will be a long, frosty Friday before you get other mills that want to locate in Alberta. I don't think you'll see anyone come up to the table for a long, long time."[36] Lost in the media's enthusiasm for Getty's reaction to the assessment report was any mention of the fact that he also called for both interdepartmental and independent assessments of the EIA review board's findings. In the latter half of March 1990, while Klein was in Vancouver, Fjordbotten held a meeting to galvanize support for proceeding with the plans for the pulp mill. Alberta-Pacific officials met with Getty, Fjordbotten, Cardinal, and Economic Development minister Peter Elzinga. From this meeting the premier emerged transformed—he now threw brickbats, not bouquets, at the review board. Hearings which Getty referred to three weeks earlier as "very unique and important" were now described as flawed and unbalanced. The review board did not exercise independent judgment but instead was a mirror which faithfully reflected the fact that a majority of the interventions heard by the board were opposed to the mill. Tougher questions should have been asked of those who opposed the mill. Following Cardinal's lead, Getty claimed that insufficient weight had been given to the support several Native political associations, particularly the Métis Association and the Janvier Indian Band, had given ALPAC. Now, the premier declared, a hunt was on in the name of balance for a second panel—this one to be composed of scientific experts of the province's own choosing—to "review the review." He owed this second review to northern Albertans who were counting on forestry to breathe new life into their communities.

Getty's remarks drew harsh responses from several review board members. The strongest rebuke came from David Schindler, a Killam Professor of Zoology at the University of Alberta. In the spring of 1991, Schindler's long-standing research into the impact of phosphates and acid rain on northern lakes gained international recognition. The Swedish Academy of Sciences, the body that selects Nobel Prize winners, selected Schindler as the winner of the Stockholm Water Prize, an international award worth $175,000. During the previous spring and summer Schindler was a very public critic of the government's efforts to minimize the environmental and health risks posed by dioxins. Some Conservative MLAs were so angry with Schindler's refusal to remain silent in the face of Getty's criticisms that they refused to allow the legislative assembly to send congratulations to Schindler for this achievement.

More importantly, the premier's second, much harsher assessment of the review board's findings did not face a serious challenge from either his cabinet or his party. Although Getty's remarks placed a surprised Klein in a very uncomfortable position and certainly contradicted many of the environment minister's earlier statements, Klein would not challenge Getty. His earlier promises to stand up to the premier on behalf of the environment fell by the wayside. Klein did not have the power base within either cabinet or caucus to challenge the premier and Fjordbotten on this issue. Moreover, even if he did enjoy influence over his colleagues, his department officials, upon whom he relied heavily, were not insisting that the minister stand up and fight for the ground claimed by the review board. Departmental comments and observations on the review board's recommendation that the project must be delayed pending further research, given to Klein near the end of March, generally concurred with the board's position. However, the department's agreement was qualified by its observations that the research called for by the board's "sweeping recommendation" was extensive, difficult to conduct, and would take a great deal of time to complete. Klein's briefing material did not come down strongly behind the position that the project should be mothballed pending the completion of river studies. Without a doubt the department felt that these studies needed to be completed but senior officials would not take the bolder step of recommending to Klein that project approval be withheld.[37] The department left the door wide open for Alberta-Pacific to propose a technological solution to the problem of chlorinated organics.

Within two weeks of criticizing the review board, Getty received a resounding endorsement for his stand from the annual convention of the provincial Progressive Conservative party. At the annual convention, the Calgary-Fish Creek constituency association asked delegates to support public reviews of all pulp mill projects, including those already under construction. The proposal was attacked by rural delegates, particularly those from areas affected by pulp mill projects. The rural delegates accused the Calgary sponsors of the resolution of hypocrisy. Why call for simply the public review of pulp mills? Why not also demand the public review of the natural gas and petrochemical projects which were integral to economic growth in Calgary and Edmonton? The proposal from the Calgary constituency went down to an overwhelming defeat, a result which was immediately interpreted as a strong indication of the party's support for the pulp mill development strategy. It also served as a strong hint of the Progressive Conservative party's growing identity with its rural base.

It did not take the province long to find a suitable pulp-mill-friendly company to conduct an independent assessment of the review board's findings. Jaakko Pöyry, a Finnish forestry consulting firm, was retained to reassess the findings of the EIA Review Board. Jaakko Pöyry was the same firm that advised the province in 1983 that a bleached kraft mill in the Athabasca area "would offer the best potential for profitable industrial utilization of the hardwood-dominated forest resources,"[38] the same firm that Lang listed as a member of Crestbrook's "very distinguished, competent team of outside advisors" when the company's initial project proposal was submitted to McDougall in July 1988. Given Jaakko Pöyry's ties to Crestbrook and its earlier enthusiasm for the concept of building a bleached kraft mill in Athabasca, Klein probably committed a Freudian slip when he arose in the legislature to say:

Certainly 2378TCDD has been identified as a very toxic dioxin. I mean, there is no secret. But there's a lot of work to be done with respect to chlorinated organics, and that is precisely why, Mr. Speaker, we have commissioned one of the most reputable firms in the world to understate . . . undertake a study of this whole issue of chlorinated organics.[39]

Jaakko Pöyry's "complementary" review, if not understating the risks associated with dioxins, certainly provided alpac's supporters with the ammunition they needed to argue that the risks associated with ALPAC's mill were tolerable. Like the original EIA Review Board, Jaakko Pöyry noted a need to gather more information about the Athabasca River system. "They indicated," one Alberta Environment official wrote sarcastically, "that not enough is known about dioxins/chlorinated organics in the river system, as did the previous panel: a $400,000 second opinion."

The crucial difference though was that, in Jaakko Pöyry's opinion, uncertainty was not a significant potential danger and therefore should not be regarded as an obstacle to the project. Instead, since uncertain risks to human health were posed by low levels of chlorinated organics Jaakko Pöyry questioned the rationality of regulatory regimes designed to reduce chlorinated organic discharges to smaller and smaller amounts. Furthermore, the firm took the offensive against those who had used scientific information to criticize the project. Jaakko Pöyry questioned the scientific methods of an important study on dioxin/furan toxicity environmentalists used at the EIA hearings; it doubted whether irreversible damage to the Athabasca River would accompany the proposed ALPAC mill; the company claimed that Native peoples, for whom the fish of the Athabasca constituted an important food source, were unlikely to face a risk of exceeding Health and Welfare Canada's maximum daily dioxin intake levels.

The Jaakko Pöyry review was only one element of the government's strategy to defuse the threat posed by the EIA Review Board's recommendations to ALPAC's plans. The government also admitted the obvious. There was little information on the state of the Peace-Athabasca river system and this important gap had to be filled. To this end, the federal and provincial governments announced a ten million dollar programme to implement the review board's wish for studies of the Peace, Athabasca, and Slave rivers. Thirdly, and most importantly, the government changed the context in which any future reviews of ALPAC would be conducted. In the summer of 1990, ALPAC revised its mill design. The company claimed the pulping process could be modified to satisfy the review board's primary worries regarding chlorinated organics. ALPAC's new process proposed to bleach pulp without using chlorine gas—a change which would reduce significantly the chlorinated organics discharged by the mill. If this process worked, it might dramatically reduce the toxicity of the mill's effluent. The company advertised its new technology as an important breakthrough from the environmental protection perspective:

Alberta-Pacific concludes that the tools to achieve environmental harmony are fully established. Indeed, from an environmental point of view, the modern mill employing modified cooking, oxygen delignification and modified bleaching is as distant from its conventional predecessors as the modern automobile is from the Model-T.[40]

From the government's point of view, ALPAC's talk of achieving environmental harmony was too risky. The focus on the environment had proven to be the political Achilles heel of the first review. To ensure that environmental protection did not get in the way of ALPAC's revised proposal, Klein removed it from the equation altogether. The three member Scientific Review Panel selected to examine ALPAC's modified pulping design was instructed only to examine the technical feasibility of ALPAC's proposal. Was it technically feasible to build and operate the type of mill now proposed by ALPAC? Would the mill's effluent have much lower levels of chorinated organics? The environmental impact of the mill—the source of demands for public hearings and the focus of the review board's investigation—was excluded altogether from the Scientific Review Panel's mandate.

This Machiavellian change to the terms of reference given to the second review panel was implemented faithfully. When the Department of Fisheries and Oceans tried to renew its earlier concerns by submitting a brief to the panel questioning whether ALPAC's new technology would reduce toxic discharges enough to protect the river's fisheries, it was not allowed to present its findings during the three days of public hearings scheduled by the panel. In explaining the decision to ignore the DFO submission the panel's chair said: "The impact of their effluent is not being considered by the panel. These are environmental issues and we're not mandated to look at them."[41] Nor would the panel consider whether the cumulative discharge of chlorinated organics into the Athabasca River, with or without any of the possible ALPAC mills, was already at an unacceptably high level. Klein's narrow terms of reference for the scientific review panel declawed environmental and health-related criticisms of ALPAC. They were irrelevant in the world Klein created.

The environmental protection issue had become a political Achilles heel largely because of the extensive public hearings held during the first review. These public hearings, stretching as they did over six weeks, offered a wonderful forum for the public to comment upon the project. Given that an impressive majority of the public submissions had opposed the mill, the government was determined to keep public examination of the new proposal to a minimum. Only three days of public hearings were scheduled. Moreover, to respect the "scientific" nature of this rematch only "expert" oral presentations and cross-examinations focussing upon "scientific evidence" would be allowed during these hearings. This look at ALPAC's new proposal, after all, was to be conducted by a "scientific" review panel, two engineers and an organic chemist. Equivalent scientific or technical credentials were demanded of those who wanted to comment upon the modified mill design. As one of the panel members was quoted as saying: "I don't think there are a lot of people out there qualified to comment on it (Alberta-Pacific's revised proposal)."[42]

With such enormous weight placed upon the technical, rather than the environmental, feasibility of the revised ALPAC proposal, there was little reason to be surprised when the Scientific Review Panel gave its stamp of approval to ALPAC's proposal.

Alberta-Pacific Gets the Green Light

In December 1990 the struggle to stop the construction of the Alberta-Pacific project was officially lost. Like a professional wrestling tag team celebrating its latest victory, Premier Getty and Mike Cardinal stood with hands clasped and arms stretched skyward before several hundred people in Athabasca and announced government approval for the mill. Mill supporters were jubilant; environmentalists and Native spokespersons were outraged. In the summer Lorraine Sinclair, the executive director of the Mother Earth Healing Society, had characterized the ALPAC review process as nothing more than a smoke screen. The public participation in such processes was just tokenism because "when you watch over a period of years and see the end result, you are able to go back and see what they started with . . . when they develop these processes, these phony processes like public consultation workshops . . . they already have the end result in mind."[43] The Jaakko Pöyry review, the scientific review panel, and the government's ultimate approval all lent measures of credibility to her cynicism.

By the time the government officially gave the project the green light, environment minister Klein's credibility among the province's environmentalists stood in tatters. Through his complicity in the government's attack upon the authority of the original review board's conclusions, Klein turned his back upon his populist reputation. Perhaps his leadership ambitions, ambitions that LeRoy Fjordbotten, his chief rival during the ALPAC controversy, scoffed at,[44] contributed to this about-face. However, a focus upon Klein's dream of becoming premier pays too little attention to his powerlessness in cabinet. His appointment to cabinet came at a moment when pulp and paper megaprojects still enjoyed strong support from cabinet, the caucus, and party members. Fjordbotten, who generally ignored advice to seek the public support of other cabinet ministers, nonetheless could count on most members of the party's forestry caucus committee to lobby actively on behalf of ALPAC and the other forestry projects. Moreover, the weight of the Progressive Conservative party, as shown when the party's 1990 convention routed a proposal that all pulp mill projects should be delayed until public reviews were conducted, was still solidly behind these megaprojects. In addition, if the political balance within the Conservatives still tilted decisively in the direction of forestry megaprojects, so too did the balance of opinion within the provincial bureaucracy. Klein's department never played a meaningful role in Forestry, Land and Wildlife's forestry planning process; trees and the environmental issues pertaining to their removal were the prerogative of the bureaucratic champions of the forestry megaproject approach. Moreover, in regards to water quality, an area where Alberta Environment enjoyed primary jurisdiction, the department had signaled its confidence in technology. Alberta Environment, by declaring that mills must incorporate the "best available technology," weighted its own decision-making criteria in a fashion which favoured accepting the company's revised proposal. There was little question that, if ALPAC's mill design worked, its effluent would be cleaner than any other bleached kraft mill in the country. The only ground left to issue a water quality challenge to the project, the ecosystem approach—the idea that the Peace-Athabasca river system could not survive another pulp mill, had been conceded by the department after it reviewed Crestbrook's initial plans in 1988.

Although environmentalists felt betrayed by the ALPAC decision, several important consequences flowed from their criticisms. Without the persistent criticisms of the Friends of the Athabasca and other environmental and Native organizations there is no doubt that a much more polluting pulp mill design would have been approved. Their criticisms were a resource Alberta Environment could use to force stricter pollution regulations upon the Alberta-Pacific project. Furthermore, the furore over pulp mills on the Athabasca-Peace river systems drove the government to create the Natural Resources Conservation Board (NRCB), an agency with the authority to review forest industry and other natural resource projects, and to decide whether, in light of their social, economic, and environmental effects, these projects serve the public interest. The irony here was that the vast majority of the province's Green Area had already been committed to the forest products industry before the NRCB was born. Finally, this environmental opposition forced the federal and Alberta governments to launch overdue studies into the cumulative impact of industrial development on the northern river systems.

While political and bureaucratic factors paved the way for the ultimate approval of the Alberta-Pacific pulp mill, the ability of government to push ahead also illustrates well the inherent limits of the predominantly scientific critiques of resource megaprojects employed by environmentalists and Native organizations. The importance of scientific critique in this episode resulted primarily from the fact that, in the twentieth century, science has been deified—alternatively described by Ursula Franklin as a "faith" or by Stan Rowe as "Humanism's chief religious sect."[45] As such, science, scientific credentials, and scientific information all bequeath important legitimizing and symbolic powers to those who use them in public policy debates. According to Schindler, for example, it had been the material submitted to a large extent by federal and provincial scientists which influenced the EIA review board's conclusions, not the "fairy stories from eco-freaks with no professional credentials." Even when the Scientific Review Panel had its scientific pedigree challenged during its brief hearings it managed to raise a scientific banner to defend its outlook on the ALPAC proposal. It responded to criticisms that ALPAC's proposed modifications would not stand up to the expectations of pure experimental science with the argument that, nonetheless, the panel approached its task in a very scientific fashion. The two issues before it, the technical feasibility of ALPAC's modifications and effluent characteristics, were "largely questions of science within the context of industrial design." Science, albeit in a different guise, was used again as an important legitimizing instrument.

There are several inherent limitations to evaluating these resource megaprojects primarily in a scientific context. First, in the words of the ecologist Stan Rowe: "Science has a secret agenda which is to deliver power."[46] Rowe's experience as an assessor of scientific research grant applications suggested to him that, when it came to government research support, the state's generosity depended upon whether or not the scientific research promised to deliver more power humans could use to control the world. Types of science and scientific projects that promised this controlling power were rewarded more generously than those that did not. Related to this observation is the point that, in this context, scientific debate invites industry to submit and government to accept the technological "cure" we saw offered in the ALPAC case since technology is one important means by which science delivers control. Consequently, the scientific debates in which many environmentalists participated enthusiastically invited the very technological responses Crestbrook subsequently made. These technological responses generally are viewed favourably because of our cultural belief that technology, Rowe's "Big T," is synonymous with progress. The government's enthusiasm for this marriage between a particular type of scientific debate and technology was illustrated in several ways. We have already seen Alberta Environment's endorsement of the "best available technology" approach to regulating this industry. Also, as we saw in the last chapter, this outlook or faith animated the responses of the province's deputy minister of economic development to questions about the environmental limits to economic growth in Alberta. The willingness of environmentalists to engage in the type of scientific arguments that often invite optimistic appraisals of technology's virtues contributed as well to the failure to stop Crestbrook's Alberta project.

1 . Frank Crawford, interview with author, Calling Lake, 28 May 1992.
2 . Dr. W.A. Fuller, interview with author, Athabasca, 28 May 1992.
3 . *The Athabasca Advocate*, 19 September 1988.
4 . Louis Schmittroth, letter to Ian Reid, 23 October 1988.
5 . *Pulp and Paper Canada*, March 1990.
6 . The presentation of the East Kootenay groups is found in Alberta, The Alberta-Pacific Environment Impact Assessment Review Board, *Public Hearings Proceedings*, 20, 2732–2790.
7 . For an examination of Mitsubishi's interests in Brazil see Yuta Harago, "Mitsubishi's Investments in Brazil: A Case Study of Eidai do Brasil Madeiras S. A." (paper prepared for Rainforest Action Network: September 1993). For information on Chile, see Japan Tropical Forest Action Network (JATAN), "Report on Eucalyptus Plantation Schemes in Brazil and Chile by Japanese Companies" (Tokyo: JATAN, May 1993).
8 . E. Wakker, "Mitsubishi's Unsustainable Timber Trade: Sarawak," *Restoration of Tropical Forest Ecosystems*, H. Lieth and M. Lohmann, eds. (Netherlands: Kluwer Academic Publishers, 1993).
9 . Eric Wakker, "No Time for Criticism? An Evaluation of Mitsubishi Corporation's Tropical Forest Policy and Practise," (report prepared for Friends of the Earth the Netherlands/Milieudefensie, May 1992).
10 . Ibid., 5. The report goes on to note that the Mitsubishi Research Institute offered a different explanation for deforestation—the industrialized world's demand for tropical timber products.
11 . D. Lamb, *Exploiting the Tropical Rain Forest: An Account of Pulpwood Logging in Papua New Guinea* (Carnforth: Parthenon Publishing Group Ltd., 1990), 218.
12 . British Columbia, Environmental Protection Branch, letter to author, 26 July 1993.
13 . Peter L. Timpany, letter to K. R. Smith, 3 June 1988.
14 . L. Noton, memorandum to F. Schulte, 15 June 1988.
15 . Bruce MacLock, memorandum to Fred Schulte, no date.
16 . Minutes of a meeting of 2 November 1988. Crestbrook; Alberta Environment; Forestry, Lands and Wildlife; and Stanley Engineering.
17 . The quote is from Mark Lisac, "Getty's Bullish Reply Difficult to Accept," *The Edmonton Journal*, 15 December 1988.
18 . Friends of the Athabasca Environmental Association, letter to Ian C. Reid, 8 January 1989. Reproduced in Friends of the Athabasca, *The FOTA Files*.
19 . W. A. Fuller, "The EIA Process" (February 1989), reproduced in *The FOTA Files*, 6.
20 . One biographical sketch of Klein claimed that "his drinking has attained the

currency of an urban folk myth. . . ." See Don Gillmor, "The People's Choice," *Saturday Night*, 104 (August 1989), 34.

21. Scott McKeen, "Klein Says He'll 'Dig for Truth' Over Pulp Mill Threat," *The Edmonton Journal*, 5 May 1989.

22. Confidential interview with author, 1 February 1994.

23. Dr. W. A. Fuller, interview with author, 28 May 1992.

24. Ralph Klein, in Alberta, Legislative Assembly, *Alberta Hansard*, 5 June 1989, 35.

25. Catherine Galliford, "Crestbrook Head Frustrated with Public Criticism," *Kootenay Advertiser*, 11 December 1989, 4.

26. *Science*, 7 May 1976.

27. The reference to "Nebulizing Ion Induced Coupled Plasma analysis techniques" is from a study of sediments in the Athabasca River delta prepared for the Athabasca Chipewyan Band.

28. Vivian Pharis, interview with author, 10 June 1992.

29. LeRoy Fjordbotten, interview with Ed Struzik, 24 August 1989.

30. Lorraine Vetsch, interview with author, 9 June 1992.

31. "Bigstone Cree Band Elder's Senate Statement" in Mother Earth Healing Society, "Bigstone Cree Nation Position Paper," presented to the Al-Pac Review Board, Wabasca/Desmarais, 5 December 1989, 1.

32. Brian Laghi, "Klein Faces Uphill Grind Inside Tory Caucus," *The Edmonton Journal*, 24 December 1989.

33. Confidential interview with author, 1 February 1994.

34. The Alberta-Pacific Environmental Impact Assessment Review Board, *The Proposed Alberta-Pacific Pulp Mill: Report of the EIA Review Board*, Executive Summary, March 1990.

35. Mark Lisac, "Tories' Conversion Signals a New Era," *The Edmonton Journal*, 3 March 1990.

36. Christopher Donville, "Minister Defends Proposal for Controversial Alberta-Pacific Mill," *The Globe and Mail*, 22 January 1990.

37. This information comes from an untitled document offering departmental comments and observations on the recommendations made by the Alberta-Pacific EIA Review Board. The document was delivered to the minister on 27 March 1990.

38. Roy Cook, "Credibility of Pulp Mill Review Doubted," *The Edmonton Journal*, 19 April 1990.

39. Alberta, Legislative Assembly of Alberta, *Alberta Hansard*, 24 April 1990, 745.

40. Alberta-Pacific Forest Industries Inc., *Mitigative Response to Concerns Regarding Chlorinated Organic Compounds* (July 1990), 52.

41. Scott McKeen, "Critical Report on Pulp Mill won't Be Heard by Al-Pac Panel," *The Edmonton Journal*, 29 August 1990.

42. Erin Ellis and Ron Cook, "Mill Review Panel Expects Few Public Submissions," *The Edmonton Journal*, 13 July 1990.

43. Lorraine Sinclair, interview with Lynn Cover, July 1990.

44 . Confidential interview with author, 1 February 1994.

45 . Ursula Franklin, "Let's Put Science Under the Microscope," *The Globe and Mail*, 20 August 1990; Stan Rowe, "Beauty and the Botanist," in Stan Rowe, *Home Place: Essays on Ecology* (Edmonton: NeWest Press, 1990), 92.

46 . Stan Rowe, "The Boreal Forest in the Global Context," in Boreal Forest Conference Committee, *Boreal Forest Conference: Proceedings* (Athabasca University: 1991), 115.

Moving Backwards into the Future

ALL MEMBERS ARE AWARE THAT THE PULP INDUSTRY IN CANADA IN THE
LAST PERHAPS 18 MONTHS HAS SUFFERED LOSSES AS HIGH AS 2 AND A
HALF BILLION DOLLARS. THIS IS NOT A WHITECOURT PROBLEM; THIS IS
NOT A NORTHERN ALBERTA PROBLEM; THIS IS NOT AN ALBERTA
PROBLEM; THIS IS NOT A CANADIAN PROBLEM. THIS IS AN
INTERNATIONAL PROBLEM.

—*KEN KOWALSKI, MINISTER OF ECONOMIC DEVELOPMENT AND TOURISM, 1 MARCH 1994*

 The Alberta-Pacific pulp mill lives up to the imagery inspired by the phrase "the world's largest single-line pulp mill." Everything about ALPAC is gigantic. It sprawls over the countryside near Prosperity. On a clear day its brown and beige towers, some twenty storeys high, are visible from up to sixteen kilometres away. The woodyard which feeds the mill is about half a kilometre long and is tended by a pair of thirteen storey cranes, cranes able to pick logging trucks clean in just three minutes. The logging trucks that work for ALPAC are controlled by "Trucknet," a computerized monitoring network which might conjure up Orwellian images of "Big Brother" for some. This system uses satellite technology and supplies the mill with around-the-clock information about the exact geographical location of the logging truck fleet and loaders. The opening of the mill was one of the few areas where gigantism was missing. When ALPAC began operating in the late summer of 1993 it did so without the fanfare, pomp, and circumstance which had attended the official opening of Daishowa's Peace River mill in September 1990. Unlike Daishowa's opening, Alberta-Pacific's inauguration was a hushed, unpublicized affair. The spectacle of Japanese dignitaries smashing open barrels of saki to symbolize a new beginning and awakening, witnessed by nearly fourteen hundred invited guests to Daishowa's opening, would not be seen when ALPAC started production. This difference had nothing to do with frugal-

ity. Instead, it recognized the political risks which now accompanied publicly celebrating pulp mill megaprojects. In 1993, the public climate to these megaprojects was cooler. Enthusiastic, extravagant displays were bound to attract uninvited guests, the environmentalists. ALPAC certainly did not want to offer its foes this media opportunity—"Why make yourself a lightning rod?" an ALPAC spokesperson asked rhetorically. This feeling was especially strong for ALPAC, given the proximity of its mill site to Athabasca and Edmonton, homes to many of the most active environmentalists. The silence surrounding ALPAC's opening symbolized then an awakening quite different from what had been heralded by the traditional Japanese ceremonies held in Peace River three years earlier. An environmental opposition had awakened, one that government and business took seriously.

As we have noted in previous chapters, the promise of another type of change stimulated the early bursts of enthusiasm for the tremendous expansion of the pulp and paper industry. Pulp and paper megaprojects promised new jobs with security and stability—scarce commodities in Alberta's "boom-bust" natural resource economy. These projects, especially during their construction stages, delivered a partial remedy to people who had been either bypassed by the energy boom or chastened by the subsequent bust. In Daishowa-Marubeni's case, dozens of Alberta contractors, engineering firms, and manufacturers cashed in on the mill's construction and supplied badly needed employment in the Peace River region; over thirteen hundred construction workers were working on this project in the summer of 1989; 57 percent of the company's construction budget was spent on the goods and services provided by Alberta-based firms. The construction of the Daishowa-Marubeni pulp mill must be credited then for a drop in the Peace River region's unemployment rate, from 8.5 percent in 1988 to 6.7 percent in 1990. A similar rush for the spoils followed ALPAC's approval. An overflow crowd, estimated at fifteen hundred, crammed into the Edmonton Convention Centre to find out how Edmonton businesses might secure some of the contracts ALPAC's construction would generate. At the peak of construction, about twenty-five hundred workers were employed at the Prosperity mill site.

The hopes that local residents would be able to secure the lion's share of the permanent, highly-skilled jobs in the mills were not realized, however. The contemporary pulp mill environment is dominated by what Shoshana Zuboff calls "smart machines," not workers.[1] During the restructuring of the Canadian pulp and paper industry which occurred during the latter stages of the 1980s mill modernizations came at the expense of jobs. New pulp mill designs produced more pulp with fewer workers and mechanized harvesting yielded more logs with fewer loggers. Moreover, not only are fewer workers required to run a state-of-the-art pulp mill but the mill's highly-computerized setting demands a very-skilled, computer-literate workforce. The high-tech flavour of this work environment is captured neatly by an ALPAC job advertisement in which the company's management information system is described in the following, reader-friendly, language:

> The state of the art network consists of approximately 200 PC's; Novell Net Wares LANs arranged in a campus network over eight buildings. IPX' LAT, and TCP/IT communication protocols; Rumba Netware/SAA and Sabre connectivity; Ascom Timeplex/Syneptics routers and hubs; 10 Base Ethernet; Level 5 copper wiring within building and fibre optics between buildings; a 56KB megaroute WAN links the plantsite with Edmonton.[2]

Few residents of the Athabasca and Peace River regions had the educational skills or the years of computing experience needed to take advantage of these opportunities. More generally, the majority of the unemployed residents of these regions did not possess the basic education background, Grade 12 or its equivalent for Daishowa-Marubeni and two years of postsecondary education for ALPAC, to qualify for the excellent in-house training programs these companies offered. Few had the capital or borrowing power needed to purchase one of the $140,000 logging trucks used to haul logs from the ALPAC FMA. NLK Consultants, a frequent consultant to the pulp and paper sector noted that, apart from clerical operations, "the pulp and paper projects will not directly employ a large number of those presently unemployed unless they upgrade their skills."[3] NLK also predicted accurately that competition between companies for skilled workers would intensify. The new mills tried to lure skilled employees away from older mills and tapped the labour pool found in the oil and gas sector. These personnel practices made it that much more difficult for local residents to secure the cream of the mill jobs. Therefore, while Daishowa-Marubeni can claim that 50 percent of its mill employees are from the local area it is likely that many, if not most, of the most skilled positions at the mill have been filled by applicants from outside the Peace River region. The end product of several factors—the end of the brief construction boom, the modern pulp mill's emphasis upon machinery rather than manpower, and the absence of a highly skilled local workforce—is an increase in local unemployment rates. In 1992, the unemployment rate in the Peace River region had climbed back to 9 percent. Moreover, smaller sawmills and other wood products manufacturers are unlikely to alleviate this unemployment situation since the timber resources in Alberta have been fully, if not over, committed.

Our intent here is not to argue that the jobs provided by the pulp mills are not important to northwestern and northeastern Alberta. Clearly, they are and unemployment in the Peace River and Athabasca areas would be higher without them. Rather, our point is that, from the perspective of reducing unemployment, simply dropping a megaproject into a region does not address the structural circumstances such as education and training which ultimately have a powerful effect upon whether local residents will be able to take advantage of the megaproject's presence. We hope, but are not optimistic, that government will finance the educational and training initiatives needed for local populations to participate more fully in these industrial projects.

As we argued in chapter 3, the success of the Alberta pulp and paper projects hinges upon their ability to remain competitive and maintain market share against global rivals. The security of the employment these mills offer Albertans depends on how these mills fare in a highly cyclical, volatile industry which is undergoing major structural changes. When pulp prices soared to $840/tonne during the heady days of 1989, it seemed unlikely that a sharp, prolonged downturn in the industry was just around the corner. In fact, on the eve of the price collapse, Koichi Kitagawa, the Canadian CEO of Daishowa Canada, was predicting steady, linear growth for the pulp and paper industry. "If you look at long-term forecasts for pulp requirements," he said, "the trend is 2–3% growth until 2025. So you require so many machines per year."[4] This over-confidence was contagious; it coloured the judgment of industry and government. Consequently, companies made, and in some cases, governments helped finance, the large capital investments needed to build modern pulp mills. Industry and government alike acted with the destructive self-indulgence the ancient Greeks called *hubris*.

Excess capacity in the industry grew, aggravating the price collapse which began with the recession in late 1989. The magnitude of the capital investments required to build state-of-the-art pulp mills plunged several companies, including Daishowa, into debt crises. Instead of steady, profitable growth, the industry has been swimming in a sea of red ink in the 1990s. Bleak financial reports from pulp and paper companies have filled the business press. In 1991,

Weyerhaeuser, the American giant, posted its first loss since it began reporting its financial results in the early 1930s, a performance linked by company officials in part to "abysmal" prices for pulp throughout the second half of 1991. Prices recovered briefly in 1992 in anticipation of a strike in the British Columbia segment of the industry, only to fall further in 1993. By November 1993, however, the average price for the premium grade of softwood pulp was reported to have sunk to four hundred dollars.[5] Struggling with excess capacity and the low prices associated with fierce global price competition, Canadian pulp and paper producers lost an estimated $750 million in 1993, a considerable portion of the $4 billion operating loss accumulated by the industry between 1991 and 1993.

The changing character of the global competition faced by the Canadian pulp and paper industry also threatens the long term viability of the new Alberta pulp and paper mills. Since the late seventies the dominance of the world's pulp and paper markets by Scandinavian and North American producers has been challenged by new plantation eucalyptus production in South America and Iberia. The economic advantage of eucalyptus, apart from certain pulping qualities, rests in the rapid growth of this species. The short rotation time of seven to twelve years for eucalyptus allows large pulp mills to be supplied by relatively small land areas. Certainly, predicting the potential impact of the fast-growing eucalyptus stocks on overall capacity and price in the market pulp industry is problematic; but the addition of low-cost production from the eucalyptus plantations of the southern hemisphere may exert further downward pressure on hardwood pulp prices and make the competitive position of Alberta mills such as Daishowa-Marubeni and ALPAC increasingly difficult.

During the pulp investment boom, the technological sophistication of the new mills had been regarded as a characteristic of the Alberta pulp and paper projects that would cushion the new firms from future recessions and global competition. However, the expensive price tag attached to technological sophistication may actually increase risk. When combined with the depth of the price collapse in pulp and paper, the embrace of expensive mill technology may hasten closures. In British Columbia, the depressed price for newsprint led Avenor Incorporated (formerly Canadian Pacific Forest Products Limited) to stop making interest and principal payments on the bank debt it assumed to build an ultramodern newsprint mill on the west coast of Vancouver Island. The mill shut down in December 1993 and, according to Avenor's president, the prospect of opening the mill in the near future was slim.[6] In the spring of 1994, the future of this mill and the two hundred workers it employed rested in the hands of the banks. In Alberta, at least some of the new, ultramodern facilities are facing similar pressures. Continuing low pulp prices prompted Millar Western Pulp Limited, already the beneficiary of a $120 million debenture from the province's Heritage Savings Trust Fund, to request more government financial assistance. The company's request for another loan from the Trust Fund was rejected. Ken Kowalski, now the deputy premier and the minister of Economic Development and Tourism, cited this decision as an example of the government's new-found desire to avoid offering financial assistance to the business community. Instead, the government helped to persuade the Canadian Imperial Bank of Commerce, the other key financier of Millar Western's Whitecourt pulp mill, to restructure its loan to the company and advance thirty million dollars to Mac Millar's venture.[7] The government can expect more visitors in the future.

There are also signs that Daishowa-Marubeni is struggling. With prices for bleached hardwood market pulp languishing in the $430 range, the Peace River pulp mill cannot be generating the $220 million in sales revenues company officials expected from this 340,000 tonne-per-year facility.[8] Like other integrated forest products companies with substantial exposure to the pulp and paper sector, Daishowa's Canadian operations began the 1990s by generating losses, not profits. In the company's 1991 fiscal year, revenues sagged and the company reported a loss of just over fifty-two million dollars. Back in Japan, the collapse of pulp and paper prices has made it extremely difficult for the scandal-plagued parent company, Daishowa Paper Manufacturing, to address its financial crisis. The parent's two chief debt-reduction measures, the sale of the Peace River pulp mill to Daishowa-Marubeni International and Ryoei Saito's purchase of more than ninety million dollars of new shares in the company, are reported to have "scarcely decreased" the company's $415 million debt.[9] The financial quagmire in which Daishowa Paper is mired plus the low prices resulting from excess capacity contributed to the decision to lend assistance of a different sort to the company's Alberta affiliate. In mid-December 1993 the government amended the Daishowa-Marubeni FMA to give the company five more years before deciding whether or not to proceed with one of the additional development possibilities the company had dangled before the government during negotiations—doubling the production of the Peace River mill, adding a 220,000 tonnes-per-year paper machine, or building a 500 tonnes-per-day CTMP pulp mill. A similar value-added provision, the construction of a paper mill, if economically feasible, is found in the Alberta-Pacific FMA and we should expect similar forgiveness for ALPAC in the future.

Developments in the industry other than the depressed market pulp prices which are fuelled by the addition of more, low-cost production also offer potential threats to the stability provided the largest of Alberta's pulp mills. In Europe, the campaigns of environmentalists against chlorine-bleached pulp have forced changes in industry behaviour and are emerging as potential threats to Alberta's pulp industry. Greenpeace Germany successfully spearheaded a campaign against paper products made from chlorine-bleached pulp. The threat of a Greenpeace-led consumer boycott forced a number of German publishers and paper manufacturers to ensure that their products were made from "TCF pulp," totally chlorine-free pulp. The growing political power of European environmentalists is such that, for now, it does not matter if TCF pulp is more benign to aquatic environments than chlorine dioxide-bleached pulp produced by a company such as ALPAC. The ability of Greenpeace and its allies to make credible boycott threats has already had an impact upon the industry's structure. Procter and Gamble's sale of its Grande Prairie complex, discussed in Chapter 4, was motivated in part by the European campaign against chlorine-bleaching. The environmentalists' campaign has forced a number of Nordic pulp and paper producers to make the expensive changes to their bleaching methods needed to produce TCF pulp. There are certainly voices from within the pulp and paper industry that do not regard the demand for TCF pulp as a passing fad. NLK Consultants predicts growing European demand for TCF pulp and argues that by 1996 TCF pulp will have captured a 25 percent share of the European market, nearly double its 1993 share.[10] Some Canadian forestry companies have already taken steps to present a "greener" image in response to these signals from Europe. One example is Canfor Corporation which formed a joint venture with Japan's Oji Paper Company and in 1990 built a $1.1 billion unchlorinated kraft pulp mill in British Columbia.

Another potential threat to the Alberta forest products industry lies in the efforts of environmentalists to tar the Canadian forest products industry with the same deforestation brush they have used against forest company operations in developing countries. To date, this tactic has been used only against the British Columbia forest industry, in particular MacMillan Bloedel, as part of the battle over the future of the temperate rainforests in Clayoquot Sound. In the United Kingdom, threats from Greenpeace that it would run an advertising campaign publicly linking Scott Paper to what Greenpeace called "Ca-

nadian rain forest destruction" prompted Scott to cancel its contract to purchase approximately five million dollars in market pulp from MacMillan
Bloedel. Two weeks later the British division of Kimberley-Clark cancelled a
$2.5 million pulp contract with the same British Columbia firm. It is certainly
possible that in the future, environmental organizations may try to develop
similar boycott strategies against Alberta pulp producers who do not produce
TCF pulp and/or clearcut the boreal forest.

There is an inescapable irony in the situation Alberta faces. The forestry
strategy was crafted to offer a measure of stability by counteracting the wild
gyrations typical of the provincial economy, dependent as it is upon the health
of unpredictable, international commodity markets. Yet, as events since 1989
have made painfully clear, jobs in the pulp and paper industry also depend
upon uncertain international commodity demand. The government's headlong rush into pulp and paper ignored the cautions offered by people such as
Peter Pearse, the well-known forestry economist from the University of British Columbia, who, after approving the principle of industrial diversification,
warned that "the forest industry slides into a recession at least as much as
other industries."[11] Ironically then, the provincial government's forestry strategy, when viewed in the context of the depressed pulp market of the early
1990s, imported another set of unstable industries to a province already familiar with the volatility and risks inherent in international commodity markets.
The province's economic future may bear a striking resemblance to its past.

For their part, the environmentalists have not presented an alternative
economic blueprint which is likely to prevent the Alberta economy from re-
visiting its turbulent past. Strong on environmental sustainability, they are
weaker when it comes to economic sustainability and their criticisms do not
offer the economic growth and jobs craved by the residents of northern Alberta. For environmentalism to expand its Alberta beachhead it must do more
than simply criticize the environmental consequences of megaprojects; it must
intensify its search for alternative models of economic growth which address
the dreams of rural Alberta, as significant as this area is to provincial politics.
This will not be an easy task since some of the alternatives bandied about to
date do not offer the short-term individual economic rewards of pulp and paper mill employment. For example, ecotourism, a favourite alternative for some
environmentalists, offers workers a fraction of what may be earned in mill or
woodlands operations. Until the new environmental economy in Alberta
strengthens its attachment to economic growth in rural Alberta it will be very

difficult for environmentalists to incorporate rural Albertans into their political coalition.

If we are right to suggest that sluggish markets and tough competition from low-cost producers cloud the future of the new generation of pulp and paper projects, it would follow that, in the years to come, we should expect to see more demands from this sector for financial, regulatory, or investment concessions. Is it likely that Alberta will intervene again on behalf of these companies? When Ralph Klein became leader of the Progressive Conservatives in December 1992 he promised Albertans, like Don Getty in his last years as premier, to balance the provincial budget. During his first few months as premier and the subsequent 1993 election campaign, Klein successfully disassociated himself from the Getty government's record and promised Albertans that he would eliminate the provincial deficit without raising taxes. In the 15 June 1993 election Klein rather easily accomplished what many pundits felt was a very difficult or impossible task nine months earlier—the reelection of the Progressive Conservatives, albeit with a smaller majority. For the right-wing newsmagazine *Alberta Report*, the election gave Klein "an overwhelming mandate for massive cuts to government programs and spending." Since the election, Klein has interpreted his mandate in exactly those terms. He has attacked the provincial deficit, and according to "negative thinkers" like ourselves, attacked the poor, the aged, and other vulnerable segments of Alberta society, through a single-minded focus upon government spending cuts. In this budget-cutting climate, the government has devalued its opinion of grants, loans, and loan guarantees. These interventionist instruments have fallen from grace. No longer are they regarded as important instruments of industrial policy; instead, they have become legitimate targets for the budget-cutter's axe. This change of heart was prompted in part by the unanticipated burden these measures placed upon the province's finances. By 1992, the more than $12 billion in outstanding loans, guarantees, and investments, $1.14 billion of which had been given to forest companies, had become a significant drain upon the public treasury. Between 1985 and 1992, the government either had written off or provided for $2.1 billion in loans and guarantees. When the Klein government unveiled its new economic development strategy, it promised to reduce or eliminate government assistance to business, and "only become directly involved in the marketplace in exceptional circumstances and when success requires public involvement."[12]

But if the troubles besieging the pulp and paper industry continue, it will be very difficult for the Klein government to stand on the sidelines. It has a direct commercial stake in most of the mills. For the government to wash its hands of these projects it would have to disavow its own role in fathering them; it would have to ignore the fact that, since the mid-1980s, it has not been neutral when it came to the issue of pulp and paper development in northern Alberta. Through its generosity, the government forced this type of economic growth upon northern Alberta. The rhetoric about eliminating government assistance to business ignores what the historical record, in this country and elsewhere, reveals about the nature of government intervention in economic life. Initial interventions breed additional intervention if and when financial troubles arise for the recipient of government largesse and business failure threatens a core political constituency. Albertans need only reflect upon the taxation treatment of the province's petroleum industry to see this pattern. The unfolding political dynamic in Alberta suggests that the government will find itself under intense pressure to intervene again if troubles continue for the pulp and paper industry. Klein's victories, in both the Conservative leadership race and the June 1993 election, were delivered by the political support he received from Calgary and rural Alberta. Klein could not have succeeded without these two constituencies and his political future depends upon his ability to retain their allegiance. Any refusal to help the pulp and paper projects if future troubles arise would threaten the important political foundation rural Alberta provides for the current Progressive Conservative party. Letting the market decide the future of the northern pulp mills may make economic, even ecological, sense but it is an option that would exact a political price that the Klein government, dependent as it is upon rural Alberta, could ill afford.

Sustainability, Sirens, and the Search for a New Politics

To focus only upon further financial assistance to the pulp and paper sector blinds us to the other interventionist paths governments will take to assist this industry. Diluting the commitment to industrial development by amending Forest Management Agreements, as has already been done for Daishowa-Marubeni, is one alternative means of lightening the financial burden and weakening the contractual obligations of pulp and paper companies. Provincial pollution regulations offer a third alternative. Since the new and upgraded pulp and paper mills came on stream, the province has ignored warnings about the health of its rivers and used its licencing powers to industry's advantage. Preliminary data assembled by the federal-provincial Northern River Basins Study, one offspring of the ALPAC EIA hearings, reinforces the scientific concerns cited by environmentalists during those hearings. These data, preliminary though they may be, sustain the suspicion that the rapid expansion of the pulp and paper industry will starve the Athabasca River of the oxygen needed for the survival of aquatic life. In light of data which suggested that pulp mill effluent was the primary contributor to this situation, the study board suggested to government that it consider issuing shorter-term licences to the mills operating on northern rivers pending the study's accumulation of further information and analysis. The chair of the study's science advisory committee suggested that regulators now had more reasons to consider a much more radical option—a total ban on all pulp mill effluents. The government's response to these suggestions which threatened the health of mills, not rivers, was predictable. Instead of opting for shorter-term licences pending the completion of additional studies, Alberta issued the customary five-year licence renewals to the mills dumping effluent into northern rivers.

This particular use of government's regulatory powers raises important questions about the environmental sustainability of these developments, about whether a healthy environment is compatible with the aggressive promotion of pulp and paper projects. It supports the argument that the type of regulatory environment governments customarily establish to accelerate these types of resource megaprojects is unlikely to be compatible with the concept of environmentally sustainable development. Listening to industry, one would get a different impression, an impression that government regulators are zealous protectors of the environment. According to this view, a lenient regulatory environment is nothing more than a relic from an earlier era. Gerry Fenner, ALPAC's chief spokesperson during the environmental impact assessment hearings, used this perspective to try to calm the water pollution fears of commercial fishermen:

People like yourself who came from the west coast, you are very familiar with the past of pulp and paper mills. I'm very familiar as well with this past of pulp and paper mills because I happen to have been in that business now for almost 30 years. So I know what we used to do. We are, in fact, notorious polluters. We did not have in-process control systems that were concerned about the effluents that we created or the emissions that we had. That was the state of the rule 30 years ago. And all those mills on the coast discharged with what we call an open pipe. There was nothing. But the new mills will be totally different because of the environmental movement, technology, and regulation.[13]

In some respects, the approval of both ALPAC and Daishowa sustained Fenner's views. The environmental movement could take credit for forcing the government to insist upon different mill technologies and tougher regulatory standards. Yet, the ultimate proof will rest in the enforcement of these regulations. The vigour of this enforcement will depend in the first instance upon the political will of government, political will that in Alberta and elsewhere is often sapped by the political forces underpinning governments that have staked their political future upon resource megaprojects. A government's competence—the knowledge, skill, and personnel which will be focussed on this issue—is equally important to the vigour of any regulatory effort which takes environmental sustainability seriously. Here too government is often lacking. In Alberta, the Northern River Basins Study was formed, quite simply, because of government's collective ignorance about northern rivers. Baseline information about these rivers and the types of aquatic life they nurture had to be gathered. Such baseline information, as we noted in Chapter 6, was not in the hands of Alberta Environment officials when they were asked for their opinion about ALPAC's proposal to put the largest pulp mill yet on the Athabasca River.

A similar tale may be told about the province's forests. For the northern boreal forest, basic information about most of its wildlife and timber resources has never been gathered. Industry and environmentalists alike worry that government has overcommitted timber in several portions of northern Alberta and that crucial timber supplies exist only on the pages of government survey records. Elsewhere, a provincial expert panel on forest management echoed the Alberta Forest Service's own doubts about whether Forestry has the human and budgetary resources needed to fulfill its resource management mandate and to reassure an environmentally conscious public that forest company operations will respect the goal of environmental protection.

How can environmental sustainability be secured when massive developments precede the gathering of needed information and the assembling of the staff needed to monitor and enforce regulations?

Answers to the sustainability issue are conspicuously absent from the current debate between industry and environmentalists over the fate of the forests. As we stumble towards the twenty-first century, the popular media is filled with battles between the forest industry and environmentalists for the hearts and minds of the public. Both protagonists specialize in inflammatory gestures and a healthy portion of the educational material they bombard the public with is better labelled propaganda. Forest industry associations laud the benefits of clearcuts to wildlife, conveniently omitting the fact that certain species such as woodland caribou, spotted owls, and some furbearing animals need old growth forests. For their part, environmentalists respond with their own propaganda barrages. News conferences proclaim the "horror" of forest clearcuts, ignoring that, under certain conditions, clearcutting is the most appropriate way to harvest even-aged species such as lodgepole pine and aspen.

Nor are the solutions to the economic and ecological dilemmas described in this book likely to come from the Alberta political system, at least as it is presently constituted. Not since the complacent, stifling 1950s when Social Credit and the American petroleum industry ran Alberta as a prosperous suburb of Houston, Texas, has the corporate culture dominated the province's politicians and their ideas as totally as it has done in the 1990s. Under Ralph Klein's right-wing populism, heavily supported in the rural parts of Alberta and, of course, in Calgary, the Tories have metamorphized into lookalike provincial siblings of the federal Reform Party, whose leader—Preston Manning— happens to be the son of the man—Ernest Manning—who led Alberta in the sunny days when it became a suburb of Houston. From his brief moment of glory in the ALPAC fight when he stood up for environmental integrity, but then thought better of it, Ralph Klein has been the hottest rising star of Alberta politics: a man, not unlike the Mannings, who set out to do good and ended up doing rather well. Klein's Conservative government has pursued a business-orchestrated agenda of deficit reduction through spending cuts, while holding down taxes, and this strategy has yet to be confronted by a credible alternative policy. Dominated as it is by rural Alberta and urban business interests, including the resource-extractive industries of oil, gas, and forestry, Klein's government cannot be expected to take unpopular but necessary policies to save an environment now endangered by decades of reckless economic growth. Nor should much be expected from the opposition Liberals, a party even less likely to rock the boat of big business than is Mr. Klein's.

If there is to be an answer to the transnationalism represented by ALPAC and Daishowa-Marubeni International, it will have to come from a different political culture than the one that dominates Alberta today. It will have to come from a popular opposition, not from the system that produced premiers Getty and Klein. The environmental movement which, as we have shown, was galvanized by the forestry and pulp mill projects, and which achieved much despite the odds, has since lost much of its impetus. It has fragmented and shrivelled. Somehow it needs to regroup and rebuild, and it must do so with a strategy that has real appeal to those individuals and groups who are looking for economic growth, for decent jobs, for better prospects for their families. We have argued in this book that Alberta's environmental movement needed stronger and more credible economic alternatives when opposing the forestry giants. Arguably, it would have found these alternatives in forging alliances with other interests who have less grandiose and less destructive visions of forest development—Native communities, smaller independent forest companies, and so on; yet such alliances were never made and the transnationals won by default. Surely the lesson is that the physical environment and the political economy are part of the same reality. We cannot hope to save the one unless we reconstruct the other.

1. Shoshana Zuboff, *In the Age of the Smart Machine: The Future of Work and Power* (New York, Basic Books Inc., 1988).
2. *The Edmonton Journal*, 9 October 1993.
3. Nystrom, Lev, Kobayashi and Associates (NKL), "Training Needs Associated with Major Forest Projects in Alberta," April 1988, 24.
4. "Japan in Canada," *Pulp and Paper Journal* 42 (September 1989), 31.
5. Casey Mahood, "Wood Pulp Prices Picking Up," *The Globe and Mail*, 20 January 1994.
6. Ann Gibbon, "CP Forest mill reopening doubtful," *The Globe and Mail*, 19 March 1994.
7. Alberta, Legislative Assembly, *Alberta Hansard*, 1 March 1994, 333.
8. James P. Morrison, "Case Study One: Daishowa—A Successful Diversification Initiative," *Focus Alberta: A Global Trade and Investment Forum* (1979), 78.
9. Yomiuri Shimbun, "Saito Arrest Clouds Daishowa Prospects," *The Daily Yomiuri*, 13 November 1993.
10. Christopher Brown-Humes, "Run-of-the-Mill Debates," *Financial Times*, 20 October 1993.
11. Henry Cybulski, "Forest for Sale," *Calgary Herald*, 5 March 1989.
12. Alberta, *Seizing Opportunity: Alberta's New Economic Development Strategy* (1993), 4.
13. Alberta, The Alberta-Pacific Environment Impact Assessment Review Board, *Public Hearings Proceedings* 6 (1989), 7.

Index

Industries, 192; rationale for review of Alberta-Pacific EIA, 190; review of Alberta-Pacific EIA, 192, 193; support for pulp mills, 192, 193

Japan and New Guinea Timber Co. Ltd. (JANT): see Honshu Paper Co.

Japan. Import-Export Bank: 140

Japan. Liberal Democratic Party (LDP): 80

Japan. Ministry of International Trade and Industry: see MITI

Japan. Sumitomo Bank Ltd.: 81

Japanese forest industry: economics of, 170-172

Jari Forest Industries: 139, 140, 141

Jobin, Reinie: 119

Johnstone, Barry: 165

Juhlin, Tim: 160n

Jujo Paper Co.: 80

Kanzaki Paper Canada: 150, 151

Keynes, John Maynard: 58, 136

Kierans, Eric: 55

Kitagawa, Koichi: 85, 95, 96, 101; March 1988 meeting with Ominayak, 115, 116

Klein, Ralph: Alberta-Pacific EIA recommendations and, 188, 189; conflict with Getty, 180; credibility with environmentalists, 179-180, 195; mayor of Calgary, 178, 179; environment minister, 163, 179-185, 189-191, 193-195; premier, 209, 210, 213, 214; refusal to challenge Getty, 191

Kostiw, Bill: 147, 149, 160

Kowalski, Ken: 98-100, 112, 201

Kraft pulp mills: 69, 84, 87, 90, 103, 138, 156, 173, 174, 176

Land Surface Reclamation Act: 98

Lang, Stuart: 135, 138, 139, 141, 143, 154, 158, 167, 192; criticism of environmental groups, 145, 146; objections to Alberta-Pacific EIA Review Board, 184; trade unions and, 146

Lennarson, Fred: 111, 116, 121

Lightweight coated paper mill: 6

Little Red River Cree: 106, 107

Loomis, Reg: 17, 18

Lougheed, Peter: 3, 4, 46, 50, 51, 55, 58, 60, 78, 149; forestry policy under Lougheed administration, 46, 55

Lubicon Cree: 7, 110-126; boycott strategy, 125; confrontation strategy, 121, 122; Daishowa EIA and, 112; direct action, 117; forest management and, 121; Grimshaw agreement, 118; land claim of, 111, 112; petroleum industry and, 111; proposed reserve, 113, 114, 118; support for, 114; support of Jan Reimer, 81; suspected arson, 119, 120

Ludwig, Daniel: 139-141

MacMillan Bloedel Ltd.: 22, 27, 31, 97, 207, 208; demands for government assistance, 19-21

Malaysia: 21, 169, 170

Manning, Ernest: 45

Marubeni Corp.: 6, 76, 83, 86, 142

MC Forest Investment Inc.: 151

McDonald, Al: 137n

McDougall, Fred: 32, 33, 36, 37, 47, 49, 59, 60, 65, 112, 139, 165, 181, 192; Weyerhaeuser and, 149

McDougall, John: 55

McInnis, John: 123

Megaprojects: 7, 12, 14, 25, 26, 39, 107, 114, 129, 137, 139, 148, 151, 164, 195-197, 202, 204, 208, 211, 212

Millar Western Industries (see also Millar Western Pulp Ltd.): 31, 67, 68

Millar Western Pulp Ltd.: 5, 6, 59, 68-71, 137; financial health of, 206

Millar, Hugh MacKenzie: 31, 32, 67, 68, 206

Millar, J. W.: 68

Ministry of International Trade and Industry (MITI): 74-76, 79, 150; attitude toward Daishowa, 79; development and import strategy (D and I), 76, 77; ecology and, 77; problem of resource scarcity, 76, 77; problem of surplus capacity, 75; promotional material, 78; resource nationalism, 77; restrictions to domestic pulp production, 77; risks involved with D and I, 76, 77

Mitsubishi Corp.: 5, 7, 9, 76, 90, 135, 139, 142, 144, 145, 148, 150, 153; boycott, 170; environmental record of, 168-170; extensive involvement with Alberta-Pacific, 142, 143

Mitsui: 76, 80

Larry Pratt and Ian Urquhart

Political scientists Larry Pratt and Ian Urquhart worked for several years on the research for *The Last Great Forest*. Both are professors at the University of Alberta.

Larry Pratt is a doctoral graduate of the London School of Economics and has written, edited, and coedited eight books, mostly on international relations, political economy, and nationalism. Among them are *The Tar Sands, Socialism and Democracy in Alberta, Social Democracy Without Illusions,* and *Prairie Capitalism* (Governor General Award nominee).

Ian Urquhart received his PhD in 1987 from the University of British Columbia, where he studied the politics of the salmon fishery. He is the author of several articles on Alberta politics and is currently studying the politics of managing environmental tasks.